The Initiates Speak

Darrell Jordan

The Initiates Speak, Compiled with graphics and edits by Darrell Jordan,
Copyright © First Edition 2024. All rights reserved.

No part of this book may be reproduced in whole or in part without the written permission from the publisher, nor stored in any retrieval system or transmitted by any means, electronic, mechanical, photocopying, recording, or other, without the written consent of the publisher.
For bulk purchases, please contact the publisher.
Enquiry@Athenaia.Co

Library of Congress Cataloging-in Publication Data
Names: The Initiates | Jordan, Darrell
Title: The Initiates Speak
Description: First U.S. edition. | Coeur D'Alene, Idaho: Athenaia [2024]
Identifiers: LCCN (pending) | ISBN 979-8-88556-048-1 (First Edition hardcover)
Subjects: OCC016000: BODY, MIND & SPIRIT / Occultism |
HI036000: PHILOSOPHY / Hermeneutics |
REL047000: RELIGION / Mysticism
LCCN record available at https://lccn. loc.gov

On the internet: Parallel47North.com/collections/esoteric-books
Managing Editor: Darrell Jordan
Original Author and Essay: The Initiates
Executive Producer: Yuka Jordan
Book Cover Art and Illustrations: Jessica Naomi
Image Credits: Darrell Jordan personal collection

Printed and bound in the United States

Publisher: Athenaia, LLC
2370 N Merritt Crk Lp, Ste 1
Coeur D'Alene, ID 83814 , The United States
Enquiry@Athenaia.Co

THE INITIATES SPEAK

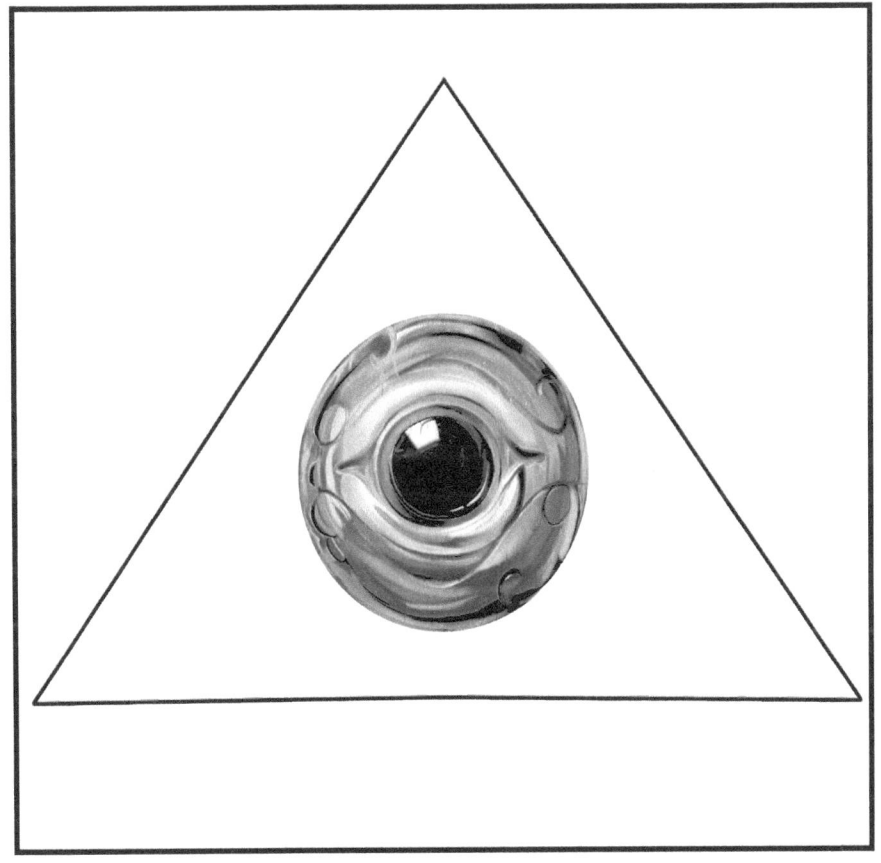

Darrell Jordan

Dedication

To those who Search for Truth and a Path with Heart.

Seat of Knowledge

An Inprint of Athenaia, LLC

"Knowing is not enough; we must apply. Willing is not enough; we must do."

Johann Wolfgang von Goethe

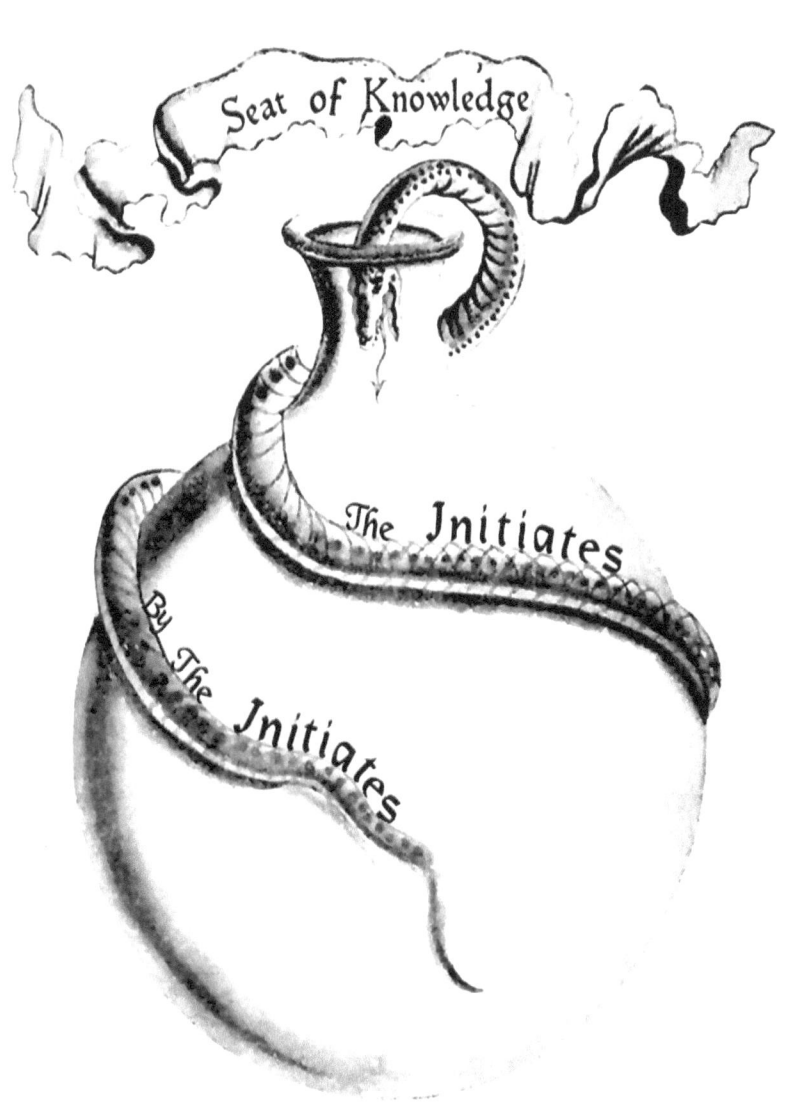

Contents

Introduction	11
THE FIRST	13
THE ANCIENT FAITH	18
PURIFIED SPIRIT IN MAN	27
THE MAGIC RITES	27
PLANES OF CONSCIOUSNESS	31
TEMPLE TALK	34
CONCERNING "LAW"	37
THE HOLY BIBLE	40
METAPHYSICS AND UNIVERSAL BROTHERHOOD	
	42
THE OCCULT AND FRAUD	46
A COMPARISON BETWEEN SOLOMON'S	50
TEMPLE AND THE "GRAND MAN"	50
THE MYSTIC AND THE OCCULT	58
CONCERNING FAITH	62
MYSTICS	65
THE OCCULT SCIENTISTS	67
CONCERNING A NEWSTATEMENT OF THEOLOGY	
	70
MYSTERIES	85
INITIATION	86
THOUGHT	88
IS THERE NEED FOR A NEW RELIGION?	90
THE NEW THEOLOGY DUALISM	94
KARMA	98
PROMETHEUS	104
THE NEW THEOLOGY-DUALISM	107
INTUITIONAL LIGHT	109
THE WORLD'S CONDITION	112
THE ROSICRUCIAN'S HISTORY	117
THE HIGHER KNOWLEDGE	127

SPIRITUAL EVOLUTION	130
THE TWELVE SONS OF JACOB	132
CONCERNING THE TRINITY	140
THE AQUARIAN AGE	144
IS MAN COMING TO HIS OWN?	146
CONCRNING THE SOUL	150
ESOTERIC PROGNOSTICATIONS	167
MYSTICAL INFLUENCE OF THE NO. 7	168
THE NEW THEOLOGY-DUALISM	170
PERSONALITY	171
FREEDOM OF THE MIND	173
WHAT IS A MASTER OR ADEPT	175
THE SUN AND THE SOUL	176
LIFE AND DEATH	180
THE SOUL'S ETERNALITY	183
CONCERNING THE TRINITY	194
IS THE SOUL PROPHETIC?	197
DISAPPOINTMENTS	201
HOW CAN WE HOPE TO ATTAIN PERFECTION	203
THE METAPHYSICAL ASPECT OP IMMORTALITY	206
KARMA AS INFINITE PATIENCE	213
THE PRE-EXISTENCE OF THE SOUL	215
FORM	218
A THINKER	221
THE OCCULT	221
THE CAUSES OF SUFFERING	225
SOUL SCIENCE	230
REFLECTIONS	238
THE RELATION OF THE INDIVIDUAL	239
TO THE UNIVERSAL MIND	239
SEED THOUGHTS	242
ONE OF THE NINE INESTIMABLES	243
THE SPIRITUAL WORLD	245

THE NEW BIRTH	252
ROOM FOR THE SOUL	255
THE FIRE MYSTERY	257
THE ELIXIR OF YOUTH	265
STORMS	268
THE ORIGIN AND THE SEAT OF EVIL	270
GOD IN MAN	278
GOD AND MAN	280
PROPHECY INTELLIGIBLE	282
METAPHYSICAL LAWS	288
CONCERNING EVIL	292
ALL THINGS WORK TOGETHER FOR GOOD	295
EQUAL TO THE OCCASION	297
THE ART OF DEFEATING ADVERSITY	300
THE MESSAGE OF THE GREAT INITIATES	307
THE SEVEN NATURAL LAWS	310
HARMONY	312
QUESTIONS AND ANSWERS	316
Author and Managing Editor	319
Books by the Author	320
The Artist and Illustrator	321

Introduction

The growing popularity of True Occultism and Mysticism throughout the whole world has at last induced us to try and issue a series, books that should be an honor to the Universal Father, to True Occultism and Mysticism, and to those who stand for all that is good in humanity. There is also another matter which has induced us to try to see whether such an effort would be appreciated.

This demand we will, therefore, meet, and "The Initiates" will be such a series of which every true student will be proud. We shall not, and will not, cater to that class of sensationalists who would make you believe that by studying a course in hypnotism, which they will sell you for a few dollars, you can be able to make men be your slaves or cause dollars to roll into your hands, for such things are impossible, and not only are they impossible, but it is this class of human ghouls who have brought down shame and disgrace upon a science which holds within itself all the religions ever known.

Not only does Mysticism hold within itself all religious teachings, but it holds the histories of such religions, and it can point the way from the lowest step upon the ladder up to the very highest, which is Imperial Initiation—the finding of the Christ. We shall stand for all that is pure and good in all religious beliefs. We shall try to give to our readers the truth concerning all religious beliefs and will at all times try to get the truth concerning all matters which concern our work. While on the one hand we shall not uphold anything, nor anyone whom we know to be a fraud, yet it will not be our desire to tear down any system of thought, but rather to build up a pure and sublime system of philosophy, which shall appeal to the heart of mankind instead of to the mind, as so many do. It is not our desire to destroy, but to build up. Ours shall be an evolution and not a revolution. We believe that we are in a position to give to our readers that which none other can give them, for we are in touch with men and orders in every civilized country in the world, and we are in a position to obtain true facts concerning these matters from any part of the globe, and at short notice. Regarding the orders of this series, we need only say that the true teachings, so far as they may be given to the profane world, will be given from time to time, and one of our greatest desires is that the old Egyptian religion may be explained in these pages, so that all men, and more especially all Christians, may know that the Egyptian priests did not teach idolatry, but that the people themselves, not understanding the greater mysteries taught, formed idol worship in spite of the teachings of the priests. These are but a few of the things that we shall hope to give to our readers, and all that we shall ask in return is that each and every one truly interested shall do all in his or her power to help and make this series a success. We all know that at the present age of commercialism, nothing can be accomplished without the current coin of the realm. It will be our duty to do the work and obtain the material, but we must ask all those who have this great work at heart to do all in their power, so that we may receive the "sinews of war" wherewith to carry on the work, and if all will help in this, we can assure each and every one that we will try to give them much more than they pay for.

The Initiates

THE FIRST

Adam was the first inventor of Arts because he had knowledge of all things as well after the fall as before. Thence he predicted the world's destruction by water. For this cause, too, it came about that his successors erected two tablets of stone, on which they engraved all Natural Arts in hieroglyphical characters, in order that their posterity might also become acquainted with this prediction, that so it might be heeded, and provision made in time of danger. Subsequently, Noah found one of these tablets under Mount Araroth, after the deluge. In this table were described the courses of the upper firmament and of the lower globe, and also of the planets. At length, this Universal Knowledge was divided into several parts, and lessened the vigor and power.

By means of this separation, one man became an astronomer, another a magician, another a cabalist, and a fourth an alchemist. Abraham, that Vulcanic Tubal-Cain, a consummate astrologer and arithmetician, carried the art out of the land of Canaan into Egypt, whereupon the Egyptians rose to so great a height and dignity that this wisdom was derived from them by other nations. The patriarch Jacob painted, as it were, the sheep with various colors; and this was done by magic; for in the theology of the Chaldeans, Hebrews, Persians and Egyptians they held these arts to be the highest philosophy, to be learned by their chief nobles and priests.

So it was in the time of Moses, when both the priests and also the physicians were chosen from among the Magi—the priests for the judgment of what related to health, especially in the knowledge of leprosy. Moses, likewise, was instructed in the Egyptian schools, at the cost of and care of Pharaoh's daughter, so that he excelled in all the wisdom and learning of that people. Thus, too, was it with Daniel, who in his youthful days imbibed the learning of the Chaldeans, so that he became a Cabalist. Witness his divine predictions and his exposition of those words, "Mene, Mene, Tecelphares." These words can be understood by the prophetic and cabalistic art. This cabalistic art was perfectly familiar to, and in constant use by, Moses and the Prophets. The Prophet Elias foretold many things by his cabalistic numbers. So did the Wise Men of old, by this natural and mystical art, learn to know God rightly. They abode in His laws, and walked in His statutes with great firmness. It is also evident in the Book of Samuel that the Berelists did not follow the devil's part, but became, by divine permission, partakers of visions and veritable apparitions, whereof we shall treat more at length.

This gift is granted by the Lord God to those priests who walk in the divine precepts. It was a custom among the Persians never to admit anyone as king unless he was a wise man, pre-eminent in reality as well as in name. This is clear from the customary names of their kings, for they were called wise men. Such were those wise men and Persian magi who came from the East to seek out the Lord Jesus, and are called natural priests. The Egyptians, also, having obtained this magic and philosophy from the Chaldeans and Persians, desired that their priests should learn the same wisdom; and they came so fruitful and successful therein that all the neighboring countries admired them. For this reason, Hermes was so truly named Trismegistus, because he was a king, a priest, a prophet, a magician, and a sophist of natural things. Such another was Zoroaster.

II

When a son of Noah possessed the third part of the world after the flood, this art broke into Chaldea and Persia, and thence spread into Egypt. The art, having been found out by the superstitious and idolatrous Greeks, some of them, who were wiser than the rest, betook themselves to the Chaldeans and Egyptians, so that they might draw the same wisdom from their schools. Since, however, the theological study of the law of Moses did not satisfy them, they trusted to their own peculiar genius, and fell away from the right foundation of those Natural Arts and Secrets.

This is evident from their fabulous conceptions, and from their errors in respecting the doctrine of Moses. It was the custom of the Egyptians to put forward the traditions of that surpassing wisdom only in enigmatical figures and abstruse histories and terms. This was afterwards followed by Homer with marvelous poetical skill; and Pythagoras, who also was acquainted with it, seeing that he comprised in his writings many things out of the law of Moses and the Old Testament.

In like manner, Hippocrates, Thales of Miletus, Anaxagoras, Democritus, and others, did not scruple to fix their minds on the same thing. And yet none of them were practiced in the true Astrology, Geometry, Arithmetic, or Medicine, because their pride prevented this, since they would not admit disciples belonging to other nations than their own. Even when they had got some insight from the Chaldeans and Egyptians, they became more arrogant still than they were before by nature, and without any diffidence propounded the subject substantially indeed, but mixed with subtle fictions or falsehoods; and then they attempted to elaborate a certain kind of philosophy which descended from them to the Latins. These in their turn, being educated herewith, adorned it with their own doctrines, and by these the philosophy was spread over Europe. Many academies were founded for the propagation of their dogmas and rules, so that the young might be instructed; and this system flourished with the Germans, and other nations, right down to the present day.

III

The Chaldeans, Persians, and Egyptians had all of them the same knowledge of the secrets of nature, and also the same religion. It was only the names that differed. The Chaldeans and Persians called their doctrine Sophia and Magic; and the Egyptians, because of the sacrifice, called their wisdom Priestcraft. The magic of the Persians, and the theology of the Egyptians were both taught in the schools of old. Though there were many schools and learned men in Arabia, Africa, and Greece, such as Albumazar, Abenzagel, Geber, Rhasis, and Avicenna among the Arabians; and among the Greeks, Machaon, Podalirius, Pythagoras, Anaxagoras, Democritus, Plato, Aristotle, and Rhodianus; still there were different opinions amongst them as to the wisdom of the Egyptians on points wherein they themselves differed, and whereupon they disagreed with it.

For this reason Pythagoras could not be called a wise man, because the Egyptian priestcraft and wisdom were not perfectly taught, although he received therefrom many mysteries and arcana; and that Anaxagoras had received a great many as well, is clear from his discussions on the subject of Sol and its Stone, which he left behind him after his death. Yet he differed in many respects from the Egyptians. Even they would not be called wise men or Magi; but, following Pythagoras, they assumed the name of philosophy.

Yet they gathered no more than a few gleams like shadows from the magic of the Persians and Egyptians. But Moses, Abraham, Solomon, Adam, and the wise men that came from the East to Christ, were true Magi, Divine Sophists and Cabalists. Of this art and wisdom, the

Greeks knew very little or nothing at all; and therefore we shall leave this philosophical wisdom of the Greeks as being a mere speculation, utterly distinct and separate from the other true arts and sciences.

IV

Many persons have endeavored to investigate and make use of the secret magic of these Wise Men; but it has not yet been accomplished. Many even of our own age, exalt Trithemius, others Bacon and Agrippa. For magic and the cabala—two things apparently quite distinct—knowing why they do so. Magic, indeed, is an art and faculty whereby the elementary bodies, their fruits, properties, virtues and hidden operations are comprehended. But the Cabala, by a subtle understanding of the Scriptures, seems to trace out the way to God for men, to show them how they may act with Him, and prophesy from Him; for the Cabala is full of divine mysteries, even as magic is full of natural secrets.

It teaches of and foretells the nature of things to come as well as of things present, since its operation consists in knowing the inner constitution of all creatures, of celestial as well as terrestrial bodies; what is latent within them; what their occult virtues are; for what they were originally designed, and with what properties they are endowed. These and the like subjects are the bonds wherewith things celestial are bound up with things of the earth, as may sometimes be seen in their operation, even with the bodily eyes.

Such a conjunction of celestial influences, whereby the heavenly virtues acted upon inferior bodies, was formerly called by the Magi a Gamahea, or the marriage of the celestial powers and properties with elementary bodies. Hence ensued the excellent commixtures of all bodies, celestial and terrestrial, namely, of the sun and planets, likewise vegetables, minerals and animals.

The devil attempted with his whole force and endeavor to darken this light; nor was he wholly frustrated in his hopes, for he deprived all Greece of it, and, in place thereof, introduced among that people human speculations and simple blasphemies against God and against His Son. Magic, it is true, had its origin in the Divine Ternary and arose from the Trinity of God. For God marked all His creatures with this Ternary and engraved its hieroglyph on them with His own finger. Nothing in the nature of things can be assigned or produced that lacks this magistery of the Divine Ternary, or that does not even ocularly prove it. The creature teaches us to understand and see the Creator Himself, as St. Paul testifies to the Romans.

This covenant of the Divine Ternary, diffused throughout the whole substance of things, is indissoluble. By this, also, we have the secrets of all nature from the four elements. For the Ternary, with the Magical Quaternary, produces a perfect Septenary, endowed with many Arcana and demonstrated by things which are known. When the Quaternary rests in the Ternary, then arises the Light of the World on the horizon of eternity, and by the assistance of God gives us the whole bond. Here also it refers to the virtues and operations of all creatures, and to their use, since they are stamped and marked with their arcana, signs, characters and figures, so that there is left in them scarcely the smallest occult point which is not made clear on examination. Then when the Quaternary and the Ternary mount to the Denary is accomplished their retrogression or reduction to unity. Herein is comprised all the occult wisdom of things which God had made plainly manifest to men, both by His Word and by the creatures of His hands, so that they may have a true knowledge of them. This shall be made more clear in another place.

V

The Magi in their wisdom-asserted that all creatures might be brought to one unified substance, which substance, they affirm, may, by purifications and purgation's, attain to so high a degree of subtlety, such divine nature and occult property, as to work wonderful results. For they considered that by returning to earth, and by a supreme magical separation, a certain perfect substance would come forth, which is at length, by many industrious and prolonged preparations, exalted and raised up above the range of vegetable substances into mineral, above mineral into metallic, and above perfect metallic substances into a perpetual and divine quintessence, including in itself the essence of all celestial and terrestrial creatures. The Arabs and Greeks, by the occult characters and hieroglyphic descriptions of the Persians and the Egyptians, attained to secret and abstruse mysteries. When these were obtained and partially understood, they saw with their own eyes, in the course of experimenting, many wonderful and strange effects. But since the super celestial operations lay more deeply hidden than their capacity could penetrate, they did not call this a super celestial Arcanum according to the institution of the Magi, but the Arcanum of the

Philosopher's Stone, according to the counsel and judgment of Pythagoras. Whoever obtained the stone overshadowed it with various enigmatical figures, deceptive resemblances, comparisons, and fictitious titles, so that its matter might remain occult. Very little or no knowledge of it, therefore, can be had from them.

It is thus why so very much is written concerning the Philosopher's Stone by the old master and so very little understood. All, or nearly all, of them were from the outside schools instead of having passed the true Egyptian initiation.

THE ANCIENT FAITH

While at this time of year the flooding condition of the Nile is such that the full beauty of these remains cannot be viewed as during July when the water no more covers the Temples, at this part of the year the tourist may view the beautiful Lotus capitals partly above the water. And as we approach closer the remains of these Ptolemaic capitals, which to us even yet stand as a lasting monument of the beauty and grandeur of that first combination of Egyptian and Greek art.

We find the mind in passing scenes of mystery and fiction trying to penetrate the obscure veils of the past in a futile attempt to picture in reality those days whose architecture we now look upon with an eye of wonder and admiration, the Lotus flowers, delicately carved petals, which alone would suggest the greatness and appreciative minds who fashioned them in the insensible rock.

Though, as has been said, much of the beauty lies hidden beneath the waters, held in check by that great engineering achievement, the Assouan Dam, yet above all and dry, stands in view the Temple of Isis. Isis who has withstood the war of the elements; whose glories at one day was the mecca of the scholar of civilization, no more are you the central shrine of wisdom and religion. Your day is past, but in passing you have served your time, yet left us a key that will eventually unlock to us much that is otherwise lost. Oh! Isis, you who have withstood the ravages of time so nobly, how soon will you too give way to the changes of progress and become a thing of the past to be covered by the waters.

But evolution works her own changes, and the world belongs to her chain of subjects. Then let her pass, no more peerless as of old, yet we know her the mother of old, the great; whose children now in the height of manhood are giving to the world but a slight departure from her motherly counsel. And yet, you stand among us to be marveled at by the sons of man. We cannot help reverting the scenes back to the time which gave her birth, and that mighty religion, though not perfect, was beautiful in its philosophy and conception of nature and her laws. Our ancient brethren out of necessity, early learning the necessity of light and heat for the preservation of all life, the people were early to note the two points in the heavens which limited the duration of the strength of the sun's rays, and hence the duration of the creative power upon the earth was the one concern of all.

For scarcely has the sun in his annual tour reached one of these points when the awakening of nature again takes place and the world becomes beautiful because from his orb there flows that power and prolific force. It was then in ancient theology that the resurrection of God took place, and His awakening so powerfully felt upon earth, and man was glad and gave thanks accordingly. But when he again reached that foremost point opposite, his powers became exceedingly feeble and nature fast asleep because of his feebleness. Here have you the mystery of Adonis wounded. The sadness felt by Venus.

Osiris precipitated into a tomb by Typhon whose generative powers the disconsolate Isis never recovered. What sign of distress more certain to render man sorrowful than each day noting the fast coming death of the "Light of the world." Slowly becoming weaker, he leaves the earth's green verdures to die.

Typhons blasts mock the children of earth. That gentle temperature which the people enjoyed now passed with the sun's passing. The flowers have died; the trees loaded with fruit, the fields with grain, have changed their dress to a sad and melancholy aspect. Earth's beauty and plenty gone, man's happiness had departed with his God. The departure having plunged the earth into sadness and gloom, only his return could free her. He was the Creator of all these blessings, for with His departure, they were taken with him. His rays the soul of vegetation, for it languished and ceased at their departure. How long will he remain away or will his departure plunge nature into eternal chaos? From whence came the powers that breathed life into it?

Again, the rise and fall of this river upon which depended the agriculture of the people whose mysteries rise and fall seemed to those early people to defy unraveling as to its cause. For its rise seemed to give no warning time of approach. Thus early unable to foretell this cause, their eyes turned heavenward (skyward). Here was the solution to be found, and a watch was set upon that coming star whose annual warnings was perfect, was beautiful in its philosophy and conception of nature and her laws.

Our ancient brethren out of necessity, early learning the necessity of light and heat for the preservation of all life, the people were early to note the two points in the heavens which limited the duration of the strength of the sun's rays, and hence the duration of the creative power upon the earth was the one concern of all. For scarcely has the sun in his annual tour reached one of these points when the awakening of nature again takes place and the world becomes beautiful because from his orb there flows that power and prolific force.

It was then in ancient theology that the resurrection of God took place, and His awakening so powerfully felt upon earth, and man was glad and gave thanks accordingly. But when he again reached that foremost point opposite, his powers became exceedingly feeble and nature fast asleep because of his feebleness. Here have you the mystery of Adonis wounded. The sadness felt by Venus. Osiris precipitated into a tomb by Typhon whose generative powers the disconsolate Isis never recovered. What sign of distress more certain to render man sorrowful than each day noting the fast coming death of the "Light of the world." Slowly becoming weaker, he leaves the earth's green verdures to die.

Typhon's blasts mock the children of earth. That gentle temperature which the people enjoyed now passed with the sun's passing. The flowers have died, the trees loaded with fruit, the fields with grain, have changed their dress to a sad and melancholy aspect. Earth's beauty and plenty gone, man's happiness had departed with his God.

The departure having plunged the earth into sadness and gloom, only his return could free her. He was the Creator of all these blessings, for with His departure they were taken-with him. His rays the soul of vegetation, for it languished and ceased at their departure. How long will he remain away or will his departure plunge nature into eternal chaos?

From whence came the powers that breathed life into it? Again the rise and fall of this river upon which depended the agriculture of the people whose mysteries rise and fall seemed to those early people to defy unraveling as to its cause. For its rise seemed to give no warning time of approach. Thus, early unable to foretell this cause, their eyes turned heavenward (skyward). Here was the solution to be found and a watch was set upon that coming star whose annual warnings was timely and certain.

Together with the mysterious east wind it served to make the people search yet farther into the mysterious and discover the nature of the heretofore unknown. Thus, as has been said, from the warning given by that star, whose name was Anubus, they were able to foretell the time of the inundation with an exactness, the people would then retire to the higher places with their herds and flocks.

How could a person whose sole protection in that day was shown them in the heavens, wisely do other than search its starry hosts for solutions other than this? And while much aside from scientific astronomy is the subject of ridicule, let it not be forgotten that the heavens have taught man many things that even the telescope in this day would fail to reveal.

Today our people, whose glory is a faded one and whose misery is not the least of mankind, scarcely remember, except in a misty legend, the origin of this star, and of the greatness of the primitive races. Yet it matters little.

No longer does the dog star's warning disturb the quietude of the common peasant. The hands of men have bridled and control this tumultuous stream much the same as you might harness and use the power of a little rivulet. And the hands of man daily meet out the required amount of water necessary for agricultural purposes.

By the order daily given from Cairo to the one man who has entire control of the dam, daily is there given, by the turn of a handle and the touch of a button, the amount of water required by the peasantry for a thousand miles. Thus, while man has destroyed the monuments of the past, he has also harnessed and controlled a stream that for thousands of years had the agriculture of a whole country at its mercy. But even this might have been accomplished without the destruction wrought. Again, let us approach the philosophical side of Osiris.

To the Initiate then as now, it is only a representative type of active generating and beneficent force of nature. Isis is the passive force of nature, the power of conceiving and bringing forth into action in the sublunary world. Yet deeper in the mysteries Osiris united to Isis conveys to the mind of the higher Initiates the works of the universal force this is the soul of all that is. As I view the interior of the Temple of Isis I imagine I see as of old the solemn ceremonies and processions, again the gayeties of feasts and festivals. At certain seasons there seems, as in the hazy past, once more to appear the vision, aside from the set one of each new moon.

The principal one, which was that of the new moon in Phamenoth, the entrance of Osiris into the moon on which planet he was supposed to fecundate. Isis in turn procuring that blessing for the earth. The other principal feast being that of the Thirtieth of Epiphi, which was celebrated with feasts and worship. Nothing is usually more confusing to the student than the many head dresses given the figure of Isis. You who have given the history of Ancient Egypt much study know the principal worship, that is, the religion was derived from astronomical observations, and considering that the divisions of time were made according to the sun's passing through the different constellations of stars according to their system, know also that in that day printing was a thing unknown and reading scarcely understood among any but the few.

It was then necessary that some more simple way of communicating time, feasts and general information had to be adopted. This was accomplished by exposing certain head dresses and other symbols to the public. Thus were the Priests not only in their day concerned in the religious worship of the people but conducted weather departments of agriculture and law as well. Of the deeper mysteries, it is not within the scope of this article to deal. First because they are forbidden, second because they would not be cherished by an idle reader and the desirous ones can always secure them, if willing to follow the path.

I am therefore not permitted to say farther than only that which tends to make man better and nobler by the instructions and contemplation of scenes peculiar to initiation has been, or is enacted before the eyes of the candidate entering these societies who rightfully can claim succession. As a conclusion, we can say that the greater mysteries but gave new birth to that divine spark smoldering within each human breast, and the soul's awaking to the true knowledge of self, our relation to the rest of mankind and creation. They no longer live for self alone, to gratify naught but their own physical wants, but seek to benefit the world. Seeking to illumine thereby that vision that has been the joy and song of the Initiates.

II

The inundation of the Nile, as has been said, lasted from ten to thirteen weeks, the waters rising from twelve to eighteen cubits, thus overflowing the land, so enriching it that seldom was a failure in crops known to our people of old. Again, you all know that the climate, aside from a few months, is delightful to dwell in, and the production of vegetables and cattle far exceeded the demands of the people.

This great blessing, so plentiful when neighboring countries had famines, served its purpose well in attracting the eyes of the world to Egypt and her religion. Returning to the original subject, it was early noticed that the rise of the Nile was always preceded by an etesian wind, which in itself served as a warning of the approaching inundation. This wind, coming from the North and flowing South, occurred about the time the sun would pass under the sign now called the crab. This again gave further proof of the theory, that all nature is governed by certain fixed laws, and understanding these laws and in living in harmony with them lays the secret of all power and greatness amongst men and nature. Having observed the etesian wind, they further learned upon close observation that the rise of waters occurred close to the time when the sun was under the stars of Leo (the Lion), near those of Cancer, following this shortly before sunrise appeared Thaut (the barker, also called Anubis). Thus born of the mother of necessity, as has been said, man early began to contemplate the starry hosts, and this gave birth to the Sacerdotal Order.

In order to ascertain the depth of the waters, a cross, marked by one or more cross bars, was employed; a circle surmounting it was frequently used to signify Providence governing the peculiar works of Nature. Thus, we have the origin of one of the most beautiful of symbols of the day, as it suggests to us the hope of the Christian. So at that time it betokened deliverance and salvation, for had not the waters reached the necessary heights no crops might be expected. But no longer does it measure the Nile; it stands alone as the Christian Pilgrims' hope, and points to Jesus, the one accredited for that religion, whose teachings of simplicity and beauty is the bosom upon which rests the head of many Pilgrims. To the Mystic Societies this cross has deeper significance, as has the different mounts and the garden of Gethsemene. These occur in the lives of each. Traveling the paths, we are sure to encounter the obstacles by the way, and many there are who are crucified upon that same cross of superstition.

Returning to the original subject, it has been charged against our ancient kin that they were morally degenerate and idolatrous. This is an error in part. Though graven images were used as symbols, the educated seen them but as attributes of that universal God whose goodness pervades all nature, and while more or less hidden (for obvious reasons) their belief in one God and immortality of the soul after death of the body was the prevalent doctrine, and idolatry in Christian lands today is equally as great, for let us not forget that idolatry properly defined does not consist alone in bowing to images, but in the worship or service to such forces or parts of nature as are not thoroughly understood but supposed to have virtue. In other language, he who bows the knee prays and knows not the meaning thereof is an idolater. Speaking of the initiation, as conducted in those early days, we can safely say the percentage of applicants were greater than today. Not this alone, but many there were, as today, who only seek initiation that they may be better enabled to succeed in the race for power and honor. In other words, many believed it a shortcut to fame and riches. How many are there today who look upon these studies much the same as did many of old, searching for the key that would unlock the storehouse of earth's treasures?

Those who begin the study of the mysteries solely for selfish purposes destroy the very fruit that would have been theirs had they started out desiring solely to benefit their race. Let us examine the lives of the Great Mystics. Note the life of the Nazarite and his teachings. Are they not all labors for the uplifting of the race, with not a selfish thought? Others seek the mysteries that they may secure greatness through prophecy. Those who desire to attain these powers should not forget that all true prophecy must be based upon a knowledge of God's law, which is at the same time natural law, and requires a complete education concerning astronomical matters, and based upon a history of the same upon which to base future predictions.

While prophecies are given to man much the same as ordinary thought, in our highest and purest conditions of mind, yet great prophecies concerning nations and realms are only revealed to the true scholar of the heavens. Forget not that the heavens are God's Chart upon which are written lessons intended for man's instruction, and the wise of all ages knew this. And you who are trying to decipher the many tangible mysteries found in the Bible, and Koran, as well as all mysterious books of old that seem to confuse the earnest seeker after truth, note this. Some are led to think these writings are only myths describing some phase of planetary life and locations. Far from it.

Each tale records a history within itself, and by computing the sum, stranger things than you yet have dreamed of will rise to your vision. But as you pass on, remember man himself is the highest and noblest production of the Gods. To live in harmony and peace with your fellow-man is to live in harmony with the Gods. It was Leigh Hunt, in "Abou Ben Adhem," who so wisely wrote:

"Abou Ben Adhem—may his tribe increase—Awoke one night from a deep dream of peace, And saw within the moonlight in his room, Making it rich, and like a lily in bloom, An angel writing in a book of gold. Exceeding peace had made Ben Adhem bold, And to the presence in the room he said: "What writest thou?" The vision raised its head, And with a voice made all of one sweet accord, Answered, "The names of those who love the Lord." "And is mine one?" said Abou. "Nay, not so," Replied the angel. . . . Abou spoke more low, But cheerily still and said, "I pray thee then, Write me as one who loves his fellow man." The angel wrote and vanished. The next night It came with a great wakening light, And showed the names whom love of God had blest. And lo, Ben Adhem's name led all the rest."

To you who are seekers after the hidden wisdom of the elect, let those words of Leigh Hunt bury themselves deep in your memory.

For he who is nearest divinity is a servant of his race. Would you meet the angel of purest light? Then visit the abode of the lowly and the poor. Mark well the place where desolation is visited upon a person, and as you approach these distressed of your race, you will see the footprints of the divine. Their works are done quietly; no trumpet announces their good deeds, but born of the "Viewless One," they find pleasure in kindly deeds amongst the needy.

Would you know the souls who are farthest from the Gods? Then listen to those who call forth from the high place, saying, "I am the great;" "Behold in me light;" "I am better than ye," etc. Look instead upon those as masters whom persecution is driving to the grave prematurely.

Watch those who having done an act of kindness say unto them that receive, "go thy way in peace, telling no man of things thou receiveth." You, who are striving and struggling for supremacy over a carnal mind and body, think no harm of any creature, for that thought once taking form will only be one enemy of your soul, for after traveling its cycle it will return to you with greater power than when you sent it forth.

Go forth, O soul, and view the beautiful, dazzling rays of the sun, feel its heat and life-giving force, and as you do so, resolve that henceforth you will endeavor to live in harmony with the secret teachings of old which, being interpreted, is, "I, Osiris (the sun), give unto you the children of earth, the herb and the insensible rock; to you all, do I give my life, my strength, that your lives may be made happier by my presence. As I give unto you freely and without reward, so do ye to one another works of mercy, that I may see your good works amongst the needy."

If you will let the soul of nature unfold to you, her bosom, and resting thy soul upon her sacred breast ever long will that "still small voice" whisper what shall be thy life's occupation. The world is full of misconceptions regarding nature and immortality. If you, reader, belong to that class who would bathe in the purer, freer air, and are searching for unfoldment and development to the end, which is freedom eternally, I say, if this be your desire, depend not wholly upon study, but, in earnest, take up the cross of your race, help bear their burdens and though in the end you be crucified, yet will you thereby advance the interests of your own soul. Every kind deed, gentle smile, or good thought is a chariot to bear you into the land of the sublime.

I have dwelt much upon this necessary habit of doing good, in order to reach the heights of "initiation," as I have met many who sought the divine powers but love not those tasks that are a part of our labor in the climb to the divine. Those who are willing to labor for the master eventually become masters. But you who are traveling the path selfishly change your life to one of unselfishness, or sooner or later you too will either return to the ranks from which you came, unsatisfied, declaring the mystic fraternities impostors, or, overcome by the forces you would otherwise have mastered, end in despair.

Hark, the still small voice speaks; obey its kindly admonitions, and soon will you discover those paths that will lead you unto the land of peace and true happiness.

PURIFIED SPIRIT IN MAN

Training and Development

Man was regarded by Paracelsus as himself in a special manner the true quintessence. After God had created all the elements, stars and every other created thing, and had disposed them according to His will, He proceeded, lastly, to the forming of man. He extracted the essence out of the four elements into one mass. He extracted also the essence of wisdom, art and reason out of the stars, and this twofold essence He congested into one mass, which mass Scripture calls the slime of earth. From that mass, two bodies were made—the sidereal and the elementary. These, according to the light of nature, are called the quintum esse.

The mass was extracted, and therein the firmament and the elements were condensed. What was extracted from the four after this manner constituted a fifth. The quintessence is the nucleus and the place of the essence and properties of all things in the universal world. All nature came into the hands of God—all potency, all property, all essence of the superior and inferior globe. All these had God joined in His hand, and from these He formed man according to His image.—Philosophia Sagax. Man, therefore, contains part of everything that was, that is, or that shall be. Herein is a mighty secret.

THE MAGIC RITES

Explaining an Ancient Mystery, which includes the becoming of man. Possibly one of the highest and most elaborate Rites, a knowledge of which has descended to us from the days of antiquity, were those of Eleusis and Bacchus of Greece, and the Saturnalia of Rome.

These, no less than the Samothracian rites were unquestionably derived from Egypt, although they were ages old before they reached Egypt, the mystery itself having come from Atlantis, and as the so called Eleusinian Mysteries probably afford the best representation of their famous Egyptian model, the Isis and Osiric Mysteries it is to a brief account of this famous pageant that we shall call the reader's attention.

So much has been written in fragments concerning these Great Mysteries, and the general tone of every description so invariably pre-supposes that the reader is already acquainted with the basic idea upon which it discourses, that we deem it not out of place to present a consecutive statement of this Mystery, the underlying principles upon which these mysteries were founded, and the solving of the mystery itself. For the first, we quote from "Taylor's Eleusinian and Bacchic Rites," published by Dr. Alexander Wilder, the greatest Platonic student living of late.

"Proserpina, the daughter of Ceres by Jupiter, as she was gathering tender flowers, in the new Spring, was ravished from her delightful abodes by Pluto, and being carried from thence through thick woods, and over a length of sea, was brought by Pluto into a cavern, the residence of departed spirits, over whom she afterwards ruled with absolute sway. But Ceres, upon discovering the loss of her daughter, with lighted torches, and begirt with a serpent, wandered over the whole earth for the purpose of finding her, till she came to Eleusis; there she found her daughter, and also taught to the Eleusinian's the cultivation of corn."

In this fable, Ceres represents the evolution of that intuitional part of our nature which we properly denominate intellect, and Proserpina that living, self-moving, and animating part which we call soul. But in order to understand the secret meaning of this fable, it will be necessary to give a more explicit detail of the particulars attending the abduction, from the beautiful poem of Claudian on this subject. From this elegant production, we learn that Ceres, who was afraid lest some violence should be offered to Proserpina, on account of her inimitable beauty, conveyed her privately to Sicily, and concealed her in a house built on purpose by the Cyclops, while she herself directs her course to the temple of Cybele, the mother of the Gods. Here, then, we see the first cause of the soul's descent, namely, the abandoning of a life wholly according to the higher intellect, which is occultly signified by the separation of Proserpina from Ceres. Afterward, we are told that Jupiter instructs Venus to go to this abode, and betray Proserpina from her retirement, that Pluto may be enabled to carry her away; and to prevent any suspicion in the virgin's mind, he commands Diana and Phallas to go in company.

The three goddesses arriving, find Proserpina at work on a scarf for her mother; in which she had embroidered the primitive chaos, and the formation of the world. Now by Venus in this part of the narration we must understand desire, which, even in the Celestial regions (for such is the residence of Proserpina till she is ravished by Pluto), begins silently and steadily to creep into the recesses of the soul. By Minerva, we must conceive the rational powers of the soul, and by Diana, nature, or the merely natural and vegetable part of our composition; both of which are now ensnared through the allurements of desire.

And lastly, the web in which Proserpina had displayed all the fair variety of the material world, beautifully represents the commencement of illusive operations through which the soul becomes ensnared with the beauty of imaginative forms. "Proserpina, forgetful of her parent's commands, is represented as venturing from her retreat, through the treacherous persuasions of Venus."

"After this we behold her issuing on the plain with Minerva and Diana, and attended by a beauteous train of nymphs, who are evident symbols of the world of generation, and are, therefore, the proper companions of the soul about to fall into its fluctuating realms." But the design of Proserpina, in venturing from her retreat, is beautifully significant of her approaching descent; for she rambles from home for the purpose of gathering flowers; and this in a lawn replete with the most enchanting variety, and exhaling the most delicious odors. This is a manifest image of the soul operating principally according to the natural and external life, and so becoming effeminated and ensnared through the delusive attractions of sensitive form.

Minerva (the rational faculty in the case), likewise gives herself wholly to the dangerous employment, and abandons the proper characteristics of her nature for the destructive revels of desire. "After this, Pluto, forcing his passage through the earth, seizes on Proserpina, and carries her away with him, notwithstanding the resistance of Minerva and Diana. They, indeed, are forbid by Jupiter, who in this place signifies fate, to attempt her deliverance. "Pluto hurries Proserpina into the infernal regions; in other words, the soul is sunk into the profound depth and darkness of a material nature. A description of her marriage next succeeds her union with the dark tenement of the body."

Night is with great beauty and propriety, introduced as standing by the nuptial couch, and confirming the oblivious league. For the soul, through her union with a material body, becomes an inhabitant of darkness, and subject to the empire of night; in consequence of which she dwells wholly with delusive phantoms, and till she breaks, her fetters is deprived of the intuitive perception of that which is real and true.

"The reader may observe how Proserpina, being represented as confined in the dark recess of a prison, and bound with fetters, confirms the explanation of the fable here given as symbolical of the descent of the soul; for such, as we have already largely proved, is the condition of the soul from its union with the body, according to the uniform testimony of the most ancient philosophers and priests.

"Throughout this mystery, it must be borne in mind that the Egyptians, Greeks, and all ancient as well as classic nations, believed in the doctrine that the soul had once existed in a purely spiritual state; that, tempted by the demands of sense, it had yearned for mortal birth—birth into a material body—descended or fallen into an earthly condition and by its probationary sufferings and trials on earth, regained the Paradisiacal bliss from which it had fallen. These ideas are represented in the Legend of Proserpina, and constitutes the chief legend of all other Ancient Mysteries."

The explanation of this legend as taught by Ancient Mystic Oriental Masonry. "Before appearing on earth, man lived in a spiritual world, similar to the one in which he lives on leaving the earth. Each awaits his turn in this world to appear on earth, an appearance necessary, a life of trials none can escape." "The life anterior, which we have all passed through, was, so to speak, a life of nothingness, of childbirth, of happiness like that which we enjoy on our exit from the earth; but this happiness cannot be comprehended, because it is not accompanied with sensations to prove its sweet reality, therefore God has deemed it fit that we should pass through these successive lives, the first, on the globes of which I speak to you—a life unknown, of beatitude, devoid of sensation—the second, the one you enjoy, a life of action, sensation; a painful life placed between the two, to demonstrate through its contrast the sweetness of, the third, the life of good and evil, without which we should not be able to appreciate the happy state reserved for us."

"That the soul is an emanation from Deity, and in its original essence is all purity, truth and wisdom, is an axiom which the disembodied learn, when the powers of memory are sufficiently awakened to perceive the states of existence anterior to mortal birth. In the Paradise of Purity and Love, souls spring up like blossoms in the All Father's garden of immortal beauty. It is the tendency of the divine nature whose chief attributes are love and wisdom, heat, and light, to repeat itself eternally, and mirror forth its own perfection in scintillations from itself."

These sparks of heavenly fire become souls, and as the effect must share in the nature of the cause, the fire which warms into life, also illuminates into light, hence the soul emanations from the divine are all love and heat, whilst the illuminations of light, which streams ever from the great Central Sun of Being, irradiates all souls with corresponding beams of light. Born of love which corresponds to divine heat and warmth, and irradiated with light, which is divine wisdom and truth, the first and most powerful souls repeated the action of the Supreme Originator, gave off emanations from their own being, some higher, some lower, the highest tending upward into spiritual essences, the lowest forming particle matter.

These denser emanations, following out the creative law, aggregated into suns, satellites, worlds, and each repeating the story of creation. Suns gave birth to systems, and every member of a system became a theatre of sub-ordinate states of spiritual or material existence. "Earths that have attained to the capacity to support organic life, necessarily attract it. Earths demand, heaven supplies it. From whence? As the earths groan for the lordship of superior beings to rule over them, the spirits in the distant Edens hear the whispers of the tempting serpent, the animal principle, the urgent intellect, which appeals to the blest souls in their distant paradises, fill them with indescribable longings (desires of Proserpina) for change, for broader vistas of knowledge, for mightier powers; they would be as the gods, and know good and evil; and in this urgent appeal of the earths for man, and this involuntary yearning of the spirit for intellectual knowledge, the union is effected between the two, and the spirit becomes precipitated into the realms of matter to undergo a pilgrimage through the probationary states of earth, and only to regain paradise again by the fulfillment of that pilgrimage."

It is well that all students should bear these teachings in mind, for it is one of the foundations of true religion. It gives that firm truth which no creed can give to you, for as we come from the gods, so must we eventually return to God.

PLANES OF CONSCIOUSNESS

Consciousness is not a thing, but a condition, a mode of the Divine Action. Consciousness says of itself: "Before creation was, I am."

Consciousness is the imminence of the Almighty in creation. Just as all power and energy in creation is an expression of His omnipotence; so all consciousness in creation is an expression of His omnipresence. It is scientifically true that, "not a sparrow falleth to the ground without the Father."

Consciousness may be compared to the great central light of the universe for without it all manifestation would be as darkness. The parable of creation says that up to a certain period, "darkness was on the face of the deep." The divine consciousness was involved (rolled up,—clothed,—hidden) in matter and, consciousness was involved for expression, creation could not become self-conscious, until a certain condition of evolvement, unfoldment or development of potentiality should be attained. Waiting the evolution of a proper vehicle, it is said that—"the Light shineth in darkness and the darkness comprehendeth it not."

Creation is the vehicle for the expression of the light of the Divine consciousness in order that it may be able to "enlighten every man that cometh into the world," and creation was instituted that out of it and through it there might be perfected individualized spiritual entities that would be fitted to dwell with God in eternal companionship.

As creation is the vehicle for the general diffusion of the light of consciousness so is the physical body the particular vehicle for its diffusion to the individual soul and, in its turn the soul is the vehicle for the individualization of the Divine Spirit which, when perfected becomes that apex and crown of creation—"Son of Man and Son of God."

The consciousness that is involved in the mineral element and which gives to it a separate and distinct character of its own and which prompts it to respond invariably to certain chemical and other affinities is evidently on a lower plane than that consciousness which dwells in the plant and prompts it to respond to what we call the laws of vegetable life. On a still higher plane of development is the consciousness that dwells in free moving life organism and which prompts them to go forth and seek that form of substance that they deem best for the prolongation of their existence. So the consciousness of the fish that dwells in the water, the bird that dwells in the air and the animal that roams the surface of the earth; each dwells in its own specific plane of consciousness.

The mineral, the plant, the fish, the bird and the animal, each one is, or may be, entirely righteous in its station of life. Its measure of rightness is the same as is measured to all creatures. The plant, the fish, the beast and the man are all measured with the same measuring rod. If the organism is in harmony with the divine mode of action on its plane of consciousness, it lives and makes progress, if not, its existence is hampered and finally terminates.

This is the divine mode of action that science calls "the survival of the fittest." The organism becomes perfect in his kind and advances in consciousness in proportion as it conforms to the harmonic law or it degenerates and deteriorates as it recedes from it. "There is one law and He that worketh is One."

The element and the plant are not self-conscious except possibly in some dim and indefinable degree. Action on their plane of consciousness is more or less automatic and action and reaction on this plane has its seat and origin in the eternal and exact nature and power of universal consciousness itself.

Above the plant, in the scale of development, comes free moving, independent living organisms and on this plane comes self-recognition. Here the light that shineth in dark¬ness begins to be apprehended, self-knowledge begins, and from this plane, looking upward, the comprehension of that light is based upon the capacity of the organism, its measure being indicated by the centralization and complexity of the physical organization.

Here, life recognizes itself and says: "I am." It also recognizes itself in relation to its environment and says, "I will become." The Divine Consciousness involved in matter is the underlying cause and energy of that orderly system of progressive development that we call by the name of "evolution." This truth is concealed in the mystic saying, viz., "Spirit clothes itself to come down and strips itself to go up."

Above the domain of Automatic Consciousness, there are four grand divisions or great planes of conscious corresponding to the four-fold nature of man, viz., Physical Self-consciousness; Mental Self-consciousness; Moral Self-consciousness; Spiritual Self-consciousness.

In conformity to the known laws of progressive development, it is evident that all organisms in the line of evolution must "emerge," or grow out of, the lower grand division before they can become capable of sustained existence in the grand division next above. This capacity is acquired by perfecting and improving the physical vehicle to such a degree that it has the ability to enter into relation with and to respond to the varied requirements of an environment of higher conscious potentiality.

The organism must not only be a condition of rightness with the plane on which it dwells, its native environment, but it must develop extra and surplus energy or power sufficient to carry it into the higher plane and begin its comprehension of the fact that something exists, in consciousness, that has more power, more freedom and possesses a more desirable outlet for its energies. This new knowledge gives the organism the necessary incentive, the stimulus, to strive for a higher attainment.

Here, as elsewhere, the mode is the same. The organism that would rise to a higher plane of existence must first overcome, it must strive to enter into the "straight gate," it must become master of the things of the lower heritage before it is entitled to become a dweller in the plane above. The Father is always saying: "To him that overcometh I will give the inheritance."

Spiritual evolution finds its counterpart and correspondence in physical evolution. Study the lower and you have the key to the mysteries of the higher. Law on one plane does not conflict with law on any other plane, for what we call "law" is the Divine Mode of Action.

"There is one law and He that worketh is One." The unfolding and perception of consciousness is the unfolding and perception of the existence of the Spirit of the Almighty, omnipresent in the manifest universe.

TEMPLE TALK

The Divine Consciousness, or Divine Thought, considered from the plane of the spiritual manifestation. In a brief paper, such as this must necessarily be, any attempt to outline a conception of what thought, in its essence and ultimate, must be will have to be confined to condensed statements which the advanced student will be obliged to consider and enlarge upon. Only the rudest outline of suggestion can be attempted.

Formerly, the world considered such subjects as unknowable, and, with a pious folding of the hands, hid their ignorance under a cloak of "resignation to the inscrutable mysteries of an all-wise providence." But progress has been rapid, many chains and shackles have been cast off, and today the thinking mass of mankind more nearly agree with the great sage who proclaimed that the grandest and greatest effort of human thought consisted in removing the boundaries of the unknown as far as possible. Without attempting an explanation, let me present to your consideration a few of the thoughts that leading minds are evolving upon this subject. A consensus among the world's thinkers will agree that the manifestation of thought is universal and omnipresent.

Its germ is in the tiniest atom, its manifestation is in orderly causation, and its realization is in the modes of action in nature whereby obedience to the central purpose is attained. Professor Oersted says: "The laws of nature are the thoughts of God." Professor Clifford says: "The universe consists of units of mind stuff." John, the beloved disciple, says: "In the beginning was the Word, and the Word was with God, and the Word was God."

The Word—the Logos—the Divine Thought—God's Thought in manifestation—Thoth, of the Egyptian—Adonai, of the Hebrew.

The general idea expressed by all theologic and theosophic systems of thought is this: The universe is the outward expression or the manifestation of a definite plan and purpose, put forth by a supreme center of perfect intelligence.

As thus manifested, the universe is the vehicle for the attainment of such purpose, and it is, and will be, sustained and controlled by the One Supreme Intelligence until the purpose of its manifestation is accomplished. This being accepted, it follows that thought must be universal and omnipresent, and that it is objectively and subjectively, the origin and the sustaining power of the universe.

Herein the scientist and the theologian agree—the laws of nature are the thoughts of God; the universe does consist of units of mind stuff; all that is at all knowable of the One Supreme Intelligence is manifested through the Logos—His thought.

Among occult students, Mystics, and Hermetists, there is a consensus of opinion expressed by the axiomatic statement, "Matter is spirit in a condition of limitation." Perfect thought is the mind of God and mind or consciousness of the one is omnipresent—thought is omnipresent.

As the consciousness of the one is a condition of perfect unity and harmony of all its attributes, it follows that perfect thought, perfect wisdom, and perfect love, must be one, and also that each attribute considered in its ultimate analysis, must contain all the others. Perfect thought, therefore, contains in itself both wisdom and love—loving wisdom—wise love.

As the seven rays of the divine light which lighted the world are all contained in the one ray, so Adoni containeth all the gods. Only by conditioning and by limitation can we conceive of thought, wisdom and love as being separate.

The divine consciousness, or the divine thought acting upon seemingly separate lines, various planes of manifestation and under different conditions of limitation, now manifesting thought as wisdom, again as power and again as love. How then was this manifestation?

The hint of a hypothesis only can be given. There are several fundamental statements that are assumed to be true in the nature of things.

1. That manifestation or creation was for an intelligent purpose and to accomplish a specific object; otherwise, the Supreme Center of Intelligence would be responsible for that which is objectless and foolish and unthinkable.

2. That this purpose for which creation was idealized was wise and beneficent; otherwise, the purpose of the Creator would be unwise, and malefic, which is contrary to His character, and therefore unthinkable.

3. That the idealization and projection of the universe into existence involved the concentration and projection of the divine thought and consciousness to the accomplishment of its object and purpose. When consciousness is in a condition of poise, or equilibrium, its concentration in one direction involves the withdrawal of consciousness in another direction; and, in this case, this would be accomplished without impoverishment of the divine substance, or being, any more than the expressed wish of an individual would impoverish the life of the individual.

This withdrawal of consciousness from one portion of the divine Logos, and its resultant concentration in another portion, would have the effect to "condition," or to produce a limitation of the consciousness so disturbed, and, this limitation in its ultimate, involves the idea of negation in the thing so limited, resulting in the manifestation of no consciousness—no wisdom—no thought—no love. Therefore, by the concentration of thought in one direction, we have a corresponding limitation which involves the manifestation of ignorance. Behold the paradox! Sin or ignorance cometh into the world, that the love of the Father might be made manifest. This is the involution of the divine thought—love—wisdom. This is the descending arc, "God immanent in creation." The divine consciousness involving itself in creation, that its purpose might be fulfilled.

If this be involution, what then is evolution? As thought, wisdom, power, love, have been involved in the "descending arc," so is it being evolved or "unrolled" in the "ascending arc." The one is the reflex of the other. The outgoing power, and the returning power are of the one. "There is one law and He that worketh is One." The divine purpose has gone out through involution, which is creation. Its return is through evolution, which is redemption.

It is a universal law in nature that all bodies that exist in a free-moving state naturally tend to a condition of equilibrium. This is expressed in the common proverb, "water seeks its own level." Now, this manifestation, this involution of spirit, mind, wisdom, power, love, in nature has disturbed the divine equilibrium of the Logos, and consequently there is a constant stress or effort on the part of nature, to restore itself to its natural condition,—that of equilibrium.

This is the returning power; this is what actuates all evolution—all progress; this is that power in the nature of things that makes for good. This is why nature groaneth and travaileth in pain, seeking the day of its deliverance.

This is the returning power: this is what actuates all evolution—"Lo, I come to do thy will, O Lord!" This is the main-spring of all that exalts and glorifies. Spirit, mind, wisdom, love, involved in matter, seeks to be evolved again into the bosom of the One. Adonai, going forth from the father, returneth, bringing with him Christos, the Divine Son.

CONCERNING "LAW"

The popular conception of the character of God and the interpretation of His mode of action in the manifest universe has been greatly modified during the last five decades and while the authorized standards of theological philosophy have not been radically changed, for the reason that such lines of thought are naturally conservative and deliberate, it still remains true that the advance in general knowledge, particularly in physics and chemistry, has induced an increased liberality of thought and expression among members of the Christian Church, as well as among all classes of investigators and thinkers. This is particularly apparent in the spread of so-called "new thought" among all classes and especially by its invasion into the ranks of the Church itself.

To such an extent is this true that very many of the most sincere and earnest Christians are open in their advocacy of a restatement of the standards of belief. Fifty years ago the statement made by LeConte, quoted in the March issue of these Talks (to which please refer), would not have been tolerated without protest and widespread criticism, yet the statement, in its essence, is only an expansion and broadening out of the avowed belief of the Church.

As you well know, the general consensus of theological philosophy, as related to this subject, and as subscribed to by all orthodox Christian churches, states that: God is omnipresent, omnipotent and omniscient, or, in other words, that God pervades the universe in perfect power and perfect wisdom. Compare this with the statement of modern science as voiced by LeConte and others, viz., "God is immanent-resident in nature! Nature is the house of many mansions in which He forever dwells."

"The forces of nature are different forms of His energy, acting directly in all times and places." Here, it will be seen that the only difference between the scientist and the theologian resolves itself into analysis of the explanation of details and their application, the general essential idea in both statements is in harmony. Therefore, it follows:

1. That the modes of action of these forces are and must be absolutely perfect, absolutely unchangeable and absolutely eternal, in conformity to the perfect and eternal nature of God. This is in full accord with the statement of material science, which affirms that "matter, energy and intelligence are indestructible and eternal."

2. That these modes of action which we designate as "laws" are in perfect harmony one with the other and that their apparent difference is one of degree only and not of kind. This statement also is accepted by investigators in the realm of physical science.

3. That the differences in such modes of action (laws), whether on the physical, mental, moral or spiritual plane, are directly proportionate to the various degrees of consciousness with which they have to deal.

4. That our statement of such modes of action (law) may be correct or incorrect proportionate to our correct or incorrect comprehension and statement of the facts inherent in our environment.

5. That the field open for the search for truth, whether on the physical, mental, moral or spiritual planes, will be found only in our physical,

mental, moral and spiritual environment.

6. That the analogies or correspondences found to exist between substances and forces on a low plane of manifestation, being as they are in relatively harmonious correspondence with substances and forces on a higher plane of consciousness, will furnish a key to the discovery of the modes of action of still higher and finer forces and their correlative action and interaction.

7. That it is a reasonable proposition to attempt the formulation of a philosophical statement of spiritual law having for its primary postulates a correct statement of the facts pertaining to the law of matter and material manifestation. To this may be added the following corollaries: First. Law is not t

God does not make laws. Law is correspondingly, as we affirm that God is. Second. Any statement of law partakes, more or less, of the nature of a discovery. When we say that Newton discovered the law of gravitation, we speak correctly for the divine mode of action that we call gravitation always existed. Franklin and others discovered electricity, yet that form of the divine energy that we call electricity might affirm of itself, "Before creation was I am."

Moses discovered and formulated the best and most complete statement of moral law ever made, yet these laws always existed. Moses was able, through education and discipline, to penetrate and realize his environment sufficiently to comprehend and grasp them. Third. Our conception of law is progressive and its progress is directly proportionate to our character progress in the development of our individual consciousness. The Master affirmed the Mosaic Law and added two statements thereto; one of duty to God and one of duty to man that spiritualized the entire Decalogue. Always keep in mind that the manifestation of the cosmos, with all its manifold complexity, has been derived from unity.

It is, therefore, proper and in the right lines of procedure that we should always look for simplicity and unity in any attempt to fathom the modes of action of the great first cause. Material creation requires diversity of elements and specialization of organization and specialization requires complexity proportionate to the degree of power, fineness, and ability of the organism; therefore, in looking for causes and reasons, we should endeavor to eliminate the idea of complexity.

As I have stated in a previous paper: Our finite minds cannot conceive of the great first cause as in action without predicating divine energy and divine substance, i.e., that which acts and that which is acted upon, hence the idea of duality is always with us in such a conception, further than this we cannot conceive of the divine in action without predicating a result of such action, consequently the idea of trinity is always with us in any conception involving the idea of manifestation.

In the phase of thought under consideration, manifest creation is the Third Person of the Trinity, hence it partakes of the divine nature, hence, also, it contains the fact of Sonship. That is to say, the Christos, the redeeming Christ Spirit, exists in our environment which man is to apprehend and appropriate for his own evolution into individualized Sonship. The ancient mystics referred to the idea of God involved in creation as "The Divine Oblation," and to the idea of the Christos or Christ Spirit in our environment as "The Lamb slain from the foundation of the world."

The divine purpose in creation is, in the nature of the case, perfect and complete and creation, as the vehicle of that purpose must of necessity be not only perfect and complete but it must be entirely and all sufficient for the accomplishment of that purpose, otherwise God would not be omniscient, which is inconceivable.

THE HOLY BIBLE

The soul that has raised itself high and above the clashing's of the day amongst churches and societies, is not to be found amongst those who are trying to destroy a single ray of hope, from whatever source it may project to enlighten the task of his brother.

The poor man, often very deficient in higher philosophical reasoning, stands aghast and hurt by the rude criticisms of his only hope, the Bible. Though it seems to furnish pleasure to those who unmercifully dissect its pages.

It matters not to the earnest soul who has written its pages. In it, he sees a code of morals the highest, a character in Jesus worthy of imitation, and a life of promise beyond the tomb. He lives, he dies, and passing into the "pale realms of shade," how often he is heard to say "all is well."

He may not know that much of the finer philosophy he reads by the evening fire is confiscated property; it matters not to him from where it was obtained. To tell him that it is a treasure of which the Church can claim a right only because of Bishop Cecil's mob in the second century having murdered the rightful owners of the Neoplatonic school of philosophy; to tell him his Bible is as a whole only a record of a greater religion of Chaldea, Egypt, yea of Atlantis; to tell him it is but a record of astronomical changes in the great fathomless space, is but to destroy his only hope, and no true knowing soul would dare be so cruel.

Should you, be one who, zealous for the cause of the better understanding of man's true mission upon earth, is led into conversation with those who have never seen the light as you have, be careful; though you work with no other hope of reward than that which your own soul repays, wound none of these who are sincere.

It is in justice to such as these that you remember that it was such as these simple trusting ones who so strangely protected this holy book through the dark period of ages, and today with all the higher criticism that has been passed upon it, it remains a grand cyclopedia of reference to the mystic student, and let it be remembered, many who in the pride of manhood and womanhood have laid it aside as secondary to other works of greater importance, only in that last parting hour to recall its shining promises, and accept its risen Christ. And after all, is it necessary that we disturb the minds of any with our favored knowledge when unasked for?

It would seem from surface indications of the great spiritual unrest so active the world over that we who have found the true happiness should do all in our power to give unto all, regardless of qualifications or preparation to receive, our cherished jewels, that they too may enjoy the happiness of a true conception of the laws of God.

But this is an error. The laws of evolution are busy preparing the dross that will eventually become pure gold, and the time is not ripe for the open and free distribution of all the knowledge that has been held under cover until the world is ready and anxious to receive and use it rightly.

But while it is not ripe and all adepts know that this old earth may undergo another great change before the people can be fully prepared to receive the unadulterated truth, yet to my soul's eye it seems not centuries distant when again upon the earth seasons and crops will be such as to prepare mankind for a more peaceful abode among one and another. But until these things are such that man no longer is in misery, want and disease itself, let not critics destroy much that is the only hope of the lonely, the Bible.

METAPHYSICS AND UNIVERSAL BROTHERHOOD

Occult (Metaphysical) Philosophy is truly the godmother and progenitor of all intellectual forces, the key to all divine obscurities, and the absolute queen of society. Behind the veil of all mystical allegories, beneath the ordeals of initiation, under the seal of all sacred writings, in the emblems of the old works of Alchemy, in the secret mysteries of the Bible, in the ceremonies of all secret societies, are found traces of a principal which is everywhere the same yet always carefully concealed.

From the remotest ages of the past true Occultism and Mysticism, both of which may be classed under the heading of Metaphysics, have been ever concealed and never revealed except through proper initiation into some secret brotherhood. All the great teachers of the past ages who have carved their names upon the very souls of humanity have spoken in parables to the multitudes and, in private, explained it to their disciples. Christ, who was an initiate of the Essenian Order, used this same method, lest he should cast pearls before swine.

Moses, who was an initiate into the Mysteries of Egypt, intended to initiate all the people into the Sacred Mysteries, but when he came down from the Mount, he found the people worshipping a golden calf and, in his wrath, and disappointment broke the tables of stone upon which were written these great secrets.

The grandest achievements in knowledge ever gained by man were originally concealed in the Ancient Mysteries. This knowledge was veiled in order to conceal it from the profane, and written in a universal language of symbolism that it might be understood by the initiates of all ages. This wisdom was never really lost as there have always lived a few who possessed the great secret.

This ancient wisdom is the fountain from which all philosophies have taken their rise and true Metaphysics is but the child of these Ancient Mysteries and upon which a universal brotherhood of Man must be founded. Numerous efforts to ascertain and interpret these mysteries have been made by men of every nation in all ages, but unless they are true initiates, possessing the key, their attempts have resulted in confusion and failure. Their interpretations have been as various and fantastic as the genius of each investigator, and numerous creeds and dogmas have arisen as the result.

Had these investigators been possessed of a key to symbolism, a complete philosophy of the secret doctrine, the result would be a true religion and a universal brotherhood of man. When investigation is guided by such a philosophy, or a complete key, the investigator has positive assurance at every step that he is on firm ground. Such a key to the mysteries cannot be bought, it cannot come from without, it must come from within. In the Far East, the great Lodge of Masters has never ceased to exist; this lodge or brotherhood, universal though not yet large, has often, though secret and unknown, shaped the course of empires and nations and controlled the fate of what we would call destiny.

To the public generally, this may be a matter of little importance, since the public, as a class, care only for themselves, but to the earnest seeker of truth, it is of the greatest interest. It will reveal to them the goal and meaning of human evolution, and give them the assurance that it is now being aided by "those who know," and it has never been for many centuries. Universal brotherhood and the teachings of true Metaphysics have now become possible, because of a cycle of liberality and enlightenment. To those who are ready to search deeper than ever before for the pearls of truth, it opens the way.

There is now a large and increasing number of people who really desire more light. Many are capable of apprehending this old philosophy or "Wisdom Religion," and at the same time, capable of understanding the responsibility incurred in misusing or abusing it. It is therefore high time that the philosophy of the East should illuminate the silence of the West and give the death blow to that imp of darkness, materialism. This work will bring about the universal brotherhood of man for which all true men are looking. It is this higher knowledge toward which all useful and rational acquirements should tend, and why should our efforts cease short of the very highest?

All education which does not tend in this direction, with the final goal in view, is incomplete and of necessity a failure. The highest knowledge is a knowledge of the soul of man. Of its origin, nature, powers, and the laws that govern its development; and this is precisely the knowledge which modern so-called science fails to afford and which it does not even believe in, for in science, so-called, there is no soul at this age. This very soul development was taught in the ancient mysteries.

All preliminary training and study led up to this—"the real nature of man." Just as all life is an evolution, so is all real knowledge an initiation; and it proceeds in a natural order and advances by "degrees." The seeker or "candidate" must be worthy and well qualified, duly and truly prepared. That is, he must perceive that such knowledge does exist; must desire to possess it, and must be willing to make whatever personal sacrifice is necessary for its acquirement. He must have passed beyond the stage of blind belief, or superstition, the bondage of fear and orthodoxism, the age of fable, and the dominion of appetite of sense.

This is the true meaning of being "duly and truly prepared." He must have proved his fitness in these directions and he must also desire to use this knowledge for the good of himself and others and not for his own selfish purposes. Man's motives, therefore, alone can determine that he is worthy and well qualified. Discerning that "knowledge is power," designing and evil men desire to possess both knowledge and power for entirely selfish purposes.

The more knowledge a purely selfish and evil-minded man possesses, the more harmful he becomes to his fellow-man. This is especially the case in regard to those deeper sciences or metaphysics which deal with the mind, and influence the thoughts and actions of others. There are latent powers and almost infinite capabilities in man, the meaning of which he has hardly dreamed of possessing. Nor will leisure or more intellectual cultivation alone reveal these powers.

It is only through a complete philosophy of the entire nature of man and the capacities and destinies of the human soul, supplemented by the use of such knowledge, that man will eventually come into possession of his birthright. The symbols of antiquity derive their real value from the universal and eternal truths which they embody.

These great truths, obscured and lost in one age by misinterpretation and selfishness, rise rejuvenated in the next. They are immortal ideals, knowing neither decay nor death. They are like a divine image concealed in a block of stone, which many artists assail with mallet and chisel, square and compass, perhaps to release a distorted idol.

Only the perfect master can so chip away the stone as to reveal in all its grandeur and beauty the divine ideal, and endow it with the breath of life. Such is the building of character. The real truth is to be found in the theme that runs through the symphony of creation; in the lofty ideals that inspire the life of man, and that lead him from the clods and lowlands, where hover the ghosts of superstition and fear, to the mountains of light, where dwell inspiration and peace.

Such ideals are the Christ and the Perfect Master, and such must be the teachers of true metaphysics and the founders of a universal brotherhood of man. The source from whence this knowledge came was Persia and India, but even before that, from ancient Atlantis. India has always been called the mother of the esoteric or concealed wisdom. To revive the ancient wisdom, which was a true religion, is to recover the lost word and to facilitate universal progress and the universal brotherhood of man. This word concerns the science of rhythmic vibrations and is the key to the equilibrium of all forces and of the harmony of eternal nature.

These secrets must be sought for by the individual himself. Every man must work out his own salvation. Dr. P.B. Randolph first taught that: There is a grand science known as magic, (call it metaphysics or the science of the mind if you will) it contemplates that all round development which liberates the intellect from the dominion of the senses and illuminates the spiritual perceptions.

All genuine initiation, like evolution and regeneration, is from within and consists in an orderly unfoldment of the natural powers of the Neophyte, so that he shall become the very thing he desires to possess. In seeking magic, he finally becomes the Magus. The Christ life and the power that made Jesus to be Christos, Master, whereby He healed the sick, cast out devils, and foretold future events, is the same life revealed by initiation in the greater Mysteries of Antiquity.

The lost word of the Master is a key to all the science of magic, and this key, or lost word, is nothing less than spiritual or soul development. Back of this science of magic lays a philosophy as boundless as cosmos, as inexhaustible as time, and as beneficent as the "Father in Heaven."

The purpose of initiation, or training in occultism, is to place the operations of the body under the dominion of the will. In freeing the ego from the dominion of the appetites, passions, and the whole lower nature. Such mastery of self by intelligent effort and willpower, produces peace, clearness of vision and spiritual discernment.

THE OCCULT AND FRAUD

The craze for occult knowledge is growing, and consequently, the story of the spider and the fly is being repeated, for many designing persons are thriving upon the ignorance and gullibility of the public. The desire for metaphysical knowledge and mental science is grand and natural, for it is one of the signs of soul-growth, but those who are seeking for the Higher knowledge and wisdom must be careful. The meaning of the word Occult is "Hidden" and its direct meaning is the hidden powers or glories of the human soul and its work and duty here and place beyond the pale. Occultism acknowledges the law of Karma, that "Whatever a man sows that shall he reap."

We believe that for our thoughts and deeds in this life, we will surely be compensated or punished hereafter. If we hurt another in thought, we will suffer tenfold more than the person or object to which it was directed. The difference between the Occult and the Church is that we believe in the law of Karma as taught by the Christ when he said: "As you sow, so shall you reap."

While the Church teaches that if a man does wrong and prays for the forgiveness of his sins, they will be forgiven, and that he must not suffer for the evil he has committed and the sufferings that he may have caused to his fellow man. The apostles taught, "Bear ye one another's burdens, and so fulfill the law of Christ." And this law was taught by Christ. "Thou shalt love thy neighbor as thyself. A new commandment I give unto you: That ye love one another."

This the Occultist believes. We aim to follow our leader and even so as to love our fellow-men and uphold them, the same as He upholds and loves us. We try to encourage and give instead of robbing and calumniating. The true follower of Occultism will forgive. No matter what wrong was committed, he will not harbor hatred in his heart toward anyone, nor will he condemn any creed or religion. He loves all, knowing that the Father of all ruleth and that it is well. Occultism is a religion in the first and its most sublime sense.

It started as a religion in the Middle Ages, when freedom of speech or thought were often considered being capital offences. The members of brotherhoods who taught the true faith were compelled to use symbols to cover their teachings and to surround their places where they taught these things for self-protection. But few of those today who claim to be teachers of the Occult say anything in regard to the religious part and the great majority of the people interested believe that it is simply a system of training, which if mastered will give them a power over their fellow beings, such as hypnotism is supposed to do.

They do not know, neither are they taught that Occultism is a religion—Christianity in its purity—and that it is necessary to first cleanse the heart and soul from all envy, hate, jealousy and immoral thoughts before they can gain any power that is not possessed by every human being. It is a sad fact that those who claim to teach the Occult, do so only to make money and their instructions are simply hypnotism clothed in mysterious rags and do not teach either morality, love, forgiveness, nor anything else that might be able to do even a little good. They are sold simply because there is a money consideration to them and all that they do is to make those taking such courses unbelievers in the true teachings.

It is also a fact that Occultism teaches the way to a power that is far beyond the comprehension of the majority of people, but these teachings only follow after a course of training whereby lust, hate and passion is completely rooted out of the soul and a peace established such as nothing can arouse and fan into anger. It is only after a man has mastered his passions that he is fit for the sublimer secrets of power, and were such instructions to be given to anyone not prepared for them he would not be able to understand them or to carry them out, and if he would, he could only bring ruin upon himself. We believe that the Christ-principle is in all.

The drunkard, the gambler, even the most depraved criminal, has the divine spark within him at birth. It may, by lying dormant, overrun by weeds and thistles, or buried deep with evil thoughts and associations, or perhaps covered by false teachings, yet, nevertheless, it is still there. But it needs the sun of love, the dew of help and charity to awaken it and bring it to active growth, so that he may have a perception of himself and his condition and turn to God within for strength and power to live and do right. It is here where the teacher of the true Occult gets into his good work.

First, to teach the student that he has the spark of immortality within himself and how and where to find it. This often takes time, patience and courage, and these things cannot be bought for any amount of money. Second, it is necessary to teach the student how to overcome his weaknesses and vices and implant love, faith and charity in their stead. In order to do this, it is necessary to learn of the student's weak points and help him to gain strength in this direction by substituting better instead, and it will be seen that no printed instructions will do this. A few or none are alike.

After the student has mastered his shortcomings and knows that God is within him, he is ready for the more advanced instructions. The Occultist knows that heaven is not a place but a condition and that this condition is harmony and love, and that love and harmony are heaven. All things that tend to be harmony, peace and happiness are of heaven; all good deeds have their inception there. Hell is but the opposite of heaven and is but another name for discord, hate, jealousy and what a great many call "crankiness."

Hate, jealousy and discord will make a perfect hell, and, as life after death is but a continuation of the earth life, we can expect that we will then be in like condition until we can forget and learn better. The Occultist knows that the Christ was an Essene, and that the Essenes were members of an occult or mystic order now known as the Rosicrucians. If people would only investigate and learn what Occultism and the teaching of the occult is, there would not be as much fraud to contend with.

Of this order of men, Sydney Beard, Esq., of England, says: "Rosicrucians are not made by passing through ceremonies, nor by studying symbolic manuals, and they recognize each other by surer signs than secret grips and passwords. Any man may become a Mason, but not one man in a hundred can become a Rosicrucian."

True Rosicrucians do not sell the priceless gems of truth which have been revealed to them—they give them without money and without price to those who are to receive them and are able to profit from them. If those who desire true Occult knowledge would only remember that the true secrets are never sold outright, but that those desiring the knowledge must first work for them and prove their fitness for them and that the true Initiation does not consist of ceremonies, rituals, etc., but of a course of training to awaken the sleeping faculties of the soul—not intellect—and that while the true teacher can guide and instruct he cannot initiate anyone, because this must be with each one himself or herself. A man can only conceive the mysteries and secrets as he advances, and no teacher of the occult would give that to one which is not fit for or which he could not understand; it would be casting "pearls before swine."

The great trouble is, that today those who desire the greater knowledge are in a hurry, and think they will be able to reach the goal by getting initiated into some so-called great Occult Order, which may take an evening, or by reading some so-called teachers instructions. Nothing could be farther from the truth. Remember that Illumination is only given to those who seek it with sincere and worthy purpose and with persevering steadfastness, and is not gained in a day or a week, for it is a process of training and growth. Mr. Beard says further: "The last misapprehension which I need to mention is one to the effect that the brotherhood is mixed up in some way with 'infidelity,' or with 'anti-Christian' tenets. This is a preposterous fallacy, for Rosicrucians are devout seekers after God, and they not only regard Jesus of Nazareth as their great exemplar and teacher, but speak of him as "The Master."

They also commemorate his great love and self-sacrifice by observing the sacramental feast he instituted for his followers. "What manner of men are they? First, they seek, after truth, aspirants after the highest wisdom attainable by mankind. They seek illumination, not for their own sakes, but that they may be better qualified to serve God and humanity and to help their fellow mortals in their struggle upwards and towards the higher planes of consciousness.

Unknown and unrecognized except by highly developed souls, dwelling in 'the shadows' cast by sin and suffering, voluntarily bearing a humble share of the burden and toil which the redemption of mankind from darkness and evil renders necessary on the part of the 'sons of God,' sorrowful because of their sympathy with pain—yet always rejoicing—they go their ways quietly and without ostentation and with the single intent to make other souls better and happier.

This is true of every Occultist, no matter what his Order, and if the true occult is to be taught, it must be in this line, and cannot be different. "We believe that God dwells in man. We believe as the Bible teaches us, and not as a priest or frauds would teach us. We believe that we are the temples of the living God, that He dwells in us, and that if we listen and obey these teachings, heaven will commence for us here on old mother earth, and that all the much lauded powers will come to man after he has awakened the inner man and knows the truth."

To do this is the work of the true teacher. The one and only work that he can do until the student is far enough advanced to receive the greater mysteries and secrets held by the greater and at the same time least known brotherhoods. The Occult teaches an immortal life—life beyond the grave—and a life of usefulness and advancement. We do not believe that man is to stand still in any state of being, but that he keeps on in one continued evolution, advancing toward perfection, or nearer to the Infinite.

The suffering through which man passed strengthens and purifies him, and his soul will be in a better state from them if he recognizes the hand of the Father in all. True occultism is not a system of Black Art, Diabolism or unearthly power, but is a grand religion in the first place and power after initiation. Greatest of all, occultism teaches us to love God and not to fear Him, but to fear the consequences of our evil acts. Man dares not do good only because he desires a future life, for to do so is selfish and cowardly, and he must do right because he loves the right, for the sake of right, truth, love and justice.

A COMPARISON BETWEEN SOLOMON'S TEMPLE AND THE "GRAND MAN"

The fore part of the year, it was suggested that lectures on hygiene would prove acceptable to the young men. Hygiene of the outside, as well as the inside of the body. We started with twenty-three, this total was soon increased to fifty, sixty, eighty, ninety, and so on, up, until one evening at least one hundred were present.

The interest has been intense from the beginning, as was evidenced by the large attendance, and the great many questions asked. (The idea was to discuss these questions presented by the boys, because it largely voiced their condition, or subjects on which they were ignorant.) Very few in considering hygiene consider that the inside is to be taken care of as well as the outside.

Usually in speaking of hygiene reference is made to the outside of the body, to the environment, that is, the location of the person's sleeping apartments, bathing, clothing, etc. Very little attention has been paid and is paid to the inside of the body, as to what we shall eat, how we shall eat it, or what effect it has on the body, either physically, mentally, morally or spiritually; no consideration at all, just eat until they cannot eat any more; then wonder and complain because they feel bad and become diseased.

About fifteen hundred years before Christ, there lived a man by the name of David, King David, he was called. A man who was respected in his time, who was a great warrior. He fought many battles and achieved great victories, as far as taking away from others was concerned, but when it came to himself, I consider him a very weak man. His hands were stained with blood from the many battles he fought. His mind, you can imagine what a condition that was in from the many battles he fought and on account of his war-like tendency and trying to subdue everything and everybody he came in contact with. His hands, as well as his mind, were stained with blood, and as a result of that, he was not permitted to do what he desired the most to do.

He was told, whether it be by his conscience, the intuitional force that was within him, or as is stated in the Bible, God speaking to him, I leave to you to think about. Spiritualists of the present day would probably say that the old Masters were speaking to him and telling him what to do, and he was guided entirely by unseen forces. This man, as he grew older, committed sin. He was victorious over armies, yet he was not master of himself, and on account of this crime or sin, he was not allowed to do what he wished to do. It was suggested to him that as he had a palace of his own, and had everything his heart could desire, that there was no place to worship God in.

He conceived the idea of building a temple, but was informed by Nathan the prophet that he could not do so because his hands were stained with blood, and no one who has blood on his hands, or has committed murder, can enter the temple. He was not a master of himself. It was prophesied that Solomon, his son, should be king instead. Before passing away, King David accumulated gold and silver in large quantities.

If you read the account in the Old Testament in Chronicles, first and second Samuel, first and second Kings, you will find the whole account of Solomon's temple and David, his father. He accumulated large quantities of brass, iron, in fact he drew from the four corners of the earth for his needs. He drew on the mineral kingdom, on the vegetable kingdom, and animal kingdom (man). In those times, they had some of the best astronomers and astrologers ever known. They computed time by the stars, and it was found that the stars represented, or the planets, represented certain seasons of the year. It was also found that those born under certain planets had certain characteristics, and were divided according to the twelve months of the year.

It was found that there were twelve planets that interested them more than any of the others, and it was found that those who were born under those planets were born in certain times of the year and it covered the entire twelve months. David, in selecting the material for the temple, which he was not to build, considered that he would have to call on the many people whom he governed to help build that temple.

He selected from the twelve tribes according to the months, those who were best adapted to aid in this work. It turned out that all those he selected as heads, and representing the twelve tribes, were masters in their respective lines; some could do one thing, some another; some could do this work best, some that work best. However, the twelve tribes were represented. In looking around among the twelve tribes, he found there were none that could take the control of the building of this temple to his entire satisfaction. At that time he became weak and his son Solomon became king in his stead, and David was gathered to his forefathers. Solomon was said to be a very wise man; one of the wisest of the times, and in fact the wisest of the times in which he lived, which was about nine hundred and seventy years before Christ.

Solomon, at that time was not a master. He had not proven himself. He was a mere novice, you might say, but in the work that he undertook, he first had to become an apprentice as it were. Solomon had a friend who was also a friend of King David, who was considered a good and wise man, who was a master, King Hiram of Tyre. Solomon requested King Hiram to send him a man who was versed, well versed, in the arts and sciences, who could work brass, iron, gold and silver.

King Hiram selected a namesake of his, Hiram Abiff. (You will find it recorded in the Bible.) This man was considered the finest workman in his line in the kingdom. Solomon drew on King Hiram not only for this man, Hiram Abiff, but for other masters of that city who were proficient in this class of work. He drew on the forests of Lebanon for cedar, for all kinds of woods; for stone, limestone in abundance, the finest of minerals. Chroniclers of the Bible state that it was a very fine limestone that was used. It could have been marble just as well as limestone.

However, all these different materials came from different sections of the country. All the wood-work; the stone-work. First, we take the stone-work because we must have a foundation. All the stones were cut, chiseled and made ready for the temple away from Jerusalem; all the wood-work was cut, seasoned and trimmed and finally prepared so that it could be taken to Jerusalem to be fitted together properly.

All the images they had, vessels, the pillars, everything that they required for use in the temple in a sacred way, or otherwise, were made away from Jerusalem and when finally all this material was brought to

Jerusalem, Hiram Abiff was there to direct the work. He was the master, the mechanic, or you might call him a Master Mason, for he was a mason, a stonemason. All this material was brought to Jerusalem. The foundation was laid oblong, longer one way than it was the other, something like a table, or, ourselves, for instance; we are longer one way than the other.

This temple was built; first the masonry, stone-work, then the superstructure, the wood-work, and finally over all that, to cover entirely on the inside, it was lined with gold. Solomon's temple comprised not only one building but several, but the one we speak of tonight (we will consider only one) is the main building. We find it was built in three sections, the outer, the inner and still further inside.

It was said the outer wall represented Jacob, the inner wall Isaac, and the inside Abraham, or body, soul and spirit. The temple stood facing east, that is the steps. Why? Because the sun rose in the east. When we speak of the sun, we speak of understanding. The sun rises in the east and sheds its light over the world. Facing the east on either side of the steps on the outside of the building, were two pillars I wish to call attention to, but before we consider the pillars themselves, allow me to remind you of a lecture I delivered here on "Phallic Worship."

You remember, the majority of you, my telling you how the pillars originated. How in the olden times, according to the records we have, which date back five thousand years (you see that was about four thousand years prior to Solomon's temple, or time), Ancient Phallic Worship was observed through a desire to acknowledge the divine or spiritual presence. It was noticed, like could produce like, and in those days man, or the masculine, was considered the highest product of creation. It was also noticed that the woman, or the feminine, was created as well, so both man and woman were linked together in thought and worshipped as being divine, for out of both came the highest type of creative thought.

To show their appreciation, they desired to perpetuate the idea by symbols, so they worshipped the Phallic and the Yoni, they seeing in them the cause or creation of a divine or God-like being. To bring out the idea better, pillars were erected, added to, modified, until the cross was accepted as representing both man and woman.

All these symbols were considered sacred—symbolizing the divine in man, the God or Spirit. You will remember I gave you different symbols to show you how these ideas or thoughts were carried out. It is not stated in Bible histories, as near as I can find, why these pillars were placed in front of the temple. They simply say the pillars were put there, without saying why or where they came from. It was simply to carry out an old idea, as the astrologers and the old masters knew, the idea of the masculine and feminine, and to show the divine, the entrance to the temple.

Read between the lines, gentlemen, and you can see where this all comes in. 'The entrance to the temple, the holy of holies is within'. One pillar was on the right side, and one pillar on the left. The pillar on the right side was named Jachin, the other one was called Boaz, and they both represented the masculine and feminine. The pillar of Jachin was divided into two parts, signifying the body and soul.

In the center of the pillar was a wreath finely wrought, so you could not tell where the upper blended into the lower. Surmounting that pillar of Jachin, which was hollow, symbolizing that the immortal part was within. Surmounting that pillar was a wreath, several wreaths, in fact, of pomegranates. The pomegranate is a fruit. The pomegranate, as you know, if you know anything about it, is plentifully supplied with seeds. It was placed there to show that the children of Israel were like the seed of the pomegranate; could not be counted for numbers. Surmounting that pillar again was a globe, showing the earth and typifying the earth as they knew it in those days. They lived on the earth, and they wanted to symbolize it, so they put a globe on top of the pillar.

The pillar of Boaz, which stood on the other side of the entrance, we find was divided into three parts (representing the body, soul and spirit), and so arranged you could not tell where one blended with the other. Surmounting that were wreaths of lilies, signifying purity, and surmounting that again we find another globe, which depicted the heavens, showing that as it was above, so it is below and vice versa. As it is within, so it is without.

These two pillars signify also strength and beauty, the strength of Judea. The pillar of Jachin representing strength, the pillar of Boaz beauty. Before we go into the temple, we find we have three steps. We go up these steps and find that we have to go one at a time. We have to go by degrees to get where we want to be. We stop again, and we find we have still seven more steps. We go on a little bit further, finally we get inside the temple; we find we have rooms there. We also find there is an upper story with rooms in it and leading up into these rooms was a ladder with many rounds.

We have to travel still further and finally get to where we want to be. These rooms were used for a storehouse of the sacred vessels and also for the use of the priests, and for various other purposes. We find as we get into the holy of holies that the room was divided from another room with a veil, supposed to be white. An emblem of purity, the room was lined with gold, signifying that all was pure within.

It all had to be eighteen carat gold, or probably they did not know anything about eighteen carat gold in those times, but in other words it had to be pure gold. It signified that the holy of holies was absolutely pure. (Some will say eighteen carat is not pure gold—but so-called commercial gold, twenty-four carat being absolutely pure, and so fine cannot be used; to be of use, it is mixed with another metal, but still remains pure.) To be perfectly developed, we must maintain an equilibrium on all three planes, spirit, soul and body. We must not go to extremes.

We find in coming down the times that there were other temples built, Ezekiel's temple being one, and so on until we come down to Herod's time, or the time of the Christian era. We leave Solomon's temple for a few moments and will take up the "grand man." You remember I said this temple of Solomon was built without the sound of noise, without the sound of a hammer; it was made the proper dimensions.

I think there must have been unions at that time for the simple reason that they divided the twenty-four hours into three parts of eight hours each, and I think they must have used the two-foot rule there also for that was divided into twenty-four parts, signifying an hour for each part, or twenty-four hours in the day, and, divided into three, showing that the day was to be divided into three parts, eight hours to worship God, eight hours to work and eight hours for sleep and recreation. Taking ourselves, we find that we are divided into three parts as well as Solomon's temple, these temples of ours.

We had nothing to say about our building, about our creation; it was simply thought, and in a great many cases, there is no thought attached to it; we are the result of thought; it is true, but very little thought was given to us at the time we were created. This temple was built without sound or noise; we were put together; we were drawn from the forces of the earth, from the four corners.

We were born some of us in one month, some in another. We were divided, we are divided according to the twelve months of the year; each section of our body affected according to the month in which we were born, each month affected according to the planet controlling at the time of birth. MAN, STUDY AND KNOW THYSELF!

We were drawn from the four corners of the earth, or the four seasons of the year. We are divided into temperaments. There are twelve pairs of nerves in the body which control the rooms of this temple, the workings of it; how everything shall go, how everything shall be placed just so, no noise about it. Everything is put into its proper place. We have the outside shell, or wall, we have the inside; the mind and the spiritual, the holy of holies, the body, soul and spirit. We have the external pillar or pillars the same as Solomon's temple did. We have strength and beauty.

We have the three steps the same as the temple, the three virtues that go with that. We have to have faith that is supplemented by hope and finally surmounted by love; we have to climb up as it were degree by degree until we finally get to where we want to be, until we get up to the five steps, that is the five senses. We go up still a little higher and we find that we have seven steps also. Two steps added to the five that are already there; they are reason and intuition, making seven. We find this temple is like Solomon's temple in a great many respects. We find in Solomon's temple the floor was paved with blocks. It looked like a checkerboard. Is not our life, the temple, the same, just like a checkerboard, varied?

We finally come to the inside of the temple, the brain. In the rooms that surround the temple we find there are a great many rooms that correspond to the different characteristics, the different temperaments of the body and some of them are musty like some of these rooms; they are musty with impure thoughts, malice, selfishness, hatred—injustice toward our brothers. (Who is our brother?) Some are clean. They can all be clean, pure in thought.

These twelve nerves that supply the twelve sections of our body can be so controlled that each section of the body, each room in the body, can be just what we wish it to be, what we will it to be, or what we think it to be. We are the result of thought; this temple is the result of thought. If we allow unclean things to enter our body (i.e., impure food—food? tainted animal, that has unhealthy vibrations—we take its life—its blood is on our hands, and we put it in the temple), the temple is defiled; it is impure and I am afraid that instead of having pure gold in the holy of holies there will be something like brass or lead. We must learn how to transmute (using the material—or body-mixing as it were the two) these baser metals into the pure gold and finally reach what we want.

We have to climb the ladder round by round; we must have faith; we must have hope; we must have charity or love for our fellow man. We must be pure in thought; we must have friendship; we must have love and truth. These links in the chain bind us together; one cannot exist without the other; each is dependent upon the other for strength. We find as we go along still further that these twelve nerves or disciples work and supply these bodies of ours. Solomon had the twelve tribes in the olden times.

Jesus had the twelve disciples, who were masters of themselves; everyone was a master, and the head, Jesus. Jesus selected twelve masters. Jesus means the flesh (that is the interpretation), and until we can overcome this flesh by aiding the twelve disciples with thought, we cannot become masters. If there is one section that is impure, the balance had as well be impure, because you cannot be a master until you have mastered all of the body, the twelve different sections of the body.

I have given samples tonight of the effect of paying attention to the appetite, allowing the appetites to control this body or temple (i.e., eating food that controls our bodies to such an extent that our brains or will-power is impaired, allowing the body [or appetite] to control the brain [or will-power] instead of vice versa).

The disciples were masters also and finally they overcame, and became true masters in every sense of the word. We have to go step by step; we have to use our senses in every particular and develop ourselves degree by degree and finally we reach the pinnacle or the apex of the pyramid. A great many do not understand what the pyramid represents. There are many rooms in that pyramid that we can dispose of. (How like ourselves.)

It seems hard at times to climb along life's journey, but day after day we build, add to our characters—every stone perfect, until finally, like Hiram, we look around and find the temple almost completed; we reach the apex, and as we pass over into the higher life, the temple is finished. After we have crucified and buried self, we can become masters, the Christ (or truth) shines forth. Then comes the resurrection of the new life, the spiritual life, and as we follow that line of thought out we become transfigured as it were, and find there all the glory there is and we become masters of ourselves. Masters of ourselves in every sense of the word.

I have not gone as deeply as I might into the comparison of Solomon's temple and ourselves, the "grand man," which is symbolic of that temple and is symbolic of the heavens; you find the three, the heavens, the temple and ourselves, or the heavens, the earth and ourselves. We are the trinity, three in one and one in three. As it is above, so it is below, and as it is within, so it is without. You can't get away from it.

The purpose of this has been to give you an idea of how to take care of your bodies on the inside so that the outside will be all right. You are not responsible, as I have told you, for your being here, but you are responsible for these temples at the present time as they are, as they will be in the future and also for the new creation or the new life that you bring into this world. We speak of creation. New worlds are being created every day, and we are responsible for those we are bringing into this world.

That is what these lectures are for, to show you and to teach you how to take care of yourselves and those born in the future; if they are born under new conditions, new life, new thought permeating their brain, they in turn will likewise bring into the world their kind and so on down through eternity, making the world better and better until finally creation will derive the benefit of our doing our duty.

While here, we must eat, eat to live, why not eat those foods which will produce the best results, those foods that have the purest vibrations?

Our bodies—our brains or thoughts, will be pure also. If we (fathers and mothers) are pure in thought, pure in body, it stands to reason we will produce pure children—physically, mentally and consequently pure morally. Everyone wants the best, why then don't you think right? In living this perfect life, we bring forth into the outer, the temple of the living God (Jehovah), and we will be guided as were the children of Israel, "The Cloud by day and the Pillar of Fire by night."

THE MYSTIC AND THE OCCULT

In all my researches in Occultism and Mysticism in the past, I have found but two authors who have given us a clear definition of the words "Occultism" and "Mysticism." Nearly all others use the two words as though they meant the same thing. While they are truly connected with each other and while Occultism should be the first to be studied, yet, there is a great difference between the two. In the seething changes of our mixed conditions, terms and names very often bother us.

We too often make a lump sum of things which cannot be contacted. As an illustration, we have the words "Occultism" and "Mysticism."

Ask a student far on the path for a definition. The answer generally is: Oh, they mean about the same thing. An Occultist or Mystic has always had strange powers and can perform supernatural things. In this answer are two misstatements; one that Occult and Mystic are similar in meaning; the other that there is anything perceived by physical sense, that is supernatural. The un-manifested is superior to the manifested and limiting or supernatural. No mortal or natural man can act in a supernatural manner.

So long has he been born under the law, or nature, that he must act according to the law. Dr. Phelon, of the Hermetic Brotherhood, says: "Occult is the doing of things by laws little known, in a secret, hidden manner. An Occult student strives constantly to learn concerning matters not generally understood. The discoverers and inventors of this and other ages are of this class. So long as these students can keep their studies and results to themselves, they are Occultists. As soon as they make the world their confident, so far they cease to be Occultists. This is true of all who act in this manner, on either the spiritual or material plane."

Occultism does not stop here, however, but leads on to the realm of religion and the deeper spiritual things. Usually, it deals with these deeper subjects in a material, scientific and investigating way, and always leads the world to a better understanding of the laws that give life. It is always, except in very rare eases, the forerunner of the true Mysticism.

Edward Maitland, in his grand work, "The Story of the New Gospel of Interpretation," one of the greatest books ever written, says: "Occultism deals with transcendental physics, and is of the intellectual, belonging to science." There is but a slight difference in the wording in the definition of Occultism by these two great men, but the meaning is the same in both cases and shows that the minds or intuitions of all those who have passed through the true initiation is the same, and must always be thus, as such knowledge is never of the brain or intellect, but ever of the soul-intuition.

Of Mysticism, Dr. Maitland says: "Mysticism deals with transcendental metaphysics, and is of the spiritual, belonging to the religions. Occultism, therefore, has for its domain the region which, lying between the body and the soul, is interior to the body but exterior to the soul;

while Mysticism has for its domain the region which, comprising the soul and the spirit, is interior to the soul, and belongs to the divine."

This definition is so plain that all can understand it, and in a few words, we may say that Occultism is transcendental physics, while Mysticism is transcendental metaphysics.

ONE THE SCIENCE OF PHYSICS, WHICH LEADS UP TO MYSTICISM, WHILE THE OTHER IS THE SCIENCE OF METAPHYSICS WHICH LEADS UP TO GOD—ALL.

In defining Mysticism, Dr. Phelon says: "A Mystic is one who desires to know God and His truth. He seeks first to perceive the kingdom of heaven and its righteousness, (rightness,) striving with intense desire to enter closely into the relations of the seen and unseen." The two words of themselves show their difference, if the light of the Cabala is thrown upon them. Occult commences with desire for all knowledge, and it is twice limited by the keeping secret or hiding quality of the word.

As a repository of knowledge, it seeks to quicken wisdom with the innate force of understanding. Mystic, at its opening, presents only silence, which is golden. "In the beginning, God created the heaven and the earth."

Out of the silence came the vibrating sound that created. Its circumstances claim for it facility of expression to attract outer support. Clearness of perception doubles the power of ready use as a whole. At the end is the limit or sign of enclosure preventing the holiest and most sacred things of the spirit from being made a mark for the worldly-wise to carp at. There may be many Occultists, but few Mystics.

Dr. Maitland, in speaking of that which he had intuitionally received, says: "The science of the mysteries can be understood only by one who has studied the physical sciences, because it is the climax and crown of all things, and must be learned last and not first. Unless thou understand the physical sciences, thou canst not comprehend the doctrine of vehicles, which is the basic doctrine of Occult science. 'If thou understood not earthly things, how shall I make thee understand heavenly things?' Wherefore, get knowledge, and be greedy for knowledge, ever more and more. It is idle for thee to seek the inner chamber until thou hast passed through the outer. This, also, is another reason why occult science cannot be unveiled to the horde. To the unlearned, no truth can be demonstrated. The science of the realization of man's potential divinity;—the process, that is, of the Christ,—is the royal science. If thou would reach the king's presence chamber, there is no way save through the outer rooms and galleries of the palace."

It is a fact that in my past writings, I have used the word "Occultism" to define that which is really Mysticism, but I have been forced to do this in order to be understood as but few of those who are far advanced in the deeper and higher science know the difference for the reason that the two have never been defined except by the authors quoted and therefore it really made but very little difference whether the word "Occultism" or "Mysticism" was used. Another thing, I never wrote on metaphysical or mystical subjects unless I clearly defined what I was trying to impress on the reader and never wrote on physical sciences under the guise of Occultism.

Occultism may be successfully studied and investigated by the materialist as it is in truth but intellectual science, but Mysticism can never be thus investigated, as it is purely spiritual but gives material results. Man, in order to become a true Mystic, must forget self and think only of the things that he may do for humanity. He does not think of saving his own soul, but thinks of the saving of others and, by saving others, he saves his own. "He that tries to gain life shall lose it," but "He that is willing to give his life shall gain it."

It is ever thus, and the true Mystic knows this only too well and follows that which he knows is true and which the materialist very often scorns. To be a Mystic one must live a moral life, not only in acting, but in thinking and living as well. The body must be kept clean by right eating and drinking. The drunkard and glutton can never become a Mystic. There are those today who claim to be teachers of Mysticism who believe in all the fads from the deadly vaccination and filling the blood with foul and filthy matter, to the eating of raw meat and the drinking of blood.

Such are the ones who, under the guise of being teachers of the grandest system of life science, are really teaching and practicing black, deadly magic in its fullest sense, and the worst of it is that they are under the impression that they are doing good to humanity, while in reality they are supplying their scholars with charts that show the direct way to a plane that is for worse than the hell that used to be taught by the church in the past.

"Seek ye first the kingdom of God and God's righteousness; and all these things shall be added unto you." This means all that it says and to be a Mystic, it must be obeyed. Beware of those that would make you a Mystic by teaching you a broad and easy way for a given sum of money. Initiation is of the self, ceremony does not enter into it, but morality does.

CONCERNING FAITH

The rapid advance in scientific knowledge has been very largely accomplished by aid of the free use of the mental faculty that we call the imagination. Following the accumulation of a vast array of facts relative to any one given subject, the next step of the investigator is to call into use all his mental powers in order to discover the hidden, or underlying meaning or principle that correlates and explains these facts. In doing so, he projects his imaginative faculties into the unknown, searching in all directions conceivable for the truth or principle that shall make understandable, the known phenomena. Theory after theory is proposed, examined and rejected, until at last, the weary search is ended and the long sought for principle is discovered.

Regarding such a consumption, the late Prof. John Tyndall says: "There is no more wonderful performance of the intellect than this, and we can render no account of it. Like the scriptural 'gift of the spirit,' no man can tell whence it cometh. The passage from fact to principle is sometimes slow, sometimes rapid, but at all times a source of intellectual joy." On the same subject I quote Prof. Ray Lankester, who says: "We boldly admit the truth of the assertion, that 'we biologists are largely occupied with speculation and hypothesis,' and we acknowledge as its most valued servant, its indispensable ally and helpmate, that faculty that we call imagination."

Following the line of investigation indicated in previous papers, let us institute a correspondence between the known and that which we seek to know, bearing in mind the axiom: "law on one plane does not conflict with law on any other plane," and beginning at the base and working upward, following the factors necessary to growth, and on the physical plane we find desire, which may be described as a physical inherency which prompts the individual to search for that which will minister to his physical comfort, sustenance and growth.

On the mental plane we shall find that the individual calls in the aid of the imagination assisted by that mental discriminative power which enables him to picture out the ideals and to accept those which he deems most desirable to aid him in his mental and moral sustenance and growth.

On the spiritual plane, this office is largely functioned by the spiritual faculty that we call faith; for faith embodies both desire and imaginative ideals, and, similarly, as desire is projected into the environment in search for physical food; and, as imagination is projected into the environment in search for mental and ethical food, so the spiritualized soul of man, in search for that truth which shall be as food and sustenance and which shall minister to its upward growth and progress.

The projections from the higher plane may or may not be comprehended by the capacities of the lower plane, but it is certain that the higher will fully comprehend the lower because it had to come through all the lower planes in order to reach its advanced altitude. This is the reason the "voice of the spirit" coming through the spiritually individualized soul is referred to as the final court of arbitration in matters pertaining to all decisions affecting the formation of human character. The higher self must dominate the so-called lower self, for otherwise, the upward progress of the ego is seemingly impossible.

Correspondingly, as desire, on the physical plane, may be educated, cultivated and transformed from an erratic, incoherent condition into a refined, coherent and rational state, and, as imagination on the mental plane can be trained, educated and cultivated and thus be made both serviceable and reliable, so faith can be educated and trained and thereby be brought into a reasonable and substantial condition of service for the spiritual, mental and physical progress of the individual. The degree of correctness and reliability of this function is proportional to the correctness and scope of the individual conception of the divine modes of action in manifestation, and also to a degree to which the lower faculties on the physical and mental planes are spiritualized and transformed.

Faith has its seat in self-confidence, which is the realization of self-contained power and ability. This self-confidence exists on the physical, mental and spiritual planes and it is the primate of courage and valor; without which there is no advancement, and self-confidence can be developed from the lower to the higher planes in the same way in which all other powers can be made to "come up higher."

Self-confidence has two factors, namely: Perception, which is the rudimentary apprehension or idea that something desirable exists in the immediate environment; and confidence, which is the conviction of the individual that he has the power and ability to grasp and retain the thing desired. Self-confidence is progressive and the attainment of the object sought in progress, has the effect of exalting the potency of all its concomitant factors and thus each new plane of attainment reached requires the further development of both perception and confidence.

Self-confidence is faith in one's self and God-confidence is faith in God, which is only a higher degree of development of the lower potentiality, and the attainment of this degree has the effect of spiritually transforming self-confidence and all its lower attending factors into a condition of God-likeness.

Wherever an individualized soul has come into a recognition of the divine and honestly and sincerely desires to cultivate the divine within himself, he can always positively reckon upon the divine assistance and protection. For this reason, the human soul is an individualized portion of the divine essence, and it partakes, according to its degree of development, of the divine nature and potencies, and therefore it must be always under the divine care and protection, otherwise God would be predicated as out of harmony with, and neglectful of, Himself, which is unthinkable.

Faith is essential to rapid spiritual progress; for, just as physical growth could be brought to a standstill without desire and its attending factors, and just as progress in knowledge, learning and scientific attainment would be hampered and hindered without the exercise of the mental faculties led by the imagination, so spiritual knowledge and progress would be crippled and retarded without faith.

The office of faith is to take the higher potentialities of the known lower display of forces, and carry them up into a higher field for use and development. It must, by the light of the past and the present, boldly and confidently walk into the future; for faith is the emotional equivalent of that inherent individualized power that enables us to advance. Faith cooperates with the will and back of will stands desire. On the higher plane, spiritualized desire partakes of that divine potency, which gives correct intuitive guidance and the act of trusting to this guidance in a new and unknown field, is of itself an act of faith.

There is reasonable ground for the assumption that faith is a factor or potentiality of universal consciousness. Viewed in this light, it may be compared to a "window" or sense opening through which the soul can inductively recognize a truth which is hidden or veiled in the environment; that it can sense there is something desirable behind the veil. Therefore, faith may be classed as one of the pre-sensory powers of the soul, whereby it detects the presence of truth before the more slow going intellect can apprehend and grasp it.

Faith precedes the understanding and gathers material for the understanding to digest and make ready for assimilation. As the physical hand gathers food for the body, so faith may be likened to the spiritual hand that gathers food for the soul.

Faith as a factor of spiritual growth must be distinguished from credulity. Faith is open-eyed and active, a vital living factor of spiritual life. Faith searches out the ideals pertaining to the higher life, the understanding interprets the living truth veiled in these ideals and the soul assimilates into its active, progressive, practical life the living truth thus apprehended, and spiritual growth and spiritual progress of the individualized divine man is the result. Thus, we are saved by faith. The mere intellectual assent to a dogmatic statement, a creed or a formula, is not an act of saving faith; although it may be to some an aid to the conception of higher and better views of personal duty.

MYSTICS

A few days since, while reading an editorial in one of our progressive daily papers, my eye caught the following words: "Plodders and human clods use the word 'visionary' as a term of derision and discredit. The man of little mind is not capable of grasping the eternal truth that the real work for advancement of the world, from the beginning of history, has been done by the seer and the dreamer," and further adds: "It is our belief that the only truly practical man is he who looks into the future, far as human eye can see. It is because of that belief that we admire no man completely who is not a man of imagination." Let us add to this that the man who, clearly seeing into the future, pushes forward with the determination to succeed, to these does the world owe its laurels. What benefactor of the race since time began, but was a dreamer?

Truly not always a seer, but well 'tis so, for many are the blessings the world would not today enjoy had the dreamer always been a seer as well. Synonymous with the word "visionary" have the "plodders and human clods" placed those grand societies they are pleased to call "Mystics." It is a word so often used by those who have but an abstract idea of its correct meaning that it often produces ridicule rather than respect in the mind of the hearer. Let us in all sanity examine the word in connection with its objects and teachings, which on its face would first denote mystery and secrecy.

There has never been a period in the history of man when certain kinds of knowledge was not dangerous to certain classes of humanity, thus these Societies having the betterment of the race in view, it would be destructive to their objects to "cast pearl before swine." The mind of man holds the key to vast powers when known. There are minds so peculiarly constituted that were they placed within reach of those keys would cause the world to "quiver and grow sick at heart," therefore the need of secrecy in conferring knowledge (and a number of these organizations I am more or less familiar and some who have existed under various names for several thousand years) except to those who are sorely tried and known to be qualified to make good and proper use of such benefits for the benefit of the race and not for selfish ends.

Let us next approach one of these "mystic" fraternities as they exist in the twentieth century, examine them in the light of twentieth century investigation, so far as this be permitted. At the outset, we discover it all but impossible to enter their circle, if the aspirant does not possess an unblemished character, possessing virtue, respectability, and a belief in a Supreme God who has created and preserves the universe. (Not such a bad lot of fellows who permit no applicant to join fellowship unless they are satisfied regarding the above.) Let us enter their halls and discover, if possible, their secret ties, the nature of those bonds that have united mankind in their faith since history began. Now, within their walls we first behold peace and harmony, viewing the ceremonies of their lesser mysteries, we see plainly the teacher's wisdom in impressing upon the mind the truths concerning man and his duty to man, and to his God, here the doctrines of immortality of the soul breathe forth a message, though but a whisper or maybe some symbolic scene, yet with a voice that makes the heart feel glad and dim mists pass from the mind as dew before a blazing sun.

Here, within this sphere are found those who bear with us the toils and cares of life, from these ranks in the hour of sickness or distress goes forth an angel unseen, unheard, whose joy is to help a brother in the hour of need. Noble, we say, but we must pass on with but a glance at each degree, higher and higher we pass each succeeding one, opening to our eyes a grander lesson and a greater mystery we are now approaching.

Here we note the neophyte's development, here the source and control of the human mind and will power unfold their greatest mysteries. But let us pass on. Hereafter trials and self-denials, and we come face to face with things too sacred to write, and reaching the higher rungs of the ladder of initiation we pierce the veil that keeps the eyes of the profane from viewing that perfect light whose radiance exceeds the August sun. We turn and looking backward see below a struggling mass of humanity, toiling, longing, and sighing toward that end they see not. Our hearts grow sick and with an affinity greater than the power of the lodestone for the steel, we are attracted to their side, here, to calm a fear, there to comfort and cheer the weary poor as he treads earth's crust in misery and want. It is useless to attempt to enumerate the many sad conditions of man, to whom a helping hand in the hour of need comes as a ministering angel from the purer heavens. It might be advanced that there are some "mystic" fraternities, who are only an imposition upon the credulity of mankind.

To this I say, there being such, is it not disrespectful to condemn and ridicule all because of the few who have strayed from the path of wisdom or that may have had their birth solely as a monetary consideration? Let those who are so ready to use the pen militant against all that appears on the surface as impure, stop long enough to see the fruit of the tree before condemning the species. Let them examine history carefully and note the mighty oaks of progress, and endeavor to discover from what soil they abstracted their nourishment and sustenance, that gave to them precedence over other men of their day.

THE OCCULT SCIENTISTS

Occultism is, as its name implies, a science which embraces the secret laws of the Universe. It has been taught among all great nations of the past, and even at the present time there is scarcely to be found any wild tribe or uncivilized nation that does not have a medicine man or priest who demonstrates some phase of occult science.

It is only among nations who have by false ideas or alleged civilization been led away from the real truth of being, that we find almost total ignorance of the hidden laws which are in fact more potent than the known laws. The name by which such knowledge is known is not material.

In the remote ages of Chaldea, India and Egypt, it was known as The Mysteries. It has since been referred to as The Movement, Magnetism, Occultism, Esoterism and Occult Science. However, the principle is the same in all cases. When Paracelsus returned from the East, he claimed to have found the philosopher's stone, which means he had received the initiation. Later Prof. F. A. Mesmer appeared in France as the exponent of magnetism, which was at that time called Mesmerism. Cagliostro was also enabled to confuse and mystify the world with a knowledge of magnetism. In all ages, the brightest minds have known and practiced Occult Science.

Yet material science has steadily refused to accept it, for the reason that it could not be examined and weighed by the ordinary methods employed in other lines. And for that matter, physical scientists can never hope to understand or examine occult phenomena unless they do so as other students; that is, by aid of the spiritual sense.

An article published in one of the dailies came to I my notice a few days ago in which the writer gleefully stated that no occult phenomena had ever stood the test of science. Such men begin in the wrong way. Like all others, they must begin by development of the spiritual self, as only by such means can they see or hear the invisible forms and sounds from the astral.

Of course, there are many who practice hypnotism without understanding the great forces and principles with which they are in touch. However, few can investigate to any extent without realizing at every turn the existence of an omnipotent and omnipresent God. When one thus realizes the truth, he is impressed with the sacred sublimity of The Absolute and the wonders of his hidden laws.

Thus, the true student of the occult soon learns to approach the temple of Isis with awe and reverence, and full knowledge of the great and awful responsibility which rests upon one who has this knowledge. When he reads that book of books, The Bible, he does so by the aid of his spiritual sense. Where others see only contradictory recitals of ancient events, he reads and understands profound lessons in regard to the sanctuary. To such a one, the crude commercial vibrations encountered on every side are inharmonious.

The orthodox teachings to him are puerile. He knows that "the blind are seeking to lead the blind." Thus we have received a grand revelation which has directed us to form a colony, in the center of which will stand the temple, wherein invitations will be given to the worthy, neophytes from all lands. We shall also have a sanitarium, where the afflicted of all kinds may be healed, with nature's finer forces in conjunction with divine mercy.

There we shall gather about us a number of congenial souls who will live according to the law, keeping ever in mind that our sojourn in the physical is to obtain that experience which will prepare us to continue our progression in higher spheres beyond the borderland. Our colony will be located in one of Nature's most beautiful spots, where harmony of climate and scenery will combine to rest and strengthen the weary pilgrim.

To be sure, dear friends, our ambition will not be realized in a day. However, this is no dream, but a reality. The requirements for admission to our community will be such that only the sincere and worthy will be attracted. Neither is this enterprise launched for commercial purposes; on the other hand, we seek to leave behind us that vibration so strongly charged with materialism and mercenary motives.

We are fully aware also of the opposition one must expect from those who have no sympathy with our work, and are therefore unable to realize our earnestness, but so long as we have the encouragement of our invisible friends, we feel certain of success. And added to this, we have the unanimous support of the great Brotherhood of Oriental Mystics.

How many persons of education and refinement are satisfied with the religious and social conditions of this age? How many pure but disturbed souls long for a place of rest, without awaiting the great change? Why should not a community of sincere men and women who would live according to the tenets of occult science become superior in physical, mental and spiritual attainments?

With right thought, right speech, right acts, why should they not become the perfect race which the Creator intended? Think these questions over carefully.

CONCERNING A NEW STATEMENT OF THEOLOGY

In the last talk there are several propositions worthy of your careful attention and study, among them I have selected the following as the subject for present consideration, viz., "That it is a reasonable proposition to attempt the formulation of a philosophical statement of spiritual law, having for its primary postulates a correct statement of the facts pertaining to the laws of matter and materialization."

In other words: Materialism, correctly stated, must he accepted as the basis on which to build a correct statement of spiritualism. Geology, chemistry, biology, and all the allied sciences must be accepted and their ascertained facts must be used as units in the construction of a correct system of theology. A knowledge of the laws of matter and of our material environment must be acquired as the rudimentary, basic knowledge that shall lead us to a correct knowledge of God. To quote the words of the writer published in 1886: "The laws of the great hereafter must find their antecedents in the laws of manifest nature: matter and life force; matter and intellect."

Matter and morals are so closely interwoven and associated in nature that there can be no system of laws for one that will not apply to the other." My comrades, there is one God, and there is and can be but one systematic statement of truth about God, for it must partake of the unity as well as the fullness of his nature. The Master tells us that God is the Alpha and the Omega, the beginning and the end. The likeness is unto the alphabet wherein God is the first and last expression and between the two, embraced within them, stands the symbols that pertain to God knowledge. Between the beginning and the end, there is manifestation and manifestation is in God, and we are in manifestation. The invitation is to acquire knowledge of God's alphabet, so that he who runs the race may have a "reason for the hope that is within him."

How correctly we can formulate this statement is altogether another thing. We are finite and the subject of our statement is infinite, and words are limitations of limited ideas, still we may indicate the line along which such study should be made, and it is our duty as well as our privilege to make the attempt, and honestly and earnestly strive to comprehend that grand science that embraces all other knowledge to the utmost extent of our finite ability. There is one temple of truth, but there are many worshippers in the temple, each one using formulas of expression adapted to his individual state of conscious perception. Reflect on this and see for yourself the absolute necessity for the broadest charity that each one should have for the opinion of others. Also recognize the rank folly of disputation over subjects that lay hold on infinity. The Master tells it all in one sentence: "let your light shine," i.e., let your knowledge, let your goodness, let your spirituality and your God-likeness be apparent without words, carry it in your aura.

The temple of truth must be built upon a rock and that rock will be found to be a perfect and complete understanding of the facts of material science. Paul, the initiate, says: "The invisible things of God, from the creation of the world are clearly seen, being understood by the things that are made." This you recognize as a re-statement of the ancient mystic axiom: "As in the microcosm, so in the macrocosm."

God's word in nature and God's revelation must harmonize. Nature is in God and nature is God's vehicle of manifestation and revelation. We are the ones in error because we do not fully understand the one or the other. Herein lies the beauty and necessity of humility; the reverential cognizance of the greatness of the object of our study is, indeed, the beginning of wisdom. The question will naturally present itself: Why has not such a statement been attempted before this seemingly late day? There are two forms or methods of reasoning, whereby intellectual conclusions are reached. One is called the deductive and the other is called inductive method. (Study these carefully.)

The deductive method has been with us from earliest history and is the system known to the vast majority of the civilized world to-day, while the inductive method is of later development, dating from the time of Lord Bacon and not coming into extensive use until within the last few decades. The difference between these two methods mark the divergence between ancient and modern science. Since the adoption of the inductive method the march of science, and the progress and diffusion of knowledge has been simply wonderful and in a very large measure this has been brought about by the inductive method of reasoning and the adoption of the scientific method of investigation.

The day of argument and disputation has passed. Partisanship has ceased. Facts are the only things admitted as evidence and one adverse fact clearly proven will destroy any theory no matter how high the standing or how learned its proposer. Briefly, the scientific method is this: An investigator in some specific line of scientific inquiry, after long study and examination, arrives at conclusions that seem to him to be reasonable; he makes a statement of his views, which he calls an "hypothesis," and he formulates his reasons in its favor, which he supports with a as units in the construction of a correct system of theology.

A knowledge of the laws of matter and of our material environment must be acquired as the rudimentary, basic knowledge that shall lead us to a correct knowledge of God. To quote the words of the writer published in 1886: "The laws of the great hereafter must find their antecedents in the laws of manifest nature: matter and life force; matter and intellect. Matter and morals are so closely interwoven and associated in nature that there can be no system of laws for one that will not apply to the other." My comrades, there is one God, and there is and can be but one systematic statement of truth about God, for it must partake of the unity as well as the fullness of his nature. The Master tells us that God is the Alpha and the Omega, the beginning and the end. The likeness is unto the alphabet wherein God is the first and last expression and between the two, embraced within them, stands the symbols that pertain to God knowledge.

Between the beginning and the end, there is manifestation and manifestation is in God, and we are in manifestation. The invitation is to acquire knowledge of God's alphabet, so that he who runs the race may have a "reason for the hope that is within him." How correctly we can formulate this statement is altogether another thing. We are finite and the subject of our statement is infinite, and words are limitations of limited ideas, still we may indicate the line along which such study should be made, and it is our duty as well as our privilege to make the attempt, and honestly and earnestly strive to comprehend that grand science that embraces all other knowledge to the utmost extent of our finite ability.

There is one temple of truth, but there are many worshippers in the temple, each one using formulas of expression adapted to his individual state of conscious perception. Reflect on this and see for yourself the absolute necessity for the broadest charity that each one should have for the opinion of others. Also recognize the rank folly of disputation over subjects that lay hold on infinity. The Master tells it all in one sentence: "let your light shine," i.e., let your knowledge, let your goodness, let your spirituality and your God-likeness be apparent without words, carry it in your aura.

The temple of truth must be built upon a rock and that statement of all the facts pertaining to the subject within the scope of his knowledge. This is presented to the world for criticism and consideration, and after full examination and debate, after all known facts have been presented, if the hypothesis still stands, if it is found to be supported by all the facts bearing upon it; if it satisfactorily correlates with all and antagonizes none, it is finally adopted as a true proposition of science and takes its place as a portion of the accumulated knowledge of the world. In this manner, the atomic theory; the doctrine on the conservation and correlation of force; the dogma of the indestructibility of matter, mind and energy; the doctrine of evolution; the undulatory theory of light and the presence and properties of the luminiferous ether, have each and every one been thrown into the arena of scientific criticism, have all survived the ordeal and are all accepted as truths of science today.

Science has found that truth has inherent life, so it is put into condition and made to fight for its own life, and if the supposed truth does not survive the ordeal, science does not accept it for her own. As you see, the inductive method collects facts and from them it builds its conclusions.

It is a system that has foundations. It is synthetic and it is safe. Gradually all branches of learning are embracing and as far as practicable, are adopting this method of thought.

Material science is now being reseated on this basis, and the study of that form of knowledge that pertains to the nonmaterial is coming into line, and for the first time in history, psychology has a substratum of proven facts on which to base its conclusions. In a rough way, it may be said that the deductive method begins at the top and works downward and that the inductive method begins at the bottom and builds upward. This may be said, however, that both methods possess points of advantage and both methods may be true and correct; the proof of this will lay in the fact that if both are correct, they will meet at the middle distance and form a solid column of truth, thus proving both methods to be what they should be; solid pillars in God's Temple of Truth. Student members of this Brotherhood use both methods, and consequently the opinions of different members are to be construed as from different viewpoints of a common truth.

I am aware that the hypothesis that I am now presenting will occasion criticism, and I sincerely trust that it will. The earnest desire of the writer is to contribute to the presentation of theological truth and to this end honest criticism is a thing to be courted in order that any incorrect or misleading statements may be corrected. Of all the departments of classified knowledge that we dignify by the name of "science" there are none that approach the science of theology in grandeur and importance, for it is a reasonable explanation of the relation that "religion" institutes between the individual human soul and the great source of all wisdom and all love.

II

For anyone to be right, he must be in harmony with the divine mode of action, on his plane of consciousness.

1. The student should be very careful to search out the meaning of words as used in the discussion of any line of thought, and especially does this apply to studies connected with the exposition of science and philosophy, as distinctions are closely drawn and words are carefully selected to be used in their exact sense, so that they may clearly express definite ideas. The word "axiom" means, "a self-evident and necessary truth," "a proposition which, of necessity, must be taken for granted."

2. All systems of philosophy are predicted on certain fundamental statements of fact or supposed fact. In the construction of the system, these statements may be likened to the foundations on which a superstructure is to be erected. The student should, therefore, thoroughly and exhaustively analyze these primary statements. He should subject them to all tests within his power and should apply to them all known methods of research in order to ascertain their reliability and correctness; for it is evident that any error in the basic condition will impair the system in direct proportion to its deviation from an absolute standard of correctness. The question then at once presents itself. Is this statement axiomatic? Is it a self-evident truth? Does your mental and emotional consciousness harmoniously recognize and consent to this statement? Is it true to you now, without debate?

Your careful analysis of this question is vital to your progress in correct thinking, for there is probably nothing in all this conscious universe as important to a spiritually self-conscious entity as a correct statement of spiritual truth, for that which is true for today is of necessity true for all time and is therefore an unfailing guide to future progress. The Master says, that "a house built on solid foundations shall stand." Look well, therefore, to this statement. Ask yourself the question: Is it true to you, today, that one individual that is in harmony with the divine mode of action is, and must be, in a state of rightness?

3. Rightness must be considered in its dual aspect; that is, rightness as it "subsists" in its omniscient, infinite and divine aspect, and rightness as it "exists" in finite manifestation. It is evident that absolute rightness

must be complete and entire. There can, of necessity, be no failure—no weak condition—no flaw or blemish in its operation; otherwise, there would be incompleteness and want of wisdom in the character of the All-Wise, which is unthinkable. It follows, that as rightness is an attribute of the divine character, and therefore a factor in the divine mode of action, a principle and a part of the actuating power behind the action itself; the action must, of itself, be absolutely right and all correlative finite action in harmony therewith, must be relatively right. Furthermore, there cannot be two standards of rightness; one for God himself, and one for God's created and objective universe, and therefore rightness as we understand it must be in relative harmony with rightness as God understands it.

The difference being in degree and not in kind. Infinite rightness "subsists" as a factor of Omniscience; it is an eternal principle, an attribute of the divine character. In manifestation, rightness "exists" in the nature of all things manifested. All modes of divine action bear fruit in rightness; otherwise, this wonderful universe would be a chaos of mismanagement.

4. The divine mode of action being absolutely right, may we not be able to comprehend what rightness is, provided we can correctly comprehend and interpret this mode of action? And that being granted, may we not be able to come into harmony with these modes of action and thus appropriately place ourselves in a condition of rightness? And, furthermore, does it not seem to be the rational and proper way to acquire a knowledge of God's rightness by undertaking an earnest and diligent investigation of his modes of action as manifested in our environment?

5. The acquisition and tabulation of the facts connected with the study of the phenomena of the divine mode of action as realized in the manifest universe is called "science," and the acquisition and tabulation of discoveries of the spiritual ethics contained as principles in the same modes of action and the application of these principles to the spiritual evolution of the individual is called "religion," and the systematic tabulation of these spiritual principles into an orderly and rational statement is called "theology" or God-knowledge. Science, in the generally accepted understanding of the term, is "exoteric," and pertains to the knowledge and understanding of the phenomena of manifestation; while religion is "esoteric" and pertains to that knowledge and understanding that leads to an interior and spiritual unfoldment.

Both are phases of the unfoldment of man's knowledge of rightness. EXOTERIC, FOR THE SATISFACTION OF THE UNDERSTANDING AND AS A FOUNDATION FOR A KNOWLEDGE OF INTERIOR AND HIDDEN PRINCIPLES; AND ESOTERIC FOR THE HARMONIZING OF THE INDIVIDUAL SOUL WITH THE DIVINE. In a universe of rightness, wherein harmony subsists, there can be no conflict between these two. The procession of truth is from one source and from one only. Religion and science are handmaidens and children of the one. This is no assumption. This is an inherent fact, "in the nature of things."

6. In the consideration of this topic as applied to the individual, there are two things that must be carefully borne in mind, i.e., the mental as distinguished from the emotional condition of the individual. The nature dominated by reason as distinguished from the nature dominated by feeling. Science makes its demands more particularly upon the mental consciousness. Religion appeals to both, but more particularly to the emotional. The harmony between religion and science depends upon a correct comprehension of the divine mode of action, both by the mental and the emotional consciousness; both by the head and the heart, and therefore the individual must come into a condition of harmony with his own dual nature before he can fully and correctly come into full harmony with the dual expression of the one reality.

7. There is an axiom handed down to us by the ancient mystics which reads as follows: "There is one law and He that worketh is One." This is a universe of reason, of sanity, and of harmony; a moment's pause and reflection will force the conclusion that this statement is, and must be true. The law of gravitation that Newton discovered by observing the fall of an apple pertains throughout all space. Huxley says, that "any law, or mode of action that is true to-day is true for all time."

The skilled astronomer can place his instrument today, and at a given time in the future he will tell you the hour, moment and second that a named star will cross its center line. There is one law!

The divine mode of action as it pertains to physical growth, does not contradict the divine mode of action as it pertains to spiritual growth. The narrative of physical growth is the allegory that contains the unfolding of the story of spiritual growth. Material science is the "container" or matrix, out of which we get the understanding that enables us to state the science of theology. The "temple not made with hands, eternal in the heavens," has for its foundation stones the hard and immutable facts of materiality.

The law that pertains to the physical plane is the same law, unfolded, developed and spiritualized, that pertains to the mental, moral and spiritual planes, or states of consciousness, and the mode, method and process of growth from the lower to the higher is correspondingly the same. If the interpretation of the law of physical growth is correctly stated by what we call the "law of evolution," then in order to correctly understand the law of spiritual growth we must observe the same law unfolded, developed and spiritualized as it works upon the higher plane; for law on one plane of consciousness does not conflict with law on any other plane of consciousness. No religion or theology can be correctly formulated that does not fully harmonize with the facts that interpret the divine modes of action on all planes of existence.

8. If it is true that rightness consists in being in a condition of harmony with the divine modes of action, it necessarily follows: That anything that is not in such a condition of harmony is not in a condition of rightness; and it also follows that this condition of un-rightness is proportional to its degree of divergence from the divine mode of action. If the first condition is one of truth, the second condition is one of error and it is self-evident that this condition of error can be eliminated or corrected by any action that will restore the harmony.

To illustrate: You can strike wrong notes upon a musical instrument and a discord will be the result, but you can correct that discord by striking the right notes and thus effect a restoration of harmony. Your mentality informs you which notes are incorrect and your emotions cooperating with your will impel you to make the correction. Thus, by your own act and choice, you place yourself in a condition of harmony.

9. Two sets of factors may be considered in this connection: Rightness as distinguished from wrongness. HARMONY AS DISTINGUISHED FROM DISCORD. TRUTH AS DISTINGUISHED FROM ERROR. The first set of factors, i.e., rightness, harmony and truth, derive their positive and fixed character by reason of their being in harmony with the divine mode of action.

The second set of factors, i.e., wrongness, discord and error, derive their descriptive condition by reason of their being divergent from such a condition of harmony and their comparative condition is to be measured by their degree of divergence. This second set of factors also has the dual aspect. Error may occur through ignorance, or it may be instituted by willful intention.

Whenever a willful divergence from the divine mode of action is instituted by a spiritually self-conscious entity, such a divergence is called "sin" and deliberate repetition of such action tends to increase the degree of divergence, consequently an individual can "grow" less harmonious or more harmonious with the divine mode of action as he may choose; His condition of harmony or in harmony depends primarily upon himself. He makes his own character by his own acts and choices. Spiritual individualization is only attained by the exercise of the conscious free will of the individual, and in order to succeed in its attainment each one must be free to direct, guide and control his own growth.

One cannot "grow" his neighbor, but one can help him to grow by extending the divine harmony into his neighbor's environment. This is the reason why the Master inculcated the broadest charity of thought and action. Charity has a reflex action. Similarly, as the physical body grows strong and healthy by a proper choice of harmonious food, so the spiritual character grows strong, healthy and permanent by its choices of harmonious actions. Its permanence being assured by the constantly added portions of the divine spirit which it receives and individualizes through and by means of these spiritual choices.

The mystery of life manifest is the allegory of the mystery of life un-manifest.

10. Proper food for moral and spiritual growth must have dual characteristics that will provide for the requirements of an entity having a dual nature. The individual having the aspect of both mentality and emotions, it follows, that food proper for uniform growth should be able to provide pabulum for growth in both directions. This is the reason why theology and religion should go hand in hand. The emotional nature may be satisfied with the effect produced by the influx of spiritual food, but the mental nature constantly calls out. Why is this? Explain its reasons? Satisfy my understanding.

The mistakes and extravagancies of so-called religious fanatics are explained by this statement. The spiritual growth of the fanatic has not been uniform and possibly not correct. The feelings, the emotional nature has been over-excited and reason and sanity has been neglected or suppressed.

11. If natural law and spiritual law are handmaidens, so, in like manner, should reason and emotion walk lovingly side by side, for the preponderance of either factor will cause a distortion of the presentation of

spiritual truth. I would therefore ask you to consider these statements very carefully and deliberately. I would have you become real students by the careful examination of every statement and with profound deliberation, by yourself and for yourself, having the sole object in view of determining whether these preliminary postulates are really correct and true. Avoid prejudice and endeavor to bring, for yourself, by yourself and with yourself, reason and emotion into harmony. Become a "free thinker" in the truest and most God-like sense of the word.

12. Reason has been described as cold and, to some natures, unattractive but always hold firmly in mind that justice, rightness and wholeness exist in the universe because the one is pure reason and that reason (omniscience) is only an attribute of one "subsistence" whose very nature and expression is harmony and love.

When you come into the full understanding; when you come to know and feel that wisdom and love are one, then will many things be made plain that are now seemingly obscure; then may you say: "My ways shall be thy ways and thy ways shall be my ways; peace cometh with understanding."

13. Let us next take into consideration the second, or modifying clause of this statement, viz., "on his plane of consciousness." Men are not equal in all their capacities and capabilities; some are highly developed along certain lines and at the same time are woefully lacking in other directions. It is a rare thing to find a person that possesses an even and well-balanced development in all dimensions. Different conditions of growth, development and environment account for many of these differences.

My personal condition of consciousness embraces the cognizance of a varied number of phenomenal contacts with my personal environment. Your personal condition of consciousness is the result of an indefinite number of contacts with your personal environment. Your environment and mine are different; our states of consciousness are therefore different.

In a general way, and to make a statement embracing the full scope of the subject, it may be said, that The conscious position of any organism, in the scale of existence depends upon the degree to which it has become master of the total environment with which it is possible for any organism to come into the life relation.

14. You see, therefore, that it is almost impossible and certainly high-

ly improbable, for any two individuals to be found that are exactly alike in their position in the scale of conscious development. There may be many that are closely approximate in their degree of development, at the same time there are others, just as honest, just as sincere and just as truly on the road of upward progress, who are widely divergent.

This is the reason why there exists a necessity for sects and parties having partly diverse standards of religious belief. Men are Catholics, Protestants, Mohamedans or Buddhists simply because they come together on planes of consciousness that give them a community of belief in certain formulas of doctrine. Sects in religion and systems in theology are necessary because there are classes of individuals that need spiritual food of different attenuations and of varied quality and quantity.

Spiritual progress does not demand the destruction of these sects and systems, but it does demand such a liberalization of the standards of belief that the growing soul may not be bound and fettered by formulas that it has outgrown.

The progressive soul must be permitted the utmost freedom to rise higher and higher in understanding and comprehension and it must be given the fullest opportunity to assimilate, in its growth, the greater and broader realization of the divine harmonies. For the want of this liberality, many devout souls have practically withdrawn from the visible church and have joined together in societies and assemblies of students that care less for assertive form than they do for the vital esoteric meaning that is veiled and concealed under and within the exoteric formulas and statements of all philosophy. Under such a view, it appears to be evident that all sects and societies whose object is looking towards the common good should exercise a kindly feeling towards one and another.

15. In the larger view, these planes of consciousness take on a grander aspect; for nature works in spirals and the progressive souls that have made a "round" or completed a spiral, comes out on a higher and more comprehensive view-point, where the same truth that was recognized on a lower plane, or round, takes on a more magnificent aspect and with it comes a deeper insight into its mystic beauty. It is evident that individuals having such experiences cannot be fully comprehended by those of more limited realizations and, therefore, they are naturally obliged to seek a kindred companionship with others of their own class.

16. The interpretation of truth has to be made in such a manner that different persons on different planes, or conditions of consciousness, can

comprehend it in quantity and quality sufficient for their specific needs of growth while they remain on that specific plane of consciousness. When they advance to a higher condition carrying with such advance a greater capacity for comprehension and assimilation of truth, there will then arise the necessity for the unfoldment of a higher conception of the same truth; the correctness and reliability of these advances will be measured by the fact that the individual has become, mentally and emotionally, more harmonized, in thought and action with the divine mode of action in manifestation.

17. It is evident that anyone, on any plane of consciousness, can, by his own act, place himself in a condition of more or less harmony with the divine mode of action, as completely and as thoroughly, as his own personal state of consciousness will permit him to understand the necessary conditions precedent to the attainment of such harmony. Truth exists in the environment for those who have the capacity to see. Spiritual blindness is not a fault! It is a want of development of the capacity for spiritual sight. Non-cognition is due more to ignorance than to willfulness. Because one's neighbor cannot see a presentation of spiritual truth in the same light that we do is no reason why he should be classed as beneath us in spiritual development, for, in point of fact, he may average in fullness and completeness of character far better than ourselves. Spiritual growth consists of advancement from a lower to a higher plane of spiritual consciousness, and those who are the most earnest, those who strive the hardest to become the best fitted, will advance the most rapidly.

18. If it be true that rightness consists in being in harmony with the divine mode of action, it follows, that individual or personal rightness consists in being in harmony with the divine mode of action as far and as completely as it lies within the power of the individual to comprehend and to place himself in such a condition of harmony, no matter what his state or condition of consciousness may be. This gives us what we need: an absolute standard of perfection in rightness. One that is beyond man's attainment in his present state of limitation and, at the same time, one that is comparatively and proportionately attainable by any man; no matter how limited his development or how meagre his moral ability was.

19. The adoption of this standard of measurement permits each one to measure his own moral and spiritual stature; but it gives him no right whatever to measure that of his neighbor; a very desirable condition, the

adoption of which would greatly hasten the general condition of spiritual progress. In point of fact it would appear, that while his criticism of himself would be approximately correct, his criticism of his neighbor would be certainly more or less wrong, for the reason that he has no means of knowing the real state or condition of his neighbor's spiritual consciousness. This standard may be used by anyone, for himself and by himself, and to its requirements he may adjust each and every action of his life. By its definition, a righteous man is: One who in every thought, word and deed qualifies and adjusts his very action so as to live up to his highest conception of that which makes for the most perfect divine harmony in himself and in his environment. Progressively this is the ultimate standard of Christian attainment and the nearer we reach the ultimate condition, the more alike in character men will be, but in the lower stages of progress a given number of men may be classed as "righteous," and still they may vary exceedingly in their personal character and one merit of this proposition is, that it discourages all comparisons between individuals as to their various degrees of personal righteousness.

20. If the foregoing statements be conceded, it then follows, as applicable to finite spiritual progress: First. That absolute and ultimate rightness, in all its divine fullness, consists in absolute, complete and entire conformity to, and cooperation with, the divine mode of action on all planes of consciousness.

Second. That individual rightness is complete or incomplete, in degree, as it approaches to, or recedes from, such a condition of harmony.

Third. That while there is a standard of ultimate rightness that all may strive to attain unto; each individual must, of necessity, have a separate and distinct standard of his own which, as compared with the ultimate standard, will be higher or lower and therefore more or less complete and perfect, according to the character, ability and personal idiosyncrasies of the individual.

Fourth. It is, therefore, manifestly impossible for any two individuals to fully and exactly agree upon all the statements that are made regarding any one system of moral or spiritual philosophy, for while they may agree upon the ultimate statements and their leading deductions, as well as upon many minor details, the very fact that there are no two individuals exactly alike, produces as many standpoints of conception and experience as there are separate individuals and therefore as many individual planes, or separate states of consciousness.

Fifth. All divergence from the divine mode of action must occasion discord, and, as distinguished from truth and right, such must be classed as "error" and "wrong" and this being a universe where cause and effect strictly pertain, it therefore follows that all right action must cause, and merit, compensation and that all wrong action must cause and incur penalty.

Sixth. Error, on the part of an individual, may be of two kinds, viz., that which occurs through ignorance and that which occurs through willfulness, and the penalty must be different in the different cases.

Seventh. The correction of errors arising through ignorance is the vehicle for the attainment of knowledge. When you recognize an error, you learn something. This is the mystic sense of the statement made by Paul the Initiate, viz., the law (divine mode of action) is the schoolmaster that leads me to Christ. (Christos knowledge.)

The correction of errors arising through willfulness is the vehicle for the attainment of character. "Blessed are the poor in spirit," means: Sanctioned by God are those who have diminished the dominance of their lower natures and have exalted the dominance of their higher selves. That which lasts, that which "passes through" and endures forever, is divine character and in human development, that is formed by the voluntary correction of error. Each act that knowingly corrects an error is an act of redemption. There are three aspects of redemption, viz., that of the redemption of the individual entity, that of the race, and, in a larger and more comprehensive view, that of the so-called world; the redemption of creation.

When creation shall have accomplished its purpose, when all things shall have been fulfilled; when all error shall have been transformed into the divine harmony; then shall be the end typified as by "fire," but the fire is the fervent heat of the divine love which shall be recognized everywhere, and which shall permeate everything. This is the Christian interpretation of the eastern doctrine called "Nirvana."

Eighth. God—by direct act or interference—does not correct the error. That which has produced error must become enlightened by "the light that shineth in darkness" and the darkness must learn to comprehend the light, and make its own corrections. Every right choice contributes to this consummation.

Ninth. The adjustment, or correction of error by the individual, while it aids and assists the growth of the individual in knowledge and character, contributes to still farther progress by bringing about a still higher condition of knowledge which is called "understanding."

Tenth. Understanding is the open door through which the individual gets his perception and comprehension of the divine wisdom. This understanding satisfies and develops his mental nature and brings peace and rest to the emotional. Righteousness and peace are united in loving embrace and consequently harmony exists in the individual; and, finally, the individual, after a long series of choices and adjustments, embracing many cycles of lives, by means of, and as a result of, his own efforts and struggles and by the development of his own potencies and potentialities becomes fitted to enter into, what is mystically called "the rest that remaineth for the people of God."

Mark the word "remaineth." After all is done, after all is passed through, after all earthly things are left behind and the victory over their power is won, there remaineth God and God-like individualized character.

21. I have indicated to you, in brief, a line of study in spiritual evolution. Study and compare it with the evolution of the physical, and you will find no want of harmony of correspondence. For, "there is one law and He that worketh it is one." Observe the fact that the individual entity makes his own character through his own acts and choices. He "grows" his own soul by the self-development of his own potentialities, by the exercise of his own will and determination.

He "overcomes" by his own efforts. He climbs the ladder of attainment by his own exertions. He makes himself. He is not created. He creates himself. In his choices, he must stand alone. In his acts, he can have all the help that he desires and will accept. The boundless resources of divine omnipotence are always in his environment for his personal aid and succor. The sheltering arms of divine omnipresence are always extended to him for his comfort and sympathy. If he will have aid, counsel, comfort or sympathy, all is subject to his request, but on him alone devolves the choice.

It lays with him to accept or to decline. In the very "nature of things" there can be no interference with the free choice of the moral self-conscious individual, for in that way alone lies the road to perfect individualization. The individual entity must be left to his own free choice so that when he does arrive at the apex, he may be able to say, "I am that I am." He must become "Son of God," and he must also become, 'Son of Man.'

MYSTERIES

Again, speaking of our mysteries, many will ask why are these things mysteries. I will answer, only because wicked men and power-loving priests usurped the rights which originally were ours of teaching man his true relations to his maker, the Great Eternal Sun. Thus, have they covered spiritual truths until in a later day, Egypt became a nation of erring peoples, "erred and fallen." How much greater would the happiness have been for the masses, how much longer might our land have continued to be the chosen, the elect, had not our work been given over to the money and power-loving priesthood?

Greece took up our remnants, that is, the remnant of what the priests taught of pure spiritual advancement. There are scholars who believe the heights of initiation were only accomplished after our doctrines were ruled by the priesthood. True, they have contributed their part to discovery and understanding of certain forces in nature, but the loss to the human family in general happiness is beyond power of reckoning.

You say why were we then under such rule and since silent workers, not as members of the Fraternity, but as individuals? The reason is plain. Who dare teach other than the accepted doctrines of the day concerning man, spirit, or matter is doomed by priests and governments to the stake or death in some form. Study history and you have your proof. What then was to be done by those who were opposed to this inhuman treatment? But two things were possible. Acknowledge your truths to the world and die, which soon would have extinguished these Fraternities, or meet silently, practicing the rites after the manner of each land or people.

Thus, pass the knowledge down the centuries of time until that day when again opportunity permitted their general diffusion, which last was done. And there another century passes, our truths will be taught as once they were in all purity to the little ones. May our great guiding light speed the day. Again, there are those who will ask if the ancient worship consisted solely in the worship of the great central spiritual Sun, why the need of the varied phenomena usually accompanying those pure religions of nature?

To this I would answer, aside of that which tends to elevation of human character and soul advancement, it matters not whether found in the category of religions practiced by domineering priests, or by charlatans to demonstrate their greatness, to secure a livelihood or otherwise, these things were a given result of certain conditions and accomplished according to the operator's knowledge of these laws which are becoming more and more the property of the general public. Examine for a moment the phenomena now known and demonstrated as electricity, magnetism, and various strange results obtained by the experienced chemist.

Many of these things would make the ancient magi look cheap. Yet these things which we understand seem to occasion little or no thought upon those who seem to think that ancient times possessed more knowledge than do we of this day. On the other hand, the powers of mind in direct application to man's needs and wants both naturally, while in this life, as well as from the soul's point of view, has not yet reached the height of ancient times, and the public is therefore ignorant of many of these powerful occult laws, they being held as secrets by our ancient fraternities, and only communicated to those who are qualified to receive and use them for good and right purposes.

INITIATION

Initiation, is there another word to be found in any tongue so full of meaning, so misconstrued? Each within him or herself has attempted to explain it and all have failed, for no man or woman has ever been found who could find words to fully express its mystic meaning, that change which takes place within one who has truly been initiated.

Many there are who shall read these words who, while having had conferred upon them the benefits of many societies and fraternities, yet have not truly been initiated. Thousands there are who have traveled the path of inner mysteries only to emerge uninitiated. You would ask me to define "initiation" my answer would be, can the finite grasp the wonders of the infinite. No, emphatically no, in our present state of evolution we may attain the heights of initiation, we cannot find words to explain exactly what it means to become an initiate. Many believe that initiation can be no other than the reception into certain rites, ceremonies, etc., upon which ceremonies is placed special benedictions, earthly or otherwise, but I would have you know, you who have not experienced an entrance to the mysteries, that initiation is indeed a great change which takes place within the person initiated, and beyond words of expression. If this be the case, the uninformed will ask why the need for so much secrecy in all ages by those societies, teaching the way of initiation?

Truth has always had its enemies. No age, to our knowledge, has existed when evil forces have not been busily at work to undo the good of the children of truth. Nothing suffers from the hands of the profane so readily and surely as when thrown broadcast to an un-appreciating and barbaric public. Did not the man of Nazareth say: "Cast not pearl before swine?" To those who look at secrecy in any form as the product of the evil one, I would say, the doors to the mysteries are ever open to those who would travel the rugged and stony path to initiation. The door is open, and the guards of the temple have bid all welcome who would come prepared. That preparation is a desire for wisdom, for oneness with the spirit, who alone can give true happiness, a happiness that words in no tongue can express. Would you enter the temple, then pray, pray from your soul for light, pray in truth and sincerity, swear by the Bible of truth that you will obey the "still small voice" that speaks to you, and you will soon realize that you have indeed found the path to tine initiation.

But prayer alone, which may be silent or loud, is but the desire and sincere and extreme desire founded on whole-soul ness is a great prayer and one that will always be answered. The critic will ask: From where but the desiring ones will understand. Many there are who will say, "If the door is prayer the Church is the true path." To this I will answer, "The Sons of Osiris (children of God) care not how the means through which the poor soul shall first see the light and 'find the Christ,' so long as they find it. Our desire is that, those who long for supreme initiation shall find it." Yet, those institutions that teach us that no life is sacred but the human, that your future evolution is dependent upon your presence at religious ceremonies and large donations to the church are all enemies of man. Beware of such false doctrines, they would lead you astray from beaten paths leading to true happiness, and oneness with the Spirit of God which we call the Christ. Enter you into the sanctuary of your own soul, after purification, and within it you will find all happiness; yea, all that is needed for your happiness now and forever. Let no one lead you to look beyond yourself for the door to initiation.

Our mystic fraternities can guide your wandering feet; they may lead you with a hand of tenderness to the shrine where you would need worship. But this is naught unless you would worship the truth concealed there, and not the shrine itself. "Man, know thyself," has been placed over the doors of many temples, yet men search for initiation, passing this sign unheeded and their search is in vain. Then set your house in order, and guests bidden then will call and sup with you. But do not expect to commune with spirit, and that by reason of your determination to learn God's purest angels until you have become truly born of the holy life. Doing unto your neighbor as you would be done by. You cannot enjoy the riches of the Master unless you have served the Master. You will not enjoy that unspeakable joy of the initiated unless you serve your race in such capacity as is within your power to do.

THOUGHT

Says one who is unknown: "If you knew all about thought, its Laws, Principles, and it's Powers, you could dissolve this earth by a single thought." Even a limited knowledge of the laws of thought, combined with the power of thought control, which is gained by observing certain occult or thought practices, will enable you to gratify your every desire, through the magic of a wish. Do you doubt it?

Evidence to substantiate this abounds everywhere. The demonstration needs not to be perfect to be convincing. It is said, that in order to be successful in business, one must keep his mind on it. Our most successful businessmen prove it beyond the slightest doubt. Our self-made men were in their early days in a position where they had to keep their thought force focused on business, and therefore, their success. They succeeded through the application of occult principles, however faulty and imperfect such application may have been.

Can you not see what great possibilities would be open to him who studies these laws of thought, and intelligently applies them in his everyday life? But that is too simple to be it—to be that potent and creative occult force you speak about! You are right, it is simple; truth is always simple and self-evident in its conclusions, provided you fully understand it.

The thinking of creative thoughts, by the awakening of the inner self, is the true method of thinking. This can be done only through occult practices. That there exists something beyond this "house of clay" is no longer a religious dogma only, but has been absolutely proven by science.

There exists a cause, which is the creator, of which the visible universe, the creation, with all its various manifestations, is only the effect. Does it seem impossible to you, that by connecting yourself with the cause, which is within you, you can produce creative effects at will and become a creator? You are a creator now: your body, environments, finances and opportunities are all of your own making. Are you fully satisfied with your life and its results as they are? Probably not.

Your health, your home and business life are perhaps not exactly as you would like them to be. Can you not see that you can change all undesirable conditions into desirable ones, simply by a process of thought? All your relations to the outside world, your health, your finances, your friends, etc., are the results of your own thought, either during this or a previous incarnation, and are subject to change at will. "Truth is stranger than fiction" is a very old and true saying, which is particularly true if applied to occult science.

We do not wish to attack religion, but we must confess the truth, that the erroneous "total depravity" and the "worm-of-the-dust" theory of the various churches have done more harm than we could enumerate. Man is by no means a "worm of the dust:" on the contrary, he possesses the quintessence of Deity, which, although a mere germ in most of us, we can develop through occult practices, until it tills our lives and we become powerful "like unto God." Does this seem impossible, or do these theories seek to belittle God? Certainly not, but on the contrary. "Imitation," it has been truly said, "is the sincerest flattery." So, man best honors God when he seeks to be like God. Does not your religion teach you that you are a son of God? Does it not follow, that the son, although a child at first, will grow and become "like unto the father?"

We can, however, become so through knowledge only. This is an age of transition of the old conditions into new and glorious ones. Destruction of the old and construction of the new is already in progress all around us. Mighty forces, mental and spiritual, good and evil, are constantly playing upon man from without and from within. The great majority of the human race is driven helplessly like leaves before a storm. Great fortunes are swept away, nations are in revolt, and all sorts of pretenders and humbugs arise and seek adherents and followers. Instead of ruling these forces, and guiding events, man is, and will remain, a slave to circumstances and environments, until he learns to know himself and the tremendous forces which are latent within and await awakening. Occult Science has not only supplied knowledge by which man can rise above his surroundings—a master—but has established beyond a doubt the connecting link between science and religion.

In the study and practice of occult principles lies your salvation. In fact, it is your only salvation from everything undesirable in life. Do you want health—good health, which makes life worth living? Do you desire "Vital Magnetism" in such a degree as will enable you to make a success? It will come to you if you adhere to the easy and pleasant methods given. Think of the doctor's and druggist's bills, which will be a thing of the past. Of course, you value business success and advancement, or perhaps prominence in a profession. Occult Science can be applied to all these things. Occult Philosophy is the godmother and progenitor of all intellectual forces, the key to all divine obscurities, and the absolute queen of society.

The grandest achievements ever gained by man were originally concealed in the ancient mysteries. This knowledge was veiled in order to conceal it from the profane but written in a universal language of symbolism that it might be understood by the true initiates of all ages. From the earliest times, those who wished to study the secret and hidden things of nature have found it necessary to band themselves together in Brotherhoods for the purpose of self-protection and to preserve their knowledge from destruction by the ignorant masses. It is asserted in the Far East that the Great Lodge of Adepts or Perfect Masters has never ceased to exist; and that this lodge has often, though secret and unknown, shaped the course of empires and controlled the fate of nations.

In modern times, all those who have reached the highest point of success have taken advantage of the laws of the higher forces. They have put themselves into close harmony with the powers of the invisible. In this manner, they were led onward and upward to that which they desired.

IS THERE NEED FOR A NEW RELIGION?

In two notable products of literature, in the novel of Martin Martens, called the New Religion, the author, a Hollander, writing in English, calls attention by means of fiction, to the health fads and sanitarium vagaries whereby people hunt for health or what is alleged to be health in the absence of a former sustained faith or conviction. The health craze, this novelist contends, is the crying of the soul for something to sustain man and to give him vision. The older faith no longer appeals and hence the substitute, this hurry and scurry from one resort to another to heal the body, whereas it is the soul or the whole of the individual that requires healing.

Another novelist, an American, in a wonderful piece of analysis, puts into the mouth of a physician, a man of science, the telling dictum of our day. We moderns need a new religion. The new religion is to restore peace within the tempestuous restlessness, the nervous agitation, the emptiness and unreality of our own civilization. The denominational statements of religions have lost their appeal and the haunting cry of an unsatisfied soul clamors anew for the sustaining vision of man's purpose and individual destiny.

Fiction, one might object, is an unworthy or an unreliable argument. But modern fiction serves the place of the philosopher. By means of fiction, the preacher sermonizes and the teacher expounds. In our better fiction is revealed the deep perplexities of our day. Here indeed is a great truth brought home. The reaction against materialism has set in. Men today are demanding a new religion through the words of their appointed spokesmen, the fictionists and novel writers.

But let us be frank. We have a right to know exactly what this need is, which is so engrossing the minds of our thinkers. The novelists are not alone in demanding a new expression for the eternal craving of the soul. Philosophy too is not negligent in requiring a fuller explanation of man and his eternal struggle. Prof. Boyce, in his Philosophy of Loyalty, has no scruples in accepting as the primary supposition, the universally refuted dogmas of older denominations.

The articles of faith once solemnly accepted are no longer tenable among the legions of thinking beings. It is agreed that all thinking men and women are no longer adherents of the old faiths, which include the articles of faith and confessions and creeds. The day is ripe; the time is here for a new expression of religion. And in this appeal lies the grandeur and majesty of the human soul. It is a fiat and imperative denial of the argument of materialism which said with more arrogance than conviction that religion is an imposition, a contrivance of deceit invented by designing men who tried to include and beguile credulous humanity. Religion is the deepest and most universal appeal of the human being. At the heart of religion is the consciousness of unity. Religion is a bond of union, a mating of the individual with that which is for that individual, the universal; an uplifting of the one into a stream of continuous life, the merging of what is mortal with that which is immortal.

However, expressed or formulated there is no denying the fact that man can no more rid himself of the need of religion than he can of the need of expression in human forms of art or letters. This, of course, is the death blow to the careless philosophy of the street, the so-called wisdom of the mere "business" man who counted religion as he did his daily sales, and looked upon it merely as a convenience of respectability or a stubborn convention which it was safest policy for him to adopt because it is the fashion.

But this cry sounds deeper depths than the mere phrases indicate. The new religion is not so glibly expounded or so readily dealt with. Religion is a development, a growth. One form is cast aside for the adoption of other and better forms of expression. And at this point of the argument it is best to say what was intended to admit in the first place—the world cry for a new religion, vocal here in. America as it is abroad, this longing for larger conceptions of man's destiny does not shock Israel of the religion of Judaism.

Let us say now openly, admitting the charge of conceit if it needs to be charged against us—that for Judaism, the need of a new religion is not apparent. For the statements of the new religious ideals voice the ethical injunctions of Judaism. In other words the new religion which is formulating its creed in our day is a roughly drafted excerpt of Judaism with the historical imperative omitted. On the adherents of the new religion is not placed the historical responsibility imposed on the Jew to continue his religion and to redeem thereby the wayward and misguided children of men.

Let not the Jew hesitate to say this: that in his religious outlook rests the salvation of the world, for he was told of old that salvation comes from the Jew. The Jewish genius is a religious one. The ethical ideals of humanity are traced to Judaism. If today the liberal and progressive thinkers of our generation proclaim the ideals and ideas which Judaism has preserved for centuries, it is the duty of the Jew to lay claim to his ancient prerogative and say boldly that he has taught these truths not for himself alone but for all people. We know that no religion can be entirely new. Reform Judaism is not new. One phase of Judaism gives way to another. The germinal thought expands. In every age, thinkers give it their bias and impulse. The original central ideal never vanishes but enlarges. Every reform in Judaism is not a departure from it, but a return to Judaism.

No one age is entirely right; no one person has all the truth there is. For truth is in the mass. What does the new religion believe? It believes in God. What does this mean? It means that there is an eternal purpose, an energy, an unending motion which works for a righteous end, and that we and all living beings are part of that divine energy, which is God. Furthermore, that our errors (or sins if you will), man's failures as well as his victories, the triumphs of his will are the manifestations of that impulse and that we are working for a larger conquest of that energy so that we as human beings may come into a fuller realization of ourselves through the various means of our mortality.

The fundamental axiom of the new religion is that there is a God who is the creator of the ends of the world. And now the new religion incorporates a distinctly Jewish thought, and it is this: that man is created in the image of God. Man is endowed with godly properties—he is a part of the divine energy and through him does God reveal himself. The heroism, the courage, the goodness and mercy which is enacted by the human being is the revelation of God's goodness and mercy and righteousness. We are not victims of chance, playthings of fate, cast thoughtlessly into the world to fume and fret, but we are parts of a larger destiny which makes us actors in the divine drama.

From us emerges the whole of the past, which we transmit to succeeding generations. After having enlarged our heritage, we go from eternity to eternity, but each eternity is within us. What does this conception of "humanity avoid"? What does the new religion upset? It upsets and uproots the notion that man is a curse instead of a blessing. It assures him that he is a divine heritage rather than the victim of sin and doom. It makes him see the beauty of earth and the beauty of his own being and urges him to abide here among his fellows, a partner with his fellow beings in the work of eventual salvation when through his demands for recognition as a human being, a child and son of God, he establishes justice here among men as the great law of equity—refusing to let another degrade him or debase the divinity inborn in him. The new religion is the exultation and exaltation of man as the son of God, all men born free and equal in the cosmic strife to rise.

This new religion demands too that man must realize his share and part in the world of struggle, not the struggle for bread alone, but the struggle to aid the nobler impulses. He must be a worker. Whatever his task, that task adds to the realization of the divine purpose. No task is too mean.

The drudgery of doing so-called menial labors is no discipline, it is a duty which shall eventually bring peace into the world. What is this peace? It is the merging of the self in the stream of life, the realization of one's essential relationship to the totality of the world. It includes everyone, this democracy of peace, this kingdom of God—none are too low, none are too mean, none cast aside as rubbish to the void—all are needed and all of life is good.

THE NEW THEOLOGY DUALISM

Dualism is written large over all nature and all manifestation. It has always been considered a difficult subject to explain and one reason of this difficulty consists in the fact that it is the attempt of a finite mind using a physical and material brain as a vehicle of expression, to comprehend and describe a condition of infinity. This factor of the investigation has led many to consider it incomprehensible and unexplainable, but students engaged in psychological investigation are well aware of the fact that the spiritualized intelligence partakes of infinity in proportion to the degree to which it has become spiritually developed and therefore it is not only fitting and proper, but it is an act of honor to the Supreme, that we make an attempt to comprehend His works. In so doing we should always recognize, with due humility, our own limitations, keeping constantly in mind the statement of the apostle, that, "The natural man knoweth not of the things of God because they are spiritually discerned."

2. The problem of dualism has always been a very prominent one in the discussion of religion, philosophy, psychology and metaphysics. It was the "keynote" of all savage and primitive religions and is prominent in the statements of all the later religions, including the Egyptian, Persian, Grecian.

Roman and the Christian. Following Pythagoras and Zoroaster, instead of Jesus, the philosophy of Paul and Augustine has incorporated into the statement of belief of the Christian Church a rigid dualism and an uncompromising and uncharitable dogmatism that has, in all probability, done more to materialize and harden the beautiful and lovable message as presented by "the Master" than any one of the original component factors of the Christian organization.

3. As said before, all ancient as well as all modern systems of philosophy recognize the (seeming) existence of two opposing forces in, and back of, all manifestations, whether material or psychic. One power that is benefic, and another that is malefic. Good in constant striving with evil. A Great Being, who is to be adored as God, opposed to another Great Being, who is to be feared and placated and whom they term "the Devil." History gives us the picture of the world as a battleground on which these two opposing forces are contending for the mastery. Good, or Rightness as engaged in a contest with Evil, or un-rightness. In a large sense, this is a true picture and it is a presentation of fact; the error consists in the 'personification' of these contending principles and therefore, in the consideration of them as consisting of two separate and distinct forces. The ancient mystic and the modern "new thought" being the true interpretation; that God, Good, Rightness only, subsists and exists and that evil is the negative condition and is only apparent where God is not. As the darkness is dispelled by the presence of light, so the "Doxa," the outshining of God's presence, dispels the shadows of ignorance and seeing evil.

4. The marvelous advance in knowledge and correct thinking of this "latter day" lies conclusively shown us that, "in the nature of things" there cannot be two opposite and contending forces in nature; that the statement of "the Master" was true when lie said that "a house divided against itself must fall." If it be true, that God is omnipresent in this universe as a sustaining and adjusting principle of harmony and rightness, it necessarily follows, that what we call evil and un-rightness, consists in the ignorance and the non-recognition of this sustaining and adjusting principle and power. Justice requires that sin cannot be imputed to one who has no conscious recognition of moral and spiritual requirement. It is evident that the creatures that exist below the plane of moral self-consciousness. live sinless lives, as measured by our standards and evidently, equal and exact justice does not require that a penalty should be placed upon this violation of moral and spiritual requirements where there is no recognition or comprehension of moral or spiritual obligation. The "new thought" now begins to recognize the statement, that creation in order to be perfect must, necessarily go to the utmost limit that was necessary to accomplish its object, and therefore, in order to fully and completely manifest God in His infinity and fullness, the outmost limit, or the "borne of impulse" of involution, must convey the idea of no-God.

To explain more definitely: If it be granted that the object of creation is redemption involving the evolution of God-like Entities, it follows that these entities must begin their life course at the extreme limit of consciousness—at a point where consciousness is so dim and undeveloped that the entity is not self-conscious and therefore not God-conscious. In this we recognize the necessity of the seeming duality which in its larger operation is shown by the outgoing or centrifugal force and the returning or centripetal force. The out-breathing and the in-breathing of the Divine breath as explained by our oriental brothers.

In the out-breathing or centrifugal expenditure of the divine energy, the divine consciousness is "involved" or "rolled up" in creation. In the in-breathing or centripetal display of the divine energy, the divine consciousness which was involved or "rolled up" in creation is unrolled or evolved in redemption. Involution being the centrifugal energy that "creates" a vehicle proper for the accomplishment of God's purpose and evolution being the centripetal energy that carries with it the accomplishment of this divine intention. As it is written: "My word shall not return unto me void, but it shall accomplish the thing whereunto I have sent it."

5. Thus, we can comprehend how the idea of duality is inherent in all manifestations. It is the idea of projection and recalls the exoteric display and the esoteric resultant projection through the centrifugal energy and recall through the centripetal desire proceeding from the loving heart of God. Therefore, we have two concepts of God, that of the centrifugal or exoteric in which rest the attributes of lovable being (the intelligence which in going out manifests infinite ability), and the emotional desire or esoteric, which in returning manifests infinite love. The divine intelligent energy that as "the Father provides for all his creatures and the divine love, that as the "Mother" "draws all men to him."

6. In our weakness of expression and in the feebleness of our language we personify the one, which is all wrong, but it seems to be necessary in order to convey our ideas, but when the language of personification is used we should always try, to the extent of oar ability, to recognize the idea attempted in the language used; language is a "vehicle" for the expression of thought, and we must get behind the language and amplify the thought conveyed. For instance, in the last paragraph I used the expression, "the heart of God;" in this I endeavor to include the idea of the boundless love of God that is manifest towards us. The wise emotional nature of the one as distinguished from the wise power; the love that is strong enough to bind the entire universe together in perfect harmony

and at the same time a love that is so gentle and tender that it is at the call of the least unit of humanity that lifts an appealing thought to Him.

7. One of the errors of the early Church consisted of the elimination of the emotional aspect of the divine manifestation. The "chosen people," through whom the records came and from whom Jesus, the liberator, had his parentage, always laid stress upon the "power" aspect of the divine manifestation. The object of their worship was, the Lord God Almighty, the God of Might, Majesty and Dominion. God the King and Sovereign Ruler; always presenting the exoteric aspect of manifestation.

The Messiah came and, contrary to their expectations, taught them the message of Love, the esoteric aspect of the same truth that they already believed in. The Ten Commandments which had been their rule of action, and which were exoteric truths beginning with the command, "Thou shalt not" were taught by him in their emotional or esoteric sense. They were made positive and living by the command, "Thou shalt love the Lord thy God with all thy heart and all thy mind and all thy strength and thou shall love thy neighbor as thou lovest thyself." "On these two commandments hang all the law and all the prophets." Here we have it positively, love is the fulfilling of the law. The law itself is a law of love. The law being God's mode of action is the method that God takes to show his love to all creation.

The esoteric or emotional aspect of the divine nature is proclaimed as the line of exploitation in spiritual development and to our shame it must be confessed that as a church and at an interval of nearly two thousand years we have failed to fully recognize the message and as yet the pillar at the gate of the outer court which stands as the exponent of the beauty and loveliness of the divine manifestation, is not recognized as the proclamation of a great and undying love to all who seek entrance through the gate. Of all the disciples who loved and followed our Lord, one only fully understood the message in its esoteric import, and in the hermetic writing given by him on Patinos, he tells of the new day that will come to the earth when mankind shall have properly developed so as to be fitted to receive it and to assimilate its great and beautiful truth. He foretells the "day of woman," the time when the emotional aspect of the divine manifestation shall be recognized. When love and harmony shall reign; when the "motherhood" side of the One shall be recognized and its teachings fully adopted. He gave to us a picture of a "Woman clothed with the sun and having the moon under her feet" as an illustration of the recognition of this esoteric truth; showing us that the light of the divine power and intelligence was only the garment of the real, and that all illusion and misunderstanding would, in the light of that truth be overcome; for the moon gives no light, it simply reflects the light of a superior outshining which is in itself but a manifestation of the esoteric reality that is behind it.

In the matter of the seeming duality of the One, we look beyond and through the exoteric and we recognize that, in truth, God is Love and that all else is but part of the manifestation of that love and necessary for our comprehension and for our spiritual progress. In this light, reason, intellect, knowledge and understanding are but the clothing of His manifestation, the means whereby He is made known to those who seek Him. God is Love.

When we consider love as in a static condition, we see unity; when we consider love as in a dynamic condition, we see the appearance of duality, for the reason that our conception of action predicates two factors, viz., that which acts and that which is acted upon. Infinite-wise-love requires that infinite power, infinite intelligence and infinite reason should he displayed in order that it may be correctly comprehended; therefore, the exhibition of the exoteric aspect as a means whereby love could be made lovable.

KARMA

The Law of Karma does not recognize either truth or fraud, both of these are alike to it. It simply pays just debts. The truth is rewarded justly by it and fraud is just as justly punished. Neither tears nor supplication can change it, for it is the law.

Karma is kind and loving to her children, but she is just as stern to those who wrong the law. She is always in robes of white, even if her judgment is punishment. It is not really her who passes judgment, but the conscience of the one who stands before her. For this reason, it is that there can be no appeal, the conscience itself is the judge, under the law of Karma, and try how we will, we cannot appease the conscience.

The Law of Karma is. It acts. As we stand before the judgment seat, so will we stand before the great law. We know whether we were right or wrong. The conscience is awakened fully and sees where wrong or justice was done. We, the soul, the conscience, read from the Astral Light, the Great Book, all our acts, we see all our promises made, we see before us all the hearts that we have broken through broken promises. We cannot appeal to God or man, for we did the thing and the law acts, for we cannot, in any way, appease the voice of our own conscience. Whether joy or sorrow is the punishment, it is swift and sure.

The law is just, it is justice absolute. There is no joy in its actions, there can be no sorrow, for the law is. When we stand before the seat of judgment, when the conscience is awakened as it will be, then we see the wrong done, the joy given. May God who is just, help us to do right while we live, for after we stand before the law there is no appeal. Prayer will help us none then. Nothing can swerve the law from doing justice. God is good, man is a part of God; as such, he is rational, he is a thinker, he knows what he promises, and he knows whether he keeps them or not. There is no chance to swerve the law, our only chance is now, in life. It is for us now to see to it that we break not a loving heart. If we do, then there is no law in the world, neither heaven nor earth, can save us from justice in the Great Beyond.

A debt. Let us hope that all our debts are light. If we err in action, let it he towards ourselves, for then we have already paid the debt and conscience is free and the law fulfilled. It pays the debts. The conscience must settle all bills. If we have loved, if that love has been cast aside by the loved one, then our debt is paid and there is much to our credit. True, we have suffered, but in the vast eternity it will help us much and the credit is good. If we have hated, justly or unjustly, Karma cannot recognize why, she simply knows that we have hated. Eternity will make us pay the bill. Let us then be on the side of love, for love is God.

It stands for the law of God, for Karma is God's one Great Law, it is the Great Book of Revelations, the book before we must all read the good and bad. Before it, we will see all our acts. It is just. God is good, but let us be likewise.

There is no escape. We cannot say that we know not when we committed the acts which stand out before us. They are there; the conscience knows that they were committed. We must bear the punishment. Then let us see to it that every page reads: This day a sorrowful heart I cheered. This day I gave the love that was asked of me. This day did I return the love which was shown to me. This day a hungry soul I fed, I cheered for the one who loves me. I made the promises anew. I live by the promises I made, for a kind heart must never be bruised even though my own heart is broken. Then smile, smile, smile, even though your heart he has broken.

Not only does the law record our deeds and the hearts we break, but every word we speak and every thought we think, it recorded as faithfully as though we broke a heart. Then let us ever remember this and be sure that each thought, outside of the thoughts we think in business life, be that of love to all humanity, friend or enemy, each alike. God is good, and all things are for our good if we recognize them as such.

None is too good, but the conscience records all his or her acts in the Astral Light. All, even though a Christ, will have a faithful record kept.

Nothing is lost. Do not think that because you do a deed of love which is not appreciated, that it has not served its purpose. Even though your life were to be forfeited for an act of justice or love, that very act will save your immortal soul when you stand before the judgment scat, and all must stand before it. He that knows most of him will be asked most. Love, then, all humanity, breaks no heart and remembers that God and his law is just and true.

"No matter how great we are, whether ruler of the earth, or but a humble worker in the field, the acts of one, count as much as the act of the other, and a little deed of kindness to the smallest of God's children will count much for you. Let it be a deed of love. Remember that your soul, before the final judgment is just as great as that of the king or emperor. You are one of God's children, there is no other soul of more value to Him than your own. Break no heart which you have sworn to love. Your promise is scaled before the throne of God; it is firmly printed on the Astral Light. You must see it ere long.

"The Law of Karma" is just. It bears the robes of white, for in the law there is no wrong. It is only the judge, the balance, and you and I, my beloved reader, no matter how heavy our hearts may be, have no excuse to wrong a single thing with life. God is good, but He is also just and, bear in mind that the law of love is the only legal tender before the judgment throne. See to it that you have plenty of it.

Karma records all and it were far better for you if she were to record nothing but tears for us if they are shed in sorrow for love and right. What matters these few short days upon mother earth? What matters even though our heart be continually broken? If we have fulfilled the law of love, so long as that love was wanted, then we have nothing to fear. It is not asked of man to throw love upon those who do not want it, but man has not the right to take it from those who want it. Man is a conscious being. God gave him a will to control his thoughts and his desires. He gave him knowledge to know what promises he makes, and neither God nor Karma will excuse us if we break the heart that is faithful to us. Man has not the right to judge another for a promise made, must be accepted by him in good faith and though it may be a false one, not upon him, rests the punishment. Not a cry from the heart escapes the heart, and man's cry of "My God, my God, why hast thou forsaken me," has just as much weight this day as it had when the Son of man broke his heart for humanity which crucified Him.

The gods approve the law for the law is just. Karma smiles on all her children who try to do the right. It has nothing to do with us whether others are unkind to us or not. It is for us to return good for evil and to bear the things which come to us. Mayhap in the past, we, too, did hurt another, and who knows but that we are paying a just bill. Let us then bear the cross with a smile, for God is good, and the law is just. Always must we bear in mind that in, but one way can we pay the bills of the law, that legal tender is love. Not from the lips, but from the heart.

The Law of Karma does not pass judgment. This is not its duty. Man, through this mighty law, passes judgment upon himself, for as he sees the thing which he did and should not have done, so does his soul pass the judgment. It is but the duty of the law to see that judgment is fulfilled, and she does it. In the Astral Light are all our deeds, good or bad, recorded and as we pass to the beyond, so do we stand face to face before that Great Book. It is then that the soul, the awakened conscience, condemns the acts of wrong, and it is then that the law sees that punishment is meted out. My God, is it a wonder that sensitive souls groan in this world of woe, where but this is not so, man wants love but for a day and then 'tis cannot aside.

The court of Karma truly needs to ask no questions, for the soul reads its own deeds, good and bad, as easily as the human court understands when the criminal confesses. Only that there can be nothing added to the story and nothing subtracted. It stands out clear and true. The astral is the confessional.

The Law needs no brief, needs no plea, none can be put in. It receives but the verdict from the soul itself, and as it receives it, so does it pass the judgment. There is no appeal to a higher court, for the judgment is from the soul itself. God forgives those who know not love.

Pure, true, good angel of light, truly thou art robed with gems and jewels for those who have loved. The philosopher was right who has said: "Tis better to have loved and lost, than never to have loved at all." The heart may be broken, but in its turn comes the understanding that after all, all is well with the soul that has loved, even though possibly too well, if not wisely.

The law is law, and nothing but the law. It has no duties but to see that justice is done. It is but the judge of the court of God. The conscience of you and I, my friend, are safe in its keeping, and we need not fear that we will receive absolute justice, no matter what the act may have been.

In the Law of Reincarnation will be the Law of Karma fulfilled. Even the soul, in its form beyond the grave, may suffer for eternities, it does not end there. The law throws it back to earth once again and then in its suffering, sufferings caused by others as he had caused suffering to others, will its punishment be completed. God forgive them, for it is more than the mind can understand.

The law is everywhere. No matter where you may try to go, no matter what you may try to do, the law is there, for where your very soul and conscience can go, there also is the law; Think not that you can appease a wrong, think not that you can flee from a broken heart. In your sleep, even in this life, will appear that soul who was so true to you. There, even though you were in the arms of another, will the law reach you and your sweetest cup will prove to be only of bitter dregs. Then be true to your vows, love the one who loves you, and whom you have sworn to love. If he or she ceases to love you, then bear your broken heart, but let it not be you who breaks the bond of love. God understands.

"The Dweller of the Threshold." My God, is there one like it? None can understand this better than such as have entered the path to supreme initiation, for these know him and, if they have been true, have overcome him. No longer is he the terror, but he has become the guardian. My friend, you who know the laws, you who have entered the path, are you faithful to your vows? Do you follow the one who has taught you? Do you return love for love, duty for duty? If not, then God pity you. For no matter what else may happen, it was your duty, and if you break your vow, the terror will be such to you. But if you are faithful, no matter what the world may say, then he becomes your guardian and you need not fear.

No, truly, it cannot miss the way, for the acts are written on the astral as faithful as the photographer can take every line in our face. There it stands, there it is, our accuser, and just it is. No matter what man may try to do to smooth over his conscience, he cannot blot out the wrong deed done. God is good, but he will not condone the deed of a broken heart. After all, it is hearts that count in this life, as well as beyond the great white way. For love brings happiness, even in sorrow, where a broken heart can bring us nothing but sorrow and pain.

'Tis the clearing house for all acts, thoughts and deeds. 'Tis no wonder that the Egyptians called their hell a Gahena. No wonder 'tis foul, for let us but think of the crimes of a day and the soul is bowed in sorrow. Let us, dear reader, not add to the filth.

The Christ: What thoughts this brings to us. He of the beautiful life. He who suffered for no wrong in that life. And yet, His Mary, who turned to him in love, was as necessary to His fulfillment of Karmic law as is love to us. Would to God that there were more such as she ready to turn to such as are ready to give such love as she gave. Though called the scarlet woman, she stood by Him unto the last, faithful in truth and love. Karma was fulfilled and neither He nor she needs to appear again. All is well. May the God bless such faithful love as hers. And He will.

In the end, when we pass from this life's stage, we must all face the law. It will then be our friend or our foe. Not that it can be either one or the other, on ourselves will depend all. The judgment is sure, there is no getting away. No matter what our station in this life, just as sure will the tiller of the soil come under its rule as does the king and emperor. None can escape, when we pass to the beyond. There stands the judge and the conscience, he whom we may have tried to bribe, is as clear as though we had never made the attempt. It were better than that we had been the poorly paid servant of a cruel king and have loved than to have been the mightiest potentate and have not known love, or having known it, have denied or "sold" it. The law is there, the book is open before us and therein we will be forced to read all things as clearly as though we were looking into a looking-glass. There is all. Neither God nor man can intercede. Let us hope, my friend, that you and I will have a large balance of the only coin, the beatitude of love.

Love for love and hate for hate. The law is just. You and I, no matter how long our life, when the time comes to pass to the beyond, will take all with us. No matter how much we may try to hide the fact, the soul within us will tell us that "As we do unto others, so will it be done by us." Love is the key to the kingdom of heaven.

If one love proves false to you, then there is humanity to love. Think not because one may prove false, that there are none who are true. There is always the one, as Mary to Christ, who will be faithful. Others may promise, your heart may be broken many times, but remember thou, that this will not be for thee to pay. He or she who, knowing the right, swears to be true to you and is not, he or she will pay the debt. You need not pay it. You may suffer here, but in the great beyond, another and a more just law holds good. That law none can escape. It is the Law of Karma, the hand-maid of the one God.

'Tis true, love is the only way; it leads to light and life. The Rosicrucian was right when he said that the only things worth living for were light and love. Man cannot ask for more, but he must bear in mind that even these may not be had in a material world without suffering. If we want these, then we must suffer. Would we rather escape suffering now and suffer throughout eternity, or suffer now, have a little of love and the heart and soul filled with it in the great beyond. We have free will, it is for us to say. May God help us to follow the right.

PROMETHEUS

The student should read the poem by Shelley on "Prometheus" in order to understand the beauty of that work. Herein is the mystery solved so that he can then understand the poem. Olive Schreiner, one of our most gifted writers, says: "In the lowest heaven sex reigns supreme, in the higher it is not noticed, but in the highest it does not exist." We are all in different stages of evolution, for the soul grows by degrees; unfoldment is slow, it is not possible to rise at one bound from the depths of selfishness and self-gratification to the highest heaven, and freedom from personal ties—maintained for selfish motives—can never fit us for that state of advancement where sex is "not noticed."

In this higher heaven, some few live by nature, owing to their past Karma they have outgrown the senses, and can only radiate purity and pure love; such are a blessing among their fellows, emanating a moral and elevating influence, which must benefit all with whom they associate; but for the mass of humanity, this step in evolution can only be gained by an unselfish effort of one kind or another, and generally by the discipline of married life. Few indeed are ready to enter the "higher heaven." This is where Astrology, studied on esoteric lines, becomes very useful, tending to develop common-sense and practical judgment, helping us to realize our own nature and the law of our own unfoldment, preventing us from becoming dreamers, or placing undue stress on ideals we have not yet acquired the experience to live, and which few are capable of understanding; and it is a fact we often create confusion in the minds of others, by insisting on life being lived according to our own standpoint of judgment. Ideals are very useful and need publicity, so that they may reach the few who are ready to understand and seek to practice them, but we must never become discouraged or disheartened when people treat our ideals with doubts, anger or ridicule. It is very often better that men deride or are blind towards an ideal that exerts a compelling power over us. When anyone's sight is weak, to tear the shade from their eyes and let in the light would mean destruction to the organ of sight, and by the same law, to force our ideals upon others becomes destructive to their inner light and unfoldment; because they are not understood, and are therefore incapable of assimilation. Ideals suitable, and so beneficial for the soul ready for them, act as an attractive power and draw the soul onward. We must be careful not to force light on any who may be unwilling to receive it. A truth eagerly received by one is repellant to another, and people act wisely when they refrain from impressing and imposing their own convictions on their neighbor's mind, even for, as they think, his or her good, for it is unconscious hypnotism: the motive may be a good one, yet the fact, remains that if we force our opinion or will upon another, we are simply retarding their evolution.

In the secret doctrine there are many paragraphs dealing with the spiritual aspect of the creative fire, which the Orientalist calls "Kryashati," that mysterious and divine power latent in the will of every man which, if not called to life, quickened and developed by a course of training remains dormant in 999,999 men out of a million, and so gets atrophied.

"Civilization" has rightly developed the physical and intellectual but at the cost of the spiritual. The command over and the guidance of one's own psychic nature, which foolish persons now associate with, use supernatural, were with early humanity innate and congenital, and came to men as naturally as walking or thinking. These psychic gifts and faculties were lost as the fall into matter became accomplished, to appear later on, when reason, the flower of humanity—comes to perfection. The preliminary, or animal stage, had what we may call physical clairvoyance. When the higher reason is gained, then spiritual intuition supersedes the physical clairvoyance. "Starting upon the long journey of life, the immaculate spirit descends into matter, having to connect itself with every atom in manifested space." The pilgrim having struggled through and suffered in every form of life and being, is at the bottom of the valley of matter and half through his cycle—as human—but the final mission of Prometheus is to awake to consciousness the light of conscience—the inner God. Awakened, self-consciousness becomes the "Christ" of the Christian Mystic, the "Warrior" of light of the path, the "Master" in the voice of the silence. The soul's awakening means the merging of the human stage of development into the Divine.

When the awakening from self-consciousness to Divine consciousness takes place, the inner fire that burns within each human heart vivifies the whole form. The Divine man then knows how to use the forces of nature. This principle of God's life is an electric, fiery, occult and fohatic power; it has two aspects, the creative and destructive, that is why the knowledge of how to develop this power is revealed only when the soul is free from desire and the personality entirely subjugated, and all selfishness disappeared. In India certain Yogic practices of meditation commenced at dawn and were intended to liberate this fiery power, but if any man was not sufficiently pure, this fire-like lightning would destroy and wreck his physical organism. "Prometheus, in the ancient legends, the tortures of matter until freed by Hercules." Hercules having slain the lion and cleansed the Augean stalls, or in other words, having slain his passions and cleansed his heart from impurity finally overcomes and drags np to the surface of the earth by main force the dog which guards the Gates of Hell. This Prometheus fire slays the vultures which gnaws at the heart of humanity and frees mankind from the Promethean curse and sets him free from matter.

Unman passions are very strong, but Nature's Divine Force is stronger, and the rousing of mind to self-consciousness means the final turning point, "spirit can only act through mind" on this plane of matter. There are two main aspects to the awakening in the cycle of evolution and experience. The first is the awakening from the animal stage, the stage of ignorance and innocence, beautifully portrayed by the story of Adam and Eve in the Garden of Eden. As they leave the stage of ignorance, pain meets them, discord, suffering, and sin. The other aspect is the soul's awakening, by experience, in time, to full self-knowledge and final realization of the unity amidst all the diversity, the realization of Universal Brotherhood, the Divine Manhood—the Christ; first the animal stage, next the human, then the Divine, for we are gods embedded in matter, self-conscious more or less from the standpoint of intellect, but not yet self-conscious through intellect of spirit. To turn this gift of Prometheus—the light-spark of self-consciousness—which in its marriage to objects and externals has become a curse, towards its Divine counterpart the Spirit, is to undertake the same task as Hercules undertook; for when Mercury is wedded to Jupiter, Sun and Venus, the Divine Marriage is drawing near. The animal mind can never understand spiritual truth. When the mind becomes rationalized, it must then be spiritualized, and if the ancient myth of Prometheus is to help us onward, then we must make herculean efforts to cleanse away the mire of the senses, and the dust of the mind, so that Mercury, the mind, may reflect only the image of the god that dwells therein. For as is stated in the secret doctrine, "each individual is a god distinct from all others, with a kind of spiritual individuality of its own" during one special "Manvantara." To unite and become one with God is the true purpose of life.

THE NEW THEOLOGY-DUALISM

In order that we may obtain a larger and more comprehensive view of the idea of dualism, as applied to ourselves, and in order that we may thereby be enabled to treat the subject practically and correctly in our daily life problem, let us consider a line of thought somewhat as follows.

Let it be taken for granted that, at least, one of the objects of creation is: That the Power, Wisdom and Love of the Infinite should be made manifest to intelligent entities for wise and beneficent purposes, and further: That man, as the object of this manifestation, should thereby be enabled to come into a comprehension of the Divine character and thus a way would be provided whereby he could appreciate and adopt the Divine likeness.

With this as a premise, it will be apparent:

1. That in order for infinity to be manifested, there must be a vehicle provided which will be fit and competent to accomplish this manifestation.

2. That the vehicle must contain within itself the idea or the lesson that is to be taught and it must also contain the potency and potenti-

ality of that which is to be manifested, and it must also be entirely able to impart a distinct and individual self-consciousness which shall be entirely independent and self-capable of comprehending the manifestation; in other words, the "entity" that is destined to become the recipient of the realization of the comprehension of infinity must be a separately and distinctly individualized "being." He must be self-independent and self-endowed with independent capacity in order to fulfill the necessary conditions.

3. In order to comprehend infinity, the education of the "entity" must begin at the zero point, the so-called "borne of impulse" wherein lies negation or the idea of nothing.

4. The process of the evolution of this individualized entity must be by growth, in which he much comprehend and master the environment through which he ascends; he must evolve himself and he must use his own powers to climb or he must accept the consequences of declining to do so. He may have help, but that help must be given because he desires it and because he solicits it, otherwise he would not grow by his own effort and by his own independent choice, for, if he had unsolicited assistance he would grow more or less automatic and he would lose his own self-competent individuality.

5. The materials out of which he forms himself and the environment out of which he is formed must contain the physical, mental, moral and spiritual "pabulum" necessary for him to apprehend, comprehend and assimilate the education sought to be conveyed.

6. In order that this individualized entity shall be able to comprehend and to form a correct judgment of that which is to be apprehended and thus make correct choices for his further advancement, he must be absolutely independent in his right of choice, for it is evident that he will never comprehend infinity until he begins to incorporate infinite ideas, infinite principles and infinite conceptions into his own character; for his ability to comprehend the infinite will be measured in direct proportion by the extent to which he becomes infinite himself.

7. Herein we see the reasonableness of the divine plan and we discern how completely it is in harmony with the facts of the material world and its environment, and how both materially and spiritually, all good things work together for good in the accomplishment of the divine purpose. We see also the absolute necessity for dualism in the growth and development of man. In our feeble conception of the character of God,

the idea of duality is only a seeming one conditioned by the limitation of our conceptive ability, but in our description of finite and progressive man, we must accept the idea of duality as a fact and as a factor of his progress and development; for he must overcome, conquer, and become the dominant Lord of every plane of his environment in order to fit himself to rise to a higher plane, and until the process of evolution is complete he will always have a "lower nature" because it is the very thing that he is obliged to "transmute" into a higher manifestation before he himself can rise.

The lower factor of the duality of man is the "Jacob's ladder" by which he rises, step by step, to the condition of infinity. The process is one of transformation; he must transmute the lower into the higher; he must be the alchemist, who, by the use of the proper solvents transforms the seemingly base metals into the pure gold. When the alchemist shall have completed his work and become a "Master," then shall the necessity of a vehicle be terminated and duality shall be absorbed into unity.

INTUITIONAL LIGHT

All doctrines contain some truth; it may be but the tiniest seed, or it may be as full of meat as a nut. To teach the ability of discrimination and to qualify the student in the ability to recognize the truth in any and all doctrinal thought, is our object and aim. The mills of the gods grind slow; the continued influences of mental forces gradually mold and modify the clay. The changes may be long in coming but as a man thinks so is he.

Nirvana (peace) is the state in which the activities and changes and polarities of the individual move with such greater rapidity than its surroundings as to produce perfect poise or equilibrium. The rapidity of its adjustments is so much greater than the events and circumstances and affairs of its environments as they occur, and adjustments to all events take place so quickly, even before the event has time to occur, whether the event is in the form of thought activity, or physical disturbances or changes. That disturbance of the individual poise occurs not. It includes also the neutralization, by compensation, and clearing up of all Karma before it can be realized; control over sense and thought and imagination and adjustment to environment more rapid than the occurrence of events; complete elevation above the material into the spiritual—of all forces. Indifference to all worldly and sensual things.

All that ever was still exists; all that is will never cease to exist. There is a law as unchangeable as the Infinite—the Law of Neutralization—whereby one condition or principle or force is balanced by the opposite state of its quality—by its other polarity of condition or action. The evil thought or deed stands for all eternity and cannot be destroyed or lost; only as it becomes inactive by being polarized by an opposite act or thought or deed of good from the same causing source does it lose the venom of its sting and the power for harm to the one causing it or to others.

Only the material Christ is revealed in the Scriptures; the Occult Christ and methods of operation of his power and the training which he received in preparation for his work were purposely omitted by the sacred writers as dangerous to give to a profane world. At the Pentecost, the sacred tire of power and illumination descends upon the assembled Apostles, opening their psychic perceptions to the Plane of All Knowledge; and they spoke in tongues and also understood all of the Occult phases in Christ's life and ministry. When any human has reached a certain stage of development mystically, his Pentecost comes as surely as it did to the Disciples of old and he can also perform miracles and speak in tongues. For he will be in conscious relationship with all knowledge. Why was it necessary for the Christ to die? Because of the Free Moral Agency given to man (and to the Jews) by his beneficent Creator; whereby it was possible for the Jews to reject his ministry and destroy his physical life (if indeed it was destroyed) even as man has ever rejected and destroyed the lofty and the sublime and the truly spiritual, and the reformer sent to regenerate him.

As the evolution of each civilization which has appeared upon the earth during the ages has reached its highest mark, the light has been offered it and the gifts of transcendency from the celestial spheres; the great Christic light and principles. These gifts have been offered every civilization; all have rejected it and been lost; plunged back into awful darkness and are buried beneath the desert where even the lonely horseman and the caravan linger not. Or buried beneath the blue waves of the Atlantic. Or relegated to the tepee and the reservation and savagery and the darkness of ignorance.

True, the light has even been presented to each in a different outer form and through differing personalities in each ease; but God and spiritual light and the Christic principles are ever the one and the same, however much the instrument and the outer symbols may change. If Christ had been given more natural ability in the flesh than other men, it would have been no test for the flesh in general, and of little value to others as a guide and example. He possessed inherently and from past incarnations the potentialities necessary to develop into the perfect human. As to the death of Christ—What of the soldier who repudiates his trust upon the field of battle or picket line? His countrymen and comrades and officers look to him to hold his position, to sacrifice his body and his life if necessary. How much more depended upon the great tragic ordeal wherein the Great Example and Master was the actor; and upon whom the vast past, the present and future depended; to whom all heaven and hell were looking; such a spectacle never before and never again could occur (for the test has been decided). For the more power and perfection endowed in the personality, the greater the ordeal imposed upon it. Christ, the greatest one and the perfect one must therefore bear the ordeal of the entire forces of heaven and hell (to prove the possibility of the flesh overcoming all).

I see the hour at hand; upon either side behold the powers of darkness and of light; they were all, there; marshalled for the great battle and all of these tremendous forces concentrated, centered, upon the Immaculate One. The real test was made during the agony of Gethsemane. Had the powers of evil won, what of the future of the truth and the light for the flesh and the world, and the white spiritual influence for humanity? It is naught to simply die; death is comparatively easy. But to give up all power over heaven and earth which Christ as a human possessed, for the humiliation, and the terrible physical and mental suffering which only such a sublime nature could know was an ordeal, in degree, such as the world has never before seen put upon flesh and spy it. Angels from the celestial spheres were there, witnesses to the tragedy. Infinite pity bent over the lonely Man of Galilee. Immeasurable Love stood at his side longing to place about him the sheltering folds of her mantle and to shield him from the terrible strain and the sorrow and the suffering. But nothing could intervene or aid, only the strength of his own soul alone must meet and conquer.

The Fraternity which had trained him were looking to him; failure meant ruin to the cause. But the eternal light upon the lofty heights of his soul never faded; no twilight settled over the scene. Through the awful hours in Gethsemane the torch glowed brighter and more bright; for the Son of Man had conquered; the light had prevailed over the darkness and would shine forever; for the Infinite Spirit of Light, down in the human flesh, had prevailed, though all the powers of heaven and hell had battled for the mastery. It was the conquering of the right and the truth in the flesh, which signified so much. The attainment by a human in the clay to perfect mastery.

The murderer in destroying the life of his victim has made no break in the continuity of the whole. No break can ever occur. The universal is one unbroken and unbreakable unit, and possesses absolute consciousness. The only free agency in the whole of creation is man's volition.

From the most remote antiquity history describes the healing of the sick through Occult and Metaphysical forces by the direction of these through influences directed by one person, or transmitted by them to another. The transmission of the special energy and influence taking place Under the more or less objective conscious supervision of the operator, and causing corresponding changes to take place in the mind or body of the person acted upon; the results obtained depending upon several factors resident in both patient and healer; facts depending to a large degree upon the susceptibility of the patient to the influences of the special operator, as well as to his definite mental attitude toward the effects of such curative agency. His relative receptivity plays an important part in the results produced upon his organism; and the character of the agent involved must convey the specific, subtle vibration required for that individual case to the structures treated as well. Disease in its manifestations is but disturbed coordination in the balance of activity between related structures. Restoration to health (cure) is but the re-establishment of proportional distribution of vital, which is magnetic balance, to such structures according to their relative requirements. There are two main important features involving the health of every individual; one is the blood circulation; the other, distribution of "nerve wave."

THE WORLD'S CONDITION

A matter of importance to all, both students and workers. The cause of the business depression may be easily understood by any person who has studied the industrial development of this country. In the Republican National Convention of 1904, Mr. Chauncey Depew made a speech in which he put the following interrogatories: "Why are we knocking at the gates of Peking and Hong Kong? Why are we spreading over the Philippines and extending into the Orient?" and he answered: "Because we have a surplus product, which must be sold abroad." Senator Beveridge, in the keynote speech of the same campaign, said in substance: "We have a surplus product, which must be sold abroad; if it is not sold, it will accumulate in our warehouses, so that the orders will cease; then the factories will close, and the workers be thrown out of employment; they can no longer buy the products of the farms, and widespread and universal stagnation and suffering will result. So we must have a continually expanding market." That was the way the Republicans justified the policy of expansion, and they were right.

Machines have enormously increased the producing power of labor; on an average, it is said that the productivity of all labor has been multiplied by 600 within 200 years. As examples which may set you thinking; in the days of Queen Elizabeth, a man made 27 pins per day. Now, one man makes and sticks on the papers, folded and ready for market, five million pins a day. One man makes as many nails as a thousand men made fifty years ago; and so on. "When we are at work, we turn out stuff with enormous not to say startling rapidity. The working people receive a wage equal to one-fifth of the value of their product; so, they can buy one-fifth of it. Three-fifths more may be sold to non-producers; and the other fifth must be sold abroad. This is the "surplus" of which Messrs. Beveridge and Depew were speaking.

To whom shall we sell this surplus? Germany, England, France, Austria and other manufacturing nations are in exactly the same situation; that is, they have the same machines, turn out practically the same products, and have each a surplus to dispose of. The necessity for expansion is equally imperative upon every manufacturing nation in the world; modern conditions in industry produce in each of them the surplus which must be sold abroad. They cannot buy our surplus; they must sell their own. Africa cannot buy it; they have no use for it. "We want a nation which is becoming civilized enough to use the goods, but which is not yet so fully civilized as to manufacture, and so have a surplus of its own."

There is but one such nation worth considering; and that is China. And that is why the manufacturing nations of the world, without exception, are "knocking at the gates of Peking and Hong Kong;" it is because China is the dumping-ground for the world's surplus, and unless she can be made to take this surplus the horrors so well described by Senator Beveridge will be visited upon every civilized people in the world.

And now come the Japanese, that wonderful people who go ahead a thousand years in one day; and they are equipped with modern machines, and turning out a larger surplus than any of us. And being on the ground, with all the conditions favorable to them, they have captured the Chinese market. And so, the thing we feared has come upon us; and all the European nations are in the same predicament. Prince Arthur, of Connaught, was hooted on the streets of Glasgow recently by a hungry mob; and the dispatch which told of the occurrence stated that 50 percent, of the working people in Great Britain are idle, and have no prospect of finding work; and a like situation must come to pass, in time, in the United States; for production cannot go on without territorial expansion, and we have no place to expand to. What next, then?

All this has been brought about through the operation of the destructive or disintegrating principle of individual self-interest. Interest against interest, class against class, man against man; the house has been divided against itself, and it cannot stand. We are being brought to a standstill by contending interests: and disintegration and National dissolution must inevitably result. The American people are lawless by habit, and violent when aroused; if the time comes when half our working population have no work and no prospect of work, every American city will become a hell compared to which Paris during the revolution would seem a paradise.

There is no lack of work to be done. There are millions of shanties and tenements which ought to be torn down and replaced by modern and sanitary dwellings; there are floors to be carpeted, bare rooms to furnish, naked bodies to clothe, roads to build, parks and playgrounds to establish—oh there is no lack of useful and beautiful work that needs doing. And there are the idle machines, ready to do the work; and the people ready to use the machines; starving because they are denied the privilege of using them. These wonderful machines and idle hands, if set at work, would build palaces for us all, and fill those palaces with useful and lovely things; labor, with modern machines, can enrich the whole world: but labor is at a standstill. Why not substitute the constructive principle of common interest for the destructive one of self-interest? If we can no longer make things to sell, why not make them to use? Why not let the unemployed go into the idle factories and make the things they so much need; make them for themselves, and for each other? What stands in the way? Nothing but the interest of those who own the factories and the machines. And how long shall this interest be allowed to hold us all standing—and starving? Gentlemen, it is up to you; start your factories, or the people will undoubtedly start them for themselves.

Do not allow yourself to become alarmed or disturbed over the business situation. It is quite true that we are in the midst of a depression which is worldwide. In Great Britain, half of the working people are out of employment, and have no prospect of finding work. Riots and public demonstrations of desperate earnestness have already begun, and the present winter will be one of much suffering and many horrors. In the countries of continental Europe, the situation is little, if any, better; and as like causes produce like effects, the United States, traveling the same industrial roads, must arrive at the same conditions. The same system is in operation here; and the same causes are at work, are the operation of the same laws; and if these causes have wrought the workers of England to idleness and beggary, and her businessmen to bankruptcy, they can produce no other effect here.

But while all this is true, there is a new world beginning. The British government is being driven to provide work for the unemployed; and this can only be done, in any permanent way, by setting them at work to produce from the abundance of nature, the wherewithal to feed, clothe, and house themselves. All the other nations are being compelled to turn their thoughts in the same direction. Through the gateway of present poverty and suffering, the world is going to enter into universal abundance. This is the last "great" panic, for it will result in a union of all mankind to abolish involuntary poverty; and involuntary poverty can be abolished by cooperative production for use.

Fix your thought on the New Time, which is beginning, and not, on the old era which is ending. Get into the vibrations of that which are increasing. Study the political, industrial and business movements of the hour, and unite with those forces of integration which are drawing men together, not those forces of disintegration which are pushing them apart.

God is building a new world. Never mind the old one which is passing; get into the new one which is taking form. Then you will be in the way of abundance and increase, for the riches of that new time will be beyond anything we can imagine now. Work with the forces of integration and increase. Pray every day for guidance, and will to do the will of God. The spirit of God is behind every movement that makes for life to all; and He will lead you into perfect safety, spiritual and financial.

God is going to produce a world of men so ordered that all shall have abundance of every good thing; and He is ready to build you into that world now, and to give you your work to do, and He will do it if you sincerely will do His will. "He that willeth to do shall know," said Jesus; and Jesus knew Get out of the old world of strife and competition: drop its methods, its ideas, its ways of thinking. It is disintegrating, and if you stay in it, you and your affairs will go to pieces along with it. Get into the New Thought; what you want for yourself, want for all. Think for all, desire for all, pray for all, work for all. You will have good business; you will not go hungry. Abundance will come to you, for you will be one of the pioneers in the new world of abundance. Watch the forces that are at work, and unite with those which are constructive. You can; and you will prosper in the midst of hard times, for the constructive principle of nature never ceases to work, and never fails in its operations. Therefore, be not afraid.

* * *

This, from "Constructive Science." is both timely and to the point, we believe in the New Thought, there can be no other way, but under present conditions, there are things which we must consider and two of the most importance are:

1st. The fact that all, both young and old are no longer satisfied to live in the country, all of them want, to live in the cities where there is excitement. No matter if it takes the very soul and belief in a Universal Law out of them, the cities they want.

2nd. This depopulating of the country has two effects. 1. It overcrowds the cities, reduces wages on the one hand, and on the other, increases not only rents, eatables, etc., but causes everything to cost more. 2nd. The country being depopulated, there is no longer the necessary production of the foods necessary for life. Everything is high and there is universal adulteration, resulting in poisoning both the mind and body of the people. Is there then, any wonder that the country and its people are in the state that they are?

There is but one way to overcome these conditions and wise men recognize this—the universal cry "Back to the country, to nature and your God."

There is cheap land to be had, the conditions are such that one can have nearly everything that we have in the cities, there is true life there. God is there, and man can find there all that he needs and need not be a slave to others; he need not do all the things that he must do in the cities in order to exist.

Count Leo Tolstoy, one of the greatest philosophers that this old world of ours has ever known, has solved this problem. Although born to riches, although born to a position in the social world such as few have the good fortune, he refused all and during his life, he has worked one-half of the day on his farm like any common laborer and the other half of the time he has given to authorship. With it all, in jumping from one to the other, he has still been able to achieve such fame as no other man ever did.

It is no use to say that he is an exception, he is not. God gave all men brains, He gave all men a soul and He gave, above all, all men the privilege to use all these things as he wished. What man has done, man can do.

True, some men are born so "tired" that they can do nothing, and in our opinion it will take a few hundred thousand incarnations to overcome this born "tiredness."

A man can, at the present time, when all products are extremely high, make a splendid living on the farm by working one-half the time and the other half he can employ for pleasure, development and study. "God is good" it is only man, poor, tired man, who is not able to recognize this fact.

Get into the current, stop kicking, recognize that God is good but that the command "Thou shalt live by the sweat of thy brow" holds good this day as ever and that it is a wise command.

Do not think that I talk without experience. I have worked day and night, not only as a professional man but as a working man at the same time, and so long as God and my star gives me life, so long shall I hope to continue to work, love and live. "God is good."

THE ROSICRUCIAN'S HISTORY

My name is Freybourg. I am, by birth, a German, though of French parentage. I was, by nature, studious; and my attention was soon directed to the marvels of natural philosophy. An eager, and even painful, thirst after novel information kept me constantly on the alert; and, as my family was good, and their resources liberal, the opportunities and facilities of acquiring were not withheld—the less as, being a younger son, it was, of course, expected that I should turn my learning to account.

"There was little, however, in the objects towards which my curiosity was directed, to which the instruction of tutors was not rather an obstacle than otherwise. I learned what they had to teach, and felt that in so doing I had made not one step towards that after which, even without knowing what it was, I inwardly panted. Something I wanted, to satisfy the ravenous appetite I felt—something to which the cumbersome frippery of learning, which I met around me, was wholly foreign. Yet where to seek for any satisfaction, I knew not.

"I grew lonely and melancholy in my habits; I sought the deepest recesses of the woods, and spent whole days sitting idly in dark and solitary brakes, or under the shade of trees by the side of dull and unmoved waters. I did this till the inanimate things among which I wandered became my sole companions and friends.

"In a chance conversation I heard mention of the Rosicrucian doctrines of the sixteenth century. To my mind, in its excited state, a spark was sufficient. I hailed the suggestion with rapture, rejoicing that a path was thus opened by which to direct and steady the wandering feverish wishes with which I was haunted.

"I acquired, without much difficulty, the writings of Hudd, Kuhlman, Rosenberg, and others who had treated of the Divine Science. I studied them incessantly. Their phraseology was, purposely, obscure, and their meaning enveloped in terms, to the right understanding of which I had no clue. But my aim was a noble one, and my perseverance unconquerable. By degrees I became master of the secrets which, hitherto, I had possessed in those volumes only—as a man who has a rich jewel secured in a casket which he cannot open.

"Still, here was one step only advanced. The philosophers who had discovered the means of acquiring the hidden and mysterious knowledge that I desired, had either never attained the end of their inquiries, or had forborne to promulgate the details of their process. I had, thus, my tools given me; but I was still to learn whether I could use them successfully, where so many before me had failed. I bent all my energies to the task, and, gained my object. In doing this I did no more than anyone may do whose will is decided and exertions undeviating.

"Before I proceed, it is necessary that I state to you some of the additional faculties which I had now acquired. The soul, of which our fleshly body is the habitation, is not, like the latter, bounded by the fetters of place, but, when freed from its tenement, possesses ubiquity. To liberate the spirit, so fully as to enable it to enjoy, completely, this omnipresence, is, indeed, beyond the power of divine science; and can be accomplished only by that mysterious process which, terminating our progress here, returns to their proper sources as well our material as spiritual constituents. But the power may still be exerted, in an inferior degree, greater or less, as the aspirant has qualified himself for the possession of the faculties he covets.

"To me it was a source of infinite and glorious delight to disentangle myself from the narrow limits to which the observation of fallen man is confined, and dismiss, as it were, a twin spirit from myself to penetrate the extremist parts of the earth, and, taking the wings of the morning, to gather from every clime, all that might he culled of fair, and beautiful, and good. Thus, I enjoyed a double existence; and, whilst I pursued my ordinary avocations at Strasbourg, was, at the same time, roaming in thickets and jungles, by the banks of the Ganges, or contemplating, at Baalbek, the prostrate Temples of the Sun, and the ravages of time on the mighty cities of the earth.

"It was one day, when rambling, in my other self, through one of those delightful valleys that sink at the foot of the Apennines, that I became, I may well say, the victim of a sensation as novel as enrapturing. I was seated in a study, chasing away the hours by the perusal of those enduring riches which the intellect and genius of antiquity have delivered down to us, and which show, strikingly, the weakness and the superiority of their authors—when a perception, which I well knew was conveyed through the medium of my distant spirit, burst upon me;— such a dream of purity, and excellence, and loveliness, as my wildest moods of enthusiasm (and I was ever a trafficker in the ideal and contemplative) had never fashioned! To you, who are yet in ignorance and thralldom, I should, in vain, endeavor to explain the manner in which this ray—for such it seemed, and a most bright one—burst upon me. It came, not as a picture conveyed by the sense—not as a remembered idea, nor as a vivid creation of the fancy—it came as an inward impulse, newly born, springing up on the mind, indefinite, uncreated, but existing and fervent.

"The object which had thus been made present to me continued not so for more than an instant; but the effect was complete. I was as one entranced—one thought alone possessed me, until I became almost unconscious even of that. A sort of lethargy of the imagination succeeded; and I hailed the hour which, bringing on the gloom of night, enabled me to seek for rest in sleep.

"Sleep came, but not with it extinction of the thoughts that, for the last few hours, had filled my waking existence. In dreams, the vision still haunted my mind—the same idea of inexpressible beauty was still present. Associated images, too, arose, in all the wild phantasms of dreaming. Bright eyes—burning kisses—all the array of passion, danced before me. Sometimes, I half started from these incoherent slumbers; and, at such time, light and aerial forms seemed to float around me. At length I became exhausted with the excitation of these restless fancies, and sank into a profound and refreshing sleep.

"On awaking, the first idea that presented itself was the one by which I had been haunted the preceding day. Wherever I went, whatever I did, it followed me still. It became the unceasing companion of my thoughts by day and by night.

"The anxiety which I underwent affected my constitution; and, by the advice of my family, I left home to travel in search of health. The first place I visited was the valley of the Apennines, which was so strangely connected with me. Here I wandered for some days; but could learn nothing to direct me in my quest after the unknown object of my thoughts.

"Why need I detain you with a long and useless detail of the pains I suffered, the countries I traversed, and the disappointments I endured. Two years elapsed;—and, weary of myself, of the knowledge I had labored so hard to acquire, and, in short, of the world and everything in it, I determined to take the vows and habits of a Capuchin, and, rooting from my breast every remembrance of the past, to devote my future life to the meditation of noble and more enduring subjects. "Vain were the expectations that prompted me to take this step. I soon found that, if there be any place peculiarly consecrated to peace and content, it is not within the walls of a monastery. There is, there, no exclusion of the evil passions of the world; and, as poison acts more vigorously within a narrow compass, so it is in these societies. Besides, the uniformity of our life—the uninterrupted stream of existence in which we flowed along—threw me more forcibly than ever back upon myself—the very evil to have been avoided. Amid the exercises of devotion, I found-my thoughts still chained to another subject. I strove against them—the irritation induced by the conflict increased my calamity.

"My brethren were, with few exceptions, men of coarse and vulgar minds—indolent, proud, and malicious—the natural infections of the monastic atmosphere. Everything conspired to induce me to avoid their society—my present feelings and the habits of my past life. They perceived it, and were not long in manifesting their sense of it.

"I was, however, too much involved in those things which continually oppressed me, to regard, very greatly, the petty annoyances to which I was exposed. I endeavored to submit to these evils contentedly; and, in this manner, five years passed on, without seeing any material change in my situation, my thoughts, or my sufferings." "About this time our physician died—as, when at home, I had disguised my philosophical pursuits under the pretext of studying medicine, I had acquired a slight knowledge of the science, and was not, now un-willing to improve it. I offered my services to our Superior, and, after a few trials in trifling cases, they were accepted.

"The occupation in which I thus engaged was, necessarily, beneficial, as it occupied a portion of my thoughts, and diverted them, in some degree, from the recollections to which they incessantly veered. There was another advantage. I had occasion to make short excursions beyond the bounds of the monastery, for the sake of gathering plants and roots for my simple pharmacy. There was something of liberty in this, and the exercise was a luxury to me.

"The monastery of * * was situated upon a high and almost perpendicular rock. It was rarely visited by anyone, although a carriage path had been hewn out to it, and was tolerably passable. This road divided into two branches—one of which led to some neglected stone-quarries, as an approach to which the road had originally been constructed—and the other had been extended for the purpose of traveling. From this station, there was a magnificent view. Elevated far above the level of the earth, I have seen the storm raging, and the lightning flashing below, while the unchecked sunbeams fell around me above. Beyond the thick and tempestuous cloud that filled the valley and hung on the surrounding declivities, a smiling champagne country extended, bounded by hills, distinguishable only by a faint outline, from the sky with which they seemed to blend.

"It happened that the storm-clouds had, one day, gathered in such prodigious masses, that, though the autumn had but just commenced, the monastery, and everything around for miles, were enveloped in a thick haze, through which the rain fell slightly but incessantly. The contemplation of natural phenomena was the only thing I could call a recreation, and I came forth to enjoy the threatening of the elements.

"I was well acquainted with every foot of ground in the neighborhood; otherwise, it had been madness to have ventured beyond the walls—so easily might an incautious step have precipitated one down a precipice whose height left no possibility of escape from destruction—even, versed as I was, I found it needful to move with great care.

"Whilst I was endeavoring to distinguish the forms of rocks and trees through the gloom, and watching the dim blue fires that flashed idly at intervals, a sudden dull sound met ray ear which I was, at first, unable to account for. It was not, however, many moments before I felt convinced that a carriage was passing at no great distance. It could not be on the direct road, for I was standing on that, and the sound had passed me. At once, it struck me that the travelers, if such they were, had taken the wrong road; for, though a direction post was placed at the point where the path divided, it would be useless, in such a gloom. The thought was terrible; for, in three minutes, unless some aid offered, they would be dashed down the precipice, which the darkness, momentarily increasing, would conceal, until discovery was too late. Already the noise had ceased—so imperfectly is sound conducted, as you are aware, in those altitudes. I had nothing to guide me, but sprang forward, and, dropping a bank of about fifteen feet, found myself on the road that led to the quarries. Along this I speeded, almost in desperation. Again, I caught the rumbling of the wheels against the uneven surface of the rock. The vehicle was going, apparently, very leisurely; and this consideration seemed to add to the horrors of the situation—there was something so sickening and appalling in the idea of human creatures going thus slowly and unconsciously, step by step, to destruction. This, however, was not of long continuance. A flash of lightning blazing across the path, frightened the horses, and they set off at a rate that almost extinguished my hopes.

"One circumstance was in my favor. The road took a sweep round the base of a broad, but not very high rock of granite; and directly over this was a footpath. I crossed it, and saved so much ground as to meet the carriage within ten yards of the precipice. I endeavored to seize the reins; the horses plunged and reared almost upright; the motion of the carriage was stayed for a moment, and in that moment I sprang to the door, tore it open, and received in my arms a female, who fell senseless in the moment of her rescue. I heard the fearful cry of the expiring horses, as they were dashed under the carriage on the rocks beneath. Two human creatures—the father and fellow-traveler of the lady, and the driver—shared the same destruction.

"I lingered not, but bore her whom I had saved, as speedily as I might, to the monastery. The brethren whom I met stared with malicious surprise, as I entered. I loudly demanded our Superior; he came, and consented, on hearing my account, that the lady should have refuge, until her friends could be found, within the walls of our retirement—prison, I might better say; I was preparing, in the presence of some of the senior brethren, to administer such slight medicine as I deemed necessary to the object of my anxiety, when for the first time I saw her face. The phial which I held dropped from my hands. I lost all sense and recollections. When I recovered, I found myself in my cell, reclined on my pallet. By my side sat an old brother whom I had lately attended during a severe illness, and whose gratitude for the services I had rendered him had been proof against all the ill-nature of the many who looked upon me with an evil eye. He had undertaken the office of my nurse, and from him I made my inquiries.

"Where is the lady, Hilarus?"

"In the dormitory. They have sent for old Margaret, from the village, to attend her."

"It is well; is she sensible?"

"Quite; she has inquired for you. But what caused your illness?"

"I know not; a sudden pang—have you learned who she is?"

"No; her dress and ornaments bespeak her, probably, of wealthy connections."

"I should like much to see her. Does our abbot know that she has inquired for me?"

"I believe not."

"I would he knew; I wish to visit this patient; but not without, his knowledge."

"I will see that he knows," said brother Hilary; and he rose from his seat and left me. He returned presently.

"I have seen the father," said he.

"Moreover, I have seen your patient, and she insists, whatever Margaret says, on not retiring to rest until she has seen her preserver. You are at liberty to visit her."

"Let me then, brother, request your company."

And he conducted me to the chamber where she was whom I panted to behold.

"We arrived at the door. It was with difficulty that I could conceal from my companion the violent agitation that possessed me, and which shook every nerve to trembling—as the autumn wind shakes the quivering autumn leaves.

"We entered the apartment. She sat at one end. I approached her; she lifted up her eyes; 'Holy Virgin.!' she exclaimed, 'it is—it is he.'

She sprang from her seat as she spoke, gazed earnestly at me for a moment—sank down again—and covering her face with her hands, burst into tears.

"I was astonished and confounded. 'Does she know her father's fate?' I whispered to Hilary.

"No," he replied; she believes he is in the house, but unwell, and we have been, scarcely able to avoid her request to see him.

"What then could cause her present grief?" I drew nearer to her and spoke. I told her that I was, for the present, her physician; she interrupted me. 'I know you well,' said she—'too well.'

"'Nay, daughter'—the word stuck in my throat—'nay, how can that be?' 'Ask me not,' she replied; 'it were a strange and incredible tale.'

"'Surely,' said I, half to myself, 'the dream cannot have been mutual.'

"'How, what is it you say?' said she, eagerly.

"I looked around. Brother Hilary had left the apartment; the nurse sat at the farther end of the room. I sat down by my patient, and detailed to her what I have already made known to you. Yes—dead to the world— vowed to solitude and religion—I told her of the passion I had felt—and the pang I had suffered; knowing the while that there was now a gulf between us which no means could pass. It was like the dead recounting to the living object the history of his buried love.

"I concluded. She was still in tears, but checked them.

"'It is most wonderful,' she said; 'I too'—she stopped, blushed, and trembled. 'Yet why,' she resumed, 'this foolish weakness—why should I not confess that I, too, have loved and suffered for a hitherto unknown object. At the moment when your spirit caught the fatal infection, in the valley of the Apennines, mine, too, was on the wing, and hovered round you. I need not say more; your history will suggest the main features of mine. And, now, answer me a question sincerely: Where is my father? They told me I should see him in an hour: the time is past. Is he here? Is he ill? Heavens! Your color changes—tell me—tell me, by all we have suffered, is he dead?"

"'Oh, no—no,' I answered, hastily; but the confession of my manner have the lie to my words. She perceived it, and with a shriek, fell senseless to the ground." Freyhourg paused in his narrative.

"Excuse me," said he to Merler. "if even the remembrance of what I tell you stifles my voice, and calls forth my tears."

"Be assured," answered Merler, "I respect your grief. It is perhaps unpleasant for you to continue your narrative; if so......."

"No, it is over," said his companion: "I will proceed."

"I raised her from the ground, and directed the nurse to place her, while thus unconscious, in her bed; I retired to prepare a draught for her. That done, I threw myself on mv pallet—myself half distracted with what had passed. The vesper bell aroused me from the lethargy of misery, and summoned me—heaven knows how unprepared—to join the evening devotions. These past—in coming away from them, we had to pass the dormitory. I listened for a moment at the door. One of the friars, who more than the rest, had showed a marked dislike, whispered an observation to another upon this circumstance. I turned around; a malicious smile was on his countenance. Forgetful of all, save the indignation which I felt, I struck him to the earth.

"The consequence of this was, that I was confined strictly to my cell. I was not allowed to see my patient; word was brought to me by Hilary, of her state, from time to time; and on this information I was expected to proceed.

"She became delirious. In vain I represented that, in order to treat her malady properly, I must be admitted to visit her. Ignorance and malice were blind to everything.

"Day after day this continued. Hilary was assiduous in bringing me intelligence—for he alone pitied me. This was observed; he was forbidden my cell, and another deputed to act in his stead.

"You may probably think it was in my power easily to baffle this rigor, by using my faculty of spiritual visitation. But this faculty I had neglected for a long period to exert; and when I essayed it, I found the perturbing passions which had taken possession of me deprived me of my power. I had no longer the calm self-possession necessary for the enjoyment of the Divine Science. Like all uncommon powers, it failed me when most needed.

"Why should I linger in my tale? One morning, on awaking, I found Hilary by my side. I was about to inquire how he had obtained permission; but he motioned me, cautiously, to silence; and, placing a folded paper in my hands, withdrew on tiptoe.

"I opened it. Its contents ran thus: "you will receive this from brother Hilary; but before he gives it to you, the writer will be no more. Its only purport is to wish you farewell. The reason of your absence I have been informed. Here, we have both suffered deeply; that we shall meet again in happiness, I doubt not. Do not—but I know you will not—forget me. Once more, farewell; my last breath will bless you.

"I pass over my feelings on the receipt of this. I determined to escape from the monastery. I did so, in disguise, to Strasbourg. My parents and my elder brother were dead. A distant relative had succeeded to the family estates.

"I had known him in youth. I sought him, and he offered me an asylum which I accepted. I continued with him for two years, in concealment—for the Capuchins were in hot pursuit of their victim. At length I was liberated. The revolution commenced, and the friars were no longer powerful.

"My relation addressed me, one day, thus: 'Freybourg, I am about to join the royal party. In this bag is a sum which, with your habits, will supply your wants; however the struggle ends, I shall not need it.'

"I retired hither. With some occasional interruptions during the troubles, I have lived here since. Now we are again at peace; and I abide solitary and unknown, having resumed, as you have seen, my ancient studies." Such was the story told by the Rosicrucian.

THE HIGHER KNOWLEDGE

As in our previous lesson we explained that every thought of the human being enters the astral world and there finds a companion, either good or bad, according to its own nature, thus a good thought is perpetuated as an active power for good; a perverted thought becomes in reality a living demon. In this manner mankind is continually populating space according to his desires, impulses and passions. The creations react according to their intensity. The Buddhists call this result Shandra. The Hindu calls it Karma. The adept consciously creates these forms, while other men let their thoughts escape without regard to the consequences.

The agent through which one acts on the intellectual forces is the will. The faculties of man are in themselves indifferent to good or evil. Their quality is determined by the nature of The Will. It often happens when persons are seeking development without the aid of a teacher that, having abandoned their will in the desire to get en rapport with the Invisible World, they expose themselves to a grave danger. For at such times the perverse creations, larvae and others are likely to take advantage of one who has temporarily put aside his power of resistance, the will.

These elementary spiritual creations are ever seeking to augment their feeble life-force by drawing from those humans whom they find in the negative condition. Thus, every student should be protected in such experiments by a teacher who will guard them at such times, or by a magnetic chain whose members will aid them by concentration.

In some instances the soul of the experimenter leaves its physical tenement in the trance state and is replaced by one of these perverse spirits. The individual then becomes a sorcerer instead of a magus. As a demonstration of this, many readers will recall friends who have suddenly developed clairvoyant power while sitting at home, alone. A closer observation of such mediums will often disclose a suddenly changed character and disposition. And it sometimes happens that such mediums will, without apparent cause, become estranged from their relatives, friends or even families.

The reader should carefully consider these facts, so as to protect himself, as well as to warn others of this great danger. The difference between a magus and a sorcerer is that the former knows what he is about to do and what results are likely, while the sorcerer works with great forces which he does not understand, and often obtains results far different than he expects.

The most important possession of one who has attained developments is the Will. Therefore, the student should constantly seek to develop a strong and powerful will.

As Plato said, when teaching the mysteries to his followers: The will, strengthened by faith, can subjugate necessity itself, command nature, and effect miracles. It was the one great lesson taught by Zoroaster to his disciples. Jesus also said allegorically: "If ye have faith, ye can move mountains."

"Righteousness of heart and faith triumphs over all obstacles," said the great Confucius.

"All men may become the equal of sages or heroes if they so but will," said Mencius. These ideas of Chinese philosophy may be also found in the records of the Indians. It is the source of light of, the magus who creates something from nothing.

The will, backed by faith, can model it into proper form for the spirit. From it, the soul may receive power to communicate with another soul. By the will, man can raise himself up to a divine plane; in short, he may overcome all things.

There is an intimate relation between the visible and the invisible worlds. And to the great ruling or planetary angels the magi have given names.

These sacred names are used in all evocations. If for no other reason such names assist the adept in concentrating the greatest amount of universal force. The results produced are always in proportion to the force and intensity of the psychical faculties. The human brain is a generator of cosmic force of the most refined quality, which controls the inferior energy of brute nature.

The adept creates by faith a radiant center from which his soul traverses the ages to come. This is the key to the mysterious power which he possesses of projecting and materializing in the material world, the forms which his imagination has created in the invisible worlds from inert cosmic matter.

The adept knows there is nothing new in the universe; he simply employs and manipulates the materials found in nature's magazine; or, in other words, primitive matter which endures eternally and is constantly undergoing the change from various forms. He has but to choose that which is required, and call into objective existence that upon which he concentrates.

The relation of the invisible to the visible has been understood from the earliest days by a chosen few who have been found worthy to receive such profound knowledge. Yet withal an adept cannot create an effect contrary to nature.

According to the ordinary conception, there are no miracles. All phenomena are the results of eternal laws, unchangeable and ever active. As a great scientist once said, phenomena result from the known laws of nature acting one against the other.

In respect to this statement, it is well to remember that some of the most important laws are entirely unknown to modern science. Nature is triune; that is, in every series we find a trinity. Nature may be visible, objective, and nature is also invisible and occult. Spirit is the source of force, which is eternal and indestructible. Visible nature changes constantly, while the latter never changes.

Man is also composed of a trinity. The physical body is objective man. The astral body which covers the soul may also change. The soul, however, is the real man. The whole is illuminated by the Immortal Spirit. When man realizes his grand and sublime constitution, he becomes an immortal entity. Magic considered as a science is the knowledge of those occult principles in nature, by which one understands the omniscience and omnipotence of the spirit.

This knowledge, which gives the power to control, may be acquired by the individual while yet in the body. Considered as an art, magic is the practical application of occult knowledge. One who misapplies such secret knowledge is termed a sorcerer. One who uses such power for good purposes only is a magus. The medium is the opposite of a magus, as the former is but the passive instrument of unseen influences, which magus actively controls the invisible forces.

All things that are, that have been or will come, are impressed in the astral light. Thus, the true initiate can see and foretell all things, whether of the past or future. Among the races of mankind a difference of color, stature and so on exists. In the same manner, there is a difference in the state of spiritual development. Some have by nature more or less of spiritual development, while others must work long and earnestly for the attainment.

There are families in the Orient who transmit the secret methods of development from father to son. By such training, they are able to produce phenomena more or less grand.

SPIRITUAL EVOLUTION

For anyone to be right, he must be in harmony with the Divine Mode of Action, on his plane of consciousness." If it be conceded that this statement is true; it then follows: First. That absolute and ultimate right, in all its Divine Fullness, consists in absolute, complete and entire conformity and cooperation with the Divine Mode of Action, and,

Second. That individual rightness is complete or incomplete, in degree, as it approaches to, or recedes from such condition of harmony.

Third. That while there is a standard of ultimate rightness that all may strive to attain unto; each individual must, of necessity, have a separate and distinct standard of his own which, as compared with the ultimate standard, will be higher or lower, and therefore more or less complete and perfect according to the character, ability and personal idiosyncrasies of the individual.

Fourth. It is therefore manifestly impossible for any two individuals to fully and exactly agree upon all the statements that are made regarding any one system of moral or spiritual philosophy, for while they may agree upon the ultimate statements and their leading deductions is well as upon many minor details, the very fact, that there are no two individuals alike produces as many points of conception and experience as there are separate individuals and therefore as many individual "planes" or separate states of consciousness.

Fifth. All divergence from the Divine Mode of Action must occasion discord, and as distinguished from truth and right, must be classed as "wrong" and "error," and this being a universe where cause and effect strictly pertains, it therefore follows that all right actions must cause compensation and therefore wrong actions must incur penalty.

Sixth. Error on part of an individual may be of two kinds, viz., that which occurs through ignorance and that which occurs through willfulness, and the penalty to be paid by the individual must be different in the different cases.

Seventh. The correction of errors arising through ignorance is the vehicle for the attainment of knowledge. When you recognize an error, you learn something. This is the mystic sense of the statement made by Paul the Initiate, viz., The law (Divine Mode of Action) is the schoolmaster that leads me to Christ (Christos Knowledge). The correction of errors arising through willfulness is the vehicle for the attainment of character. "Blessed are the poor in spirit" means Sanctioned of God are those who have diminished the dominance of their lower nature and have exalted the dominance of the higher. That which lasts, that which "passes through" and endures forever is Divine Character and it is formed by the voluntary correction of error. Every act that corrects an error is an act of redemption.

There are three aspects of redemption. That of the redemption of the Individual entity; that of the race, and in the larger aspect that of the redemption of Creation. When creation shall have accomplished its purpose, when all things shall have been fulfilled; when all error shall have been transformed into the Divine Harmony, then shall the end of the world, typified by fire, be at hand; but the fire is the fervent heat of the Divine Hove which shall be recognized everywhere and shall permeate everything. God—by direct act—does not correct error, that which produced error must, become enlightened by "the light that shineth in darkness" and the darkness must slowly learn to comprehend the light and make its own corrections. Every right choice contributes to this consummation.

Eighth. The adjustment, or correction of error by the individual while if aids the growth of the individual in knowledge and character, contributes to still further progress by bringing about, a higher condition of knowledge which, is called Understanding.

Ninth. Understanding is the open door through which the individual gets his perception, and comprehension of Divine Wisdom. This satisfies and develops his mental nature and brings peace to the emotional. Righteousness and Peace are united in loving embrace and harmony exists in the individual; and finally, the individual after a long series of choices and adjustments embracing many cycles of lives, by means of, and as a result of, his own efforts and struggles and by the development of his own potencies and potentialities becomes fitted to enter into what is mystically called "The Best that remaineth for the people of God." Mark the word "remaineth" after all is done, after all, is passed through, after all things else are left behind, there remaineth God and God-like individualized characters. I have indicated to you, in brief, a line of study in Spiritual Evolution.

Study and compare it with the Evolution of the physical and you will find no want, of harmony of correspondence—for there is one law and He that worketh is one. Observe the fact that the individual entity makes his own character by his own acts and choice; he "grows" his own "soul" by the self-development of his own potentialities; by the exercise of his own will and determination; he "over comes" by his own efforts; he climbs the ladder of attainment by his own exertions. He makes himself. He is not created. He creates himself. In his choice, he must standalone. In his acts he can have all the help that he desires and will accept. The boundless resources of Divine Omnipotence remain in his environment for his personal aid and succor. The sheltering arms of Divine omni-presence are always extended to him for comfort and sympathy. If he will have aid, sympathy or comfort, all is subject to his request, but he must make the choice. It lays with him to accept or to decline. In the very "nature of things" there can be no interference with the free choice of the morally self-conscious individual, for in that way alone lies the road to perfect individualization. The individualized entity must be left to his own free choice, so that when lie does arrive at the apex, he may be able to say; "I am that I am." He must become "Son of God" and he must also become "Son of Man." In Mystic language this is called, the "Divine Marriage," and its final consummation is called "The Marriage Supper of the Lamb."

THE TWELVE SONS OF JACOB

We will now compound the twelve sons of Jacob with the twelve constellations of the zodiac and prove them one (according to Jacob's own language) when we weave them in with the starry myths. It seems very strange that anyone can (if they read the Bible with an eye to its spiritual significance) make a man out of one single Bible character, for the Bible is all mythical from the beginning of Genesis to the end of Revelation. We read in Numbers 23:19: "God is not a man that he should lie, nor the son of man that he should repent." In I Samuel 15:29, we read: "And also the strength (of eternity, margin) of Israel will not lie nor repent, for he is not a man that he should repent." Now if it read "Jacob is not a man that he should repent" we might infer that he was a perfect man but that one word he gives the text a very different sound, and then, too, the very same thing being said of God shows Jacob to be one with God.

We read of the God of Jacob and of Israel all through the Old Testament. What was Jacob more than other men that God should be his God. One thousand one hundred and forty years after Jacob's death, we find him breaking clods for Judah while Judah plowed. Hosea 10:11. In this Terse the Lord says "Ephraim is as heifer that is taught and loveth to tread out the corn, but I passed over upon her fair neck. I will make Ephraim to ride. Judah shall plow and Jacob shall break the clods." We would like to explain this jumbled up mess, but time and space forbid. But Ephraim, the heifer, was the younger of the three for he was at that time only nine hundred and seventy-five years old, while Judah was one thousand eight hundred and eighty years old, and Jacob was one thousand eight hundred and thirty-seven years old.

A little rough on those old men that they must plow and break clods at their age while Ephraim, the heifer, was permitted to ride. Now where is Jacob as a man, and, if he was not a man, what were his sons?

When Jacob prophesied for his sons, he began with the eldest but did not follow down in a direct line with their births, as we shall, in arranging them as the twelve sons with the months (constellations) in the platonic year. We call Reuben, the eldest, Scorpio, because of the ruby glow of the red Antares in the heart of Scorpio. Of this son Jacob said: "Reuben, thou art my first-born, my night and the beginning of my strength, my dignity, and excellency of my power. Unstable as water thou shalt not excel (shalt thou not excel, margin) because thou wentest up to thy father's bed, defilest thou it; he went up to my couch (rendered at margin my couch is gone up)."

Here Jacob says to Reuben, "You shall not excel," and the couch being gone up shows that a spiritual day has come, and no more need of a couch, and, as already shown, Scorpio (Reuben) belongs to the earth's day, or psychic age, and no more need of a couch, therefore night has evolved into day.

Of Simeon and-Levi Jacob says, "Simeon and Levi are brethren. Instruments of cruelty are in their habitation.

"O my soul, come not into their secret unto their assembly, mine honor be thou not united for in their anger they slew a man and in their self-will they digged down a wall." (The last sentence is rendered "houghed oxen" at margin.)

"Cursed be their anger for it was fierce and their wrath for it was cruel. I will divide them in Jacob and scatter them in Israel."

Why did Jacob need to tell us that Simeon and Levi were brethren since they were both children of one father and one mother? And why did not Jacob say that Reuben and Judah were also brothers, for all four were the children of the same father and the same mother?

Well, we will tell you why by showing the mythical history of Astra (Libra) and Virgo (Simeon) which story we think we have already told, but it seems necessary to repeat it here, for such a book cannot he written without many repetitions.

Mythology says that there was a time in the earth's history when the gods abode on the earth and walked and talked with men. But in time humanity became so wicked that the gods became disgusted and one after another began to leave for their heavenly home from whence they came until not one was left save the goddess Themis (Virgo), the goddess of Justice, Love and Purity, who still lingered in hope to redeem the world, but, at last, the corruption of the iron age became so disgusting to her that she, too, took her flight heavenward, grasping in her hand, as she went, the scales of Justice called in the Bible, the equal balance of the Lord which the Oriental has named Themis or Astra. Thus, we see that Virgo and Astrea are indissolubly bound together and ever will be because Justice, Love and Purity are the Trinity of the Godhead.

We believe Simeon and Levi to be Virgo and Astrea, and we see now why Jacob called them brethren. It is because of the tinseled chord of heavenly music that holds the three as one principle. But Jacob says of these brothers, "Instruments of cruelty are in their habitation."

Now while our earth was still in the habitation of these brothers about the midway of Simeon (Virgo) she was brought under the vibration of Hydra, the serpent that tempted Eve, and, therefore, under the curse or cruelty of animalism; thus we have tried to prove why the instruments of cruelty were connected with these brethren. Father Jacob says of that age:

"In their anger they slew a man and in their self-will they houghed oxen" (margin). Now let us ask, was not the spiritual man slain? But as the story of Cupid and Psyche proves the man was not slain past resurrection when the time is ripe for us to know ourselves and claim our own. Now it was the spiritual age or the spirit of universal man that was slain. The wall that they dug down broke the chain or the beauties of the psychic age and led our earth in the dark age of animalism where we are still houghing our oxen, i.e. guiding our animal instincts. Thus, we see that the man they slew was the universal spiritual man; in other words, the spiritual or psychic age which our earth is about to enter again as everything goes to show.

Now as the earth was driven from Eden while passing under Virgo (Simeon), of course she got vibrations from the old serpent and imparted them to Astrea (Levi) so that both were affected as if blended into one. In the Bible, Simeon (Virgo) is defined "that obeys or is heard" and Astrea (Levi) "that is held or associated." Here we have proof that Virgo and her scales of Justice, which she took in her hand, and which we still see at her side as if held or associated according to mythology, are one with Simeon and Levi. Jacob was made to say, "I will divide them in Jacob and scatter them in Israel." Let us remember that Jacob was only a servant of God before he wrestled with God, after which he was called Israel (Prince with God), therefore Jacob is the dark animal age, and Israel is the spiritual, psychic, or God age, and Libra and Virgo, though associated together, are the dividing line between those ages and, therefore, represent both ages; thus we find them divided in Jacob and scattered in Israel.

Of Judah (Leo) Jacob says, "Judah, thou art he whom thy brethren shall praise; thy hand shall be in the neck of thine enemies, thy father's children shall bow down before thee, Judah is a lion's whelp; from the prey, my son hath gone up: he couched as a lion and as an old lion; who shall rouse him up? The scepter shall not depart from Judah nor a lawgiver from between his feet until Shiloh come, and unto him (Shiloh) shall the gathering of the people be. Binding his foal to the vine and his ass to the choice vine, he washed his garments in wine and his clothing in the blood of grapes. His eyes shall be red with wine and his teeth white with milk."

In the face of all those symbols of animalism, darkness and drunkenness, Judah is defined the praise of the Lord, and, in the ages yet to come and not very far distant, Judah will do a work worthy of praise, in fact, he has already been doing his work in sealing up the heavens, and he must break the seals, and when the seventh seal is broken it is finished, and then comes the praise of the Lord. Read Revelation 5:5.

Now for a pen picture of all those symbols that speak so plainly from the starry myths, and speak so very plainly that we must knit them in with Jacob's prophecies. Just beside Judah (Leo) we find Hydra, the old serpent, upon whose back is perched, first, an owl, symbol of night (called a night-monster in the Bible, according to margin), and, farther along, we find a crow, symbol of perfidy, perched upon the serpent, and, near the crow is Crater, the wine cup, all of which are symbols of drunkenness. It is from this wine-cup that Judah (earth's children) drank until his eyes were red with wine (the wine of fornication) and here it was that he washed his (spiritual) garments in the blood of grapes, and, as all the mythical animals in this part of the heavens give milk, his teeth were white with milk (kind ness). The scepter that Jacob said should not depart from Judah is a little city of stars in Leo (Judah) shaped like a sickle which is symbolized as a scepter. And Hydra is the old Athenian lawgiver right at Leo's feet who, mythology tells us, was so severe as to punish every crime with death, spiritual death, of course. Of this law-giver Jacob says, "The lawgiver shall not depart from between his feet until Shiloh come." Who or what is Shiloh?

Now Shiloh is defined "peace, or abundance," which means the satisfaction gleaned from the spiritual age, so we are still under the reign of Judah's scepter as our wars clearly prove.

The next son is Dan (Judgment), or Judge, or lawgiver. Of this son Jacob says: "Dan shall judge his people as one of the twelve tribes of Israel." We must infer from the foregoing sentence that Dan was not one of the twelve tribes, after all, for Jacob said of him, "Dan is a serpent by the way, an adder in the path that biteth the horse's heels so that the rider shall fall backwards." Now in pictured astronomy, Hydra is illustrated as having three heads, and one head is pictured so near as to almost touch the heels of that constellation called the Unicorn, which is pictured as belonging to the horse family.

At this point in Jacob's prophecy, he gives a doleful moan like a father pleading for an unruly son, thus, "I have waited for thy salvation, O Lord." Here the old serpent bobs up and swallows down the Cancer influence that should have been Dan, and Dan becomes a "serpent in the way, an adder in the path," and, as Dan is defined "judgment" we find him to be the old Athenian law-giver who judged his people according to their iniquity that was the result of spiritual darkness.

Naphtali is Gemini and is defined "likeness," comparison or that struggles or fights. "Likeness or comparison" means the fact of their being twins, and mythology tells us that they were great wrestlers, also great warriors, so here we find all the symbols associated with Naphtali of whom Jacob says: "Naphtali is a bind let loose; be giveth goodly words." If Jacob had said two binds, let loose be would have spoken more correctly, for the twins were once pictured as two goats, but, even then, the comparison or likeness was the same and also the lighting, no doubt. The goodly word spoken by Naphtali means "land is in sight," for after leaving Naphtali (Gemini) our earth strikes mythical land.

Gad means Taurus. Of this son, Jacob says. "A troop shall overcome, but he shall overcome at the last." Let us here repeat that in every Bible symbol we can compound with, Taurus shows a wall, or ditch, or chains, or something hard to overcome, therefore Jacob says, "He shall overcome AT LAST," i.e., after conquering the troop. This is all that Jacob could well say in his prophecy for Gad without locating him with his troop in the starry heavens, and now for the proof that. Gad is the brazen age of Taurus. "We read Psalm 18:29, "For by thee I have run through a troop and by my God I have leaped over a wall." Again, in II Sam. 22:30, we read, "For by thee I have run through a troop and by my God I have leaped over a wall." We find two cities of stars in Taurus and a whole troop of lesser stars. In both places, this utterance was in the prophetic song of David, who saw our earth at the last was soon coming into the tabernacle of the Lord, i.e., Aries, the Christ age. Please read Ex. 33:8.

The next son is Ashur (Aries). Of this son Jacob says, "Out of Ashur his bread shall be fat and shall yield royal dainties."

Again, let us repeat that, bread or bread-stuff is a symbol of the spiritual light that came to the earth front Ashur (Aries), the Lamb of God, who was made to say, "I am the bread of life," spirit life, of course, for spirit is the only true life there is.

The next son, Issachar, is Pisces and is defined "a hire, a recompense," We find in this definition monarchy and subjection, and, as we are still influenced by Pisces, we see that the brotherly love which Christ tried to establish among men has been crucified upon the altar of mammon, and we have lost the "royal dainties" of Ashur through the strong ass, Issachar. Of this son Jacob says:

"Issachar is a strong ass couching down between two burdens. "He saw rest, that it was good and the land that it was pleasant and bowed his shoulders to bear and become a servant to tribute."

Now we see two classes upon this earth today that are controlled by an astral influx from Issachar, as Jacob has clearly shown them, viz., the

Shylock and the menial laborer. The Shylock sees rest that it is good, and the laborer bows his shoulder to bear burdens and thus becomes the subject to tribute.

Zebulun is Aquarius and is defined "dwelling," for here our earth has passed all of the large bodies of mythical waters in the starry vault, therefore Zebulun is a haven of the sea. Of this son Jacob says:

"Zebulun shall dwell at the haven of the sea and his borders shall reach unto Zidon and he shall be a haven for ships."

Zidon is defined "hunting, fishing, venison," so we see that the border reaches along the typical waters where the little fishes and Cetus, the whale, are seen swimming to the typical neck of land that reaches out from Taurus, upon which land we find Orion, the giant hunter of the celestial realms, and here we find the symbol of hunting.

Joseph is the next, of whom Jacob says,

"Joseph is a fruitful bough whose branches run over the wall by a well." (Branches here are rendered "daughters" at margin.)

"But his bow abode in strength and the arms of his hands were made strong by the hand of the mighty God of Jacob, from thence is the shepherd, the stone of Israel." (Stone Age) Here we see Joseph (Capricorn) near the well, pictured as the water-vase of Aquarius, and the wall which the branches run over is the dividing line between the animal and the psychic age, and, even now, we are struggling to plume our spiritual wings that we may rise above the worldly chaos of this age and leap the wall before us. The bow that abodes in strength belongs to Sagittarius, the next room beyond Capricorn.

You will remember that the ancient sages pictured Capricorn as a cornucopia turned down and the silver pieces are rolling out, and silver, as well as bread, means spiritual life or food. You will also remember that when Joseph sold corn to his brothers, the silver which they took with them to pay for the corn they always found in their sacks mouths on arriving at home, where Joseph had put it, for this is the same Joseph that sold corn. (Aries, the silver age in Egypt)

We read in the old translation of the Bible that Joseph had a coat of mare colors, but, in Bagster's translation, colors is rendered pieces at margin, so here we find the symbol of the born of plenty, and here we find the fruitful vine, Joseph, whose daughters run over the wall between the animal and psychic ages, and then earth's daughters will reign as Queens in the domain of sex and will be one with Jacob's Dina, the mythical Diana for whom the silver shrine was molded. Acts 19:24. "This shrine was made by Demetrius, rendered divinely touched," meaning spiritual wisdom, of course.

Benjamin, the last son, is defined "son of the right hand," which, of course, means goodness, love, power and wisdom. Of this son Jacob says:

"Benjamin shall raven like a wolf; in the morning he shall devour the prey and at night he shall divide the spoil."

Benjamin is Sagittarius, the zenith of the psychic age. And now the question arises, what is this raven and what is it all about?

Sagittarius is pictured as part man and part horse with a drawn bow in his hand, and the Scorpion's tail he has chosen for a mark, for his arrow is pointed directly that way, and mythology tells us that he shot away the string of the scorpion, and as he neared the earth's night with his booty. He divided the spoil and gave the sting over into the earth's night, but the strength of Scorpio (Benjamin) was retained in the psychic age for Scorpio is one of the strongest constellations of the zodiac, therefore, as the son of the right hand, his spiritual power is wonderful, for mythology tells that he taught Hercules his near neighbor, astronomy, and Esculapius, another near neighbor, medicine, so here we find the Bible Raphu who comes to earth with balm of healing on his wings. Here we find Benjamin surrounded by a high order of constellations, such as birds soaring through lofty altitudes, with wings wide-spread, and Esculapius and Hercules both hold in their hand the bound serpent of the Bible note. Just above Benjamin's head, so near as to almost touch, we find a crass (trouble) shielded by a miter (wisdom). This city of stars is called Sobieski's Shield or Latum. And not so far away we find Vega, the heavenly lyre.

Farther, or near Libra and Virgo, we see Corona, the Crown. So here we find in the psychic age all the symbols of elevation and harmony as pictured in the human imagination of the orthodox heaven. We saw the human imagination because they could not make a practical thing of those vibrations by associating them with the starry myths, so called. All of those beatific constellations in the coining ages proclaim spiritual elevation, joy, harmony, and wisdom, through the son of the right hand, Benjamin.

We have shown in this chapter that the twelve signs of the zodiac are the twelve sons of Jacob and proven them one by Jacob's prophecy, and in his own language, and explained the symbols as well as we could, without a chart of the heavens, and if the language should seem somewhat awkward, our readers must, have charity, for it is no small thing to follow out those twelve constellations, and the neighboring constellations with their vibration, as proven by those heavenly myths.

CONCERNING THE TRINITY

Preliminary to the contemplation of this subject, it is well for us to realize our relative condition to infinity and to understand the limitation of our own mental powers.

This attitude is necessary, not for the purpose of self-humiliation, but rather that we may get a faint idea of the immensity, the boundless scope of the object and therefore an enlarged conception of the one.

The great Father-Mother God whose "sheltering arms" are about us and in whose protection and guidance we may safely trust. When we stop to consider that the only expression of the character and attributes of the one is through manifest creation, and that this creation is only a manifestation of His wish, and that beyond and behind this manifest universe there still remains the one undiminished, perfect and complete omnipotence, omniscience and omnipresence. The human mind stands appalled and utterly powerless to grasp only the faintest outline of what the divine character must be in its entirety.

Man can weigh the sun and the planets, can tell their component elements, can calculate their distances and formulate the laws that govern their motions; yet, when we attempt to realize the fact that the star that we call "Canopus" is a blazing sun having a radiant power of ten thousand times that of the sun that warms and lights us, our finite mind utterly fails to grasp the possibility of what we know to be a material fact From this comparison let us try and realize how much more it requires to grasp the facts of infinity—thus realizing our limitations.

Let us therefore approach our subject in a spirit of humility not with a belief that we can master its details, but glad to be able to form a conception about it that shall be, to us, true and reasonable, recognizing that the subject is in the domain of infinity, and that the more closely we draw our definition the more we condition and limit our conception.

Here it is well to note that the difference of opinion that has been expressed by theologians and churchmen have largely been the result of their limitations of the subject under discussion.

The human mind insists upon close distinctions and fine-drawn definitions and this insistence has done much to confuse the subject in the minds of students, for it is evident that further we are from a full conception. Let us endeavor to consider our subject in its larger aspect and as far as possible broaden the scope of our perceptions and thereby try to get the larger and more comprehensive view.

Let us start with the best statement that we know, "God is Love." Limitless and unbounded love.

Contemplate this statement as you would contemplate the idea of space. Consider yourself as in a boundless ocean of love. No height, no depth, no boundary where love is not. God is Love.

Consider love in the abstract, in its static condition. Love as being absolute and unconditioned; here you cannot escape from the idea of unity: you are forced by the reasonableness of your own mind to say there is One God. God is Love.

Again, consider love as in the dynastic condition. Active love—living love—love with the power and the volition to make love lovable. Let it come into your mind that, love in the abstract, in the unitary condition, is endowed—has life—has power—has volition—can act.

Still holding the greater conception of the oneness of love, you will be forced to grasp the idea that love with the power to make love lovable has a dual appearance to our finite conception, because in our limited condition, one cannot conceive of action without two factors.

That which acts (power) and that which is acted upon (substance), you will see that we are obliged to form our conception of God as one with the dual aspect. God is Love. Now, carrying this conception still farther, and still holding the largest possible idea of oneness with dual appearance, let us take another step.

By the condition of our mental organization, we are obliged to recognize that whenever there exists power that acts and substance that is acted upon, there must be a result of that action. The effect must follow the cause. Here you perceive the triune aspect. Living love that has the power to make itself lovable must have an object that can relate itself to that love and that object must be the third factor of the equation.

Contemplate, meditate upon this very carefully, very devoutly and with the broadest mental conception possible. You may know God by the practical admission of His omnipresent spirit in your heart and life, but to understand what you know is the hermetic privilege, and that comes through and by means of the divine reason individualized in you as a child of the Father.

Take off the limitations, un-manifest, the physical and the psychic. It is the accomplisher and the means of accomplishment and interaction and coordination of these two, all the object are accomplished for which creation was instituted.

The results must carry the triune appearance The universe is the vehicle for the manifestation of that which the universe contains, i.e., the Logos, the Divine, Word, or in other words, the immanence of the divine wish or desire, resident in creation.

The divine omnipresence and the divine omnipotence resident in creation (unity with dual aspect), are the cause of which the individualization of beings in the "likeness" of their creator is the third "persona;" so that in one sense we are all "children of the Father." evolved into individualization in the "likeness" of the divine, and the closeness of our practical relationship is determined by the extent to which we have developed this "likeness."

Thus, all teachers, prophets and messengers for good have been and are related to the Father, each one according to his degree of likeness and each delivering his special message to his special people, according to their needs and capacities of apprehension.

All spiritually endowed men are representatives of the Christos and are endowed with Sonship to the extent to which they have assimilated and transformed their individual characters into harmony with the divine mode of action and being. In order that we may better understand and receive a key to the comprehension of this subject, let it be understood that the divine unity in creation is figured to us in a septenary manner.

The Seven Lamps, the Seven Flames: these are particularly designated as follows: The Spirit of Wisdom, the Spirit of Understanding, the Spirit of Counsel, the Spirit of Power, the Spirit of Knowledge, the Spirit of Righteousness and the Spirit of Divine Awe or Reverence. These are the potentialities of Sonship and all these must be "put on" before our Sonship is complete.

We must assimilate and incorporate these factors and make them into a condition of at-one-ment with our own individual character. God made man potentially "like" himself, but man has to "put on" this "likeness" by his own act, otherwise man would be an automaton, a creature without independent individual character.

Man must recognize the value of these Godlike qualities and he must, of his own free choice, voluntarily make them a part of himself. Now consider the value of this revelation of the septenary character of the undifferentiated Christos, for this is one of the keys to spiritual knowledge and understanding. Just as the seven rays of the color spectrum when united give perfect light, so the seven rays of the divine, the seven lamps to light our way to the throne of Adonai giving a perfect light on the character of the Christos, and they shine out as a perpetual beacon for the enlightenment of the world.

This is the greater Christos who came to the world, and the world knew him not, who came to his own and his own received him not, but to whosoever did receive him and whosoever believed on him, to them gave the power to become the sons of God. The prophecy is still true. The world has not as yet "put on" the attributes of the Christos, and practically knows him not.

The redemption of the world is still by individuals and not "en masse" and we still look forward to the millennium of peace when all shall practically know the Lord Christos, even from the least to the greatest.

The reason why the Christos is represented to us in this sevenfold aspect is to enable us to grasp the idea that it is necessary for us to assimilate all these attributes and their potentialities before we can be considered as unitary in our characters.

Perfection in all these attributes is required to constitute perfect Sonship, yet in proportion as anyone has apprehended and assimilated any of these divine attributes into his individual character and made it part of himself, just in so far, and in proportion is the entity in a condition of Sonship.

As far as this relates to the relative standing or position in divine Sonship, between different teachers, priests and prophets, God's messengers to His children, is not a question necessary for discussion.

The real vital question is one of an individual nature. What is my degree of relationship and how can I make it more perfect and complete?

During the latter days of the Master's earth manifestation, the Apostle Peter asked Him: "Lord, what shall this man do?" The reply came at once. "What is that to thee! Follow thou me."

The Church has been obliged to make specific definitions on this subject and while its wisdom in so doing is not questioned, it still seems evident that in the light of the new knowledge that the last fifty years have furnished, a broadening out of the scope of this inquiry is necessary.

Use then the new light to elucidate the old problem. Acquire a greater and more comprehensive view of God's omnipotent omnipresence, of the residence of the Christos in creation. Strip off the limitations and seek that interpretation which will give the best comprehension of the tender, loving, all-wise care of the one.

THE AQUARIAN AGE

What is Meant by the Aquarian Age? This question is asked by many people who are not conversant with "The Dial Plate of Heaven." An explanation is certainly in order. The movement of all growing, developing bodies is spiral.

The movement of all finished, or perfected bodies is cyclic. The same is true of systems of things whether they be atoms or worlds.

Our solar system came from the great Central Sun that dominates this part of the infinite domain, and as it unfolded its motion was spiral; but when its creative processes were finished, it found its true orbit and began a cyclic motion.

This Central Sun is so far from our earth that it seems to us as a star, and so we call it. It is one of the stars of the Pleiades or the so-called seven stars. The pathway of our solar system around this Central Sun is an immense circle yet our sun and his family of planets move in it with such precision that astronomers are able to calculate to the fractional part of a second the time required to make the long journey. One revolution is completed in a little less than 26,000 years.

Now, this immense orbit is divided into twelve parts of thirty degrees each. These parts are called Signs of the Zodiac and astronomers have given them the following names: Aries, Taurus, Gemini, Cancer, Leo, Virgo, Libra Scorpio, Sagittarius. Capricorn, Aquarius and Pisces. It requires a little more than 2100 years for our solar system to pass through one of these signs. It moves through them in order inverse to that given above.

THE TAURIAN AGE

In the days of our historic Adam, our sun and his family entered the sign Taurus, called at that time the sign of the White Cow, and in Egypt, and other lands, the white cow was esteemed a most sacred animal, and in many places was worshipped.

THE ARIAN AGE

In the days of Melchizedek and Abraham, our solar system entered the sign Aries, or the Ram, and the ram was offered in sacrifice, the devotees believing that the wrath of God could be thus appeased. Abraham found a ram on Mount Moriah, which he offered as a sacrifice in the place of his son Isaac. The Abrahamic, or Arian Age, was distinctly the age of sacrifice.

THE PISCEAN AGE

In the days of Jesus of Nazareth, our solar system entered the sign Pisces, or the Fishes. Pisces is a water sign, and John the harbinger, and Jesus, both introduced water baptism as a symbol of inner cleansing. Water is the true symbol of purification. Jesus himself said to the Harbinger before he was baptized: "All men must be washed, symbolic of the cleansing of the soul."

Fish was a Christian Symbol. In the earlier centuries of the Christian Dispensation the fish was everywhere used as a symbol. The fish, in the opinion of antiquarians generally, is the symbol of Jesus Christ. The fish is sculptured upon a number of Christian monuments, and more particularly upon the ancient sarcophagi. It is also upon medals, bearing the name of our Savior and also upon engraved stones, cameos and intaglios. The fish is also to be remarked upon the amulets worn suspended from the necks by children, and upon ancient glasses and sculptured lamps.

"Baptismal fonts are more particularly ornamented with the fish. The fish is constantly exhibited placed upon a dish in the middle of the table, at the Last Supper, among the loaves, knives and cups used at the banquet."

THE AQUARIAN AGE

Today our sun and his family are passing from the sign Pisces into the sign of the Water Bearer, which is called Aquarius. Astronomers call Aquarius an air sign. It is, in fact, a spirit sign, and this new age is to be preeminently a spiritual age.

Aquarius has ever been known as "the sign of the Son of Man." Referring to this period of time, Jesus said: "And then the man who bears the pitcher will walk forth across an arc of heaven; the sign and signet of the Son of Man will stand forth in the eastern sky. The wise will then lift up their heads and know that the redemption of the earth is near."

The Aquarian Age is, then, the age or dispensation of the world upon which we are now entering. It has been called the New Age, the New Time, the Divine Age, and prophets of old characterized the first half of it as the Millennium, or the thousand years of peace.

IS MAN COMING TO HIS OWN?

It seems that at last Masons, at least some of them who have given the subject study, are coming to the conclusion that after all there may be more in Masonry than the mere Ritual. Robert C. Wright, a well-known Mason, in his work "Indian Masonry," under the chapter of "Brotherhood," says: "Man loves man's company, and solitude is not natural, so he seeks a neighbor, a town, a teeming city, and it is this inborn drawing of man to man that fills him with the desire for secret societies whose object is to bring him nearer to the great Beyond. This object is and should be for all members to faithfully till the soil of the great Brotherhood, first among themselves, that they may thereafter be fit laborers in the greater field of the whole world.

The ancient Egyptian priests had their secret societies which sought the way to the unknown country, and, in modern times, Masonry has striven to fulfill this ancient yearning of man for lodges or societies having their different cults.

"Speculative Masonry teaches that there is a Grand Architect of the Universe, and points out that there must be an inner life, which goes on after what we call death or the separation of the soul from the body; that Masonry seeks to bring together all its members in the great brotherhood of man; that it strives after eternal truths.

These things are taught by symbols and story from time out of mind, and with them the Grand Orient of France lays stress upon the right of free thought. "And of these, the great brotherhood of man,—what is it? Our Masonry says: 'By the exercise of brotherly love we are taught to regard the whole human species as one family, the high and the low, the rich and the poor, who, as created by one Almighty Parent, and inhabitants of the same planet, are to aid, support and protect each other.

On this principle Masonry unites men of every country, sect and opinion and causes true friendship to exist among those who might otherwise have remained at a perpetual distance. "A very nice abstract statement; but go further, into the great world. An infant, a few-weeks old, is left upon a doorstep by the mother, who for some reason, God only knows, puts it there. She sounds an alarm and is swiftly away, eagerly watching to see if it shall be taken in from the cold blasts of winter. The door opens, the light streams forth and a man with stern, forbidding face, looks upon the bundle curiously, takes it up, hears the little cry!

Will he or his wife put that little unknown stranger helpless and alone, out into the street and into the cold, dark night again? Never. Why?

Because the brotherhood of man within him rises to the surface, commanding him to keep a human being safe until it can be cared for by others if he will no longer do so. "A great crowd of pleasure seekers are hurrying homeward, jostling, laughing, tired, cross or good-natured, as it may be.

Suddenly, above all the tumult is heard the voice of a little child, crying bitterly in that great crowd, swirling and rushing in the city's street. He is lost, lost,—and as his cry goes up in pitiful tones of agonized fear and sadness, many spring to the child's side to find out his grief and help him.

In all those thousands, there is not one in his right mind, no matter how low or vicious he might be, who would deny that child the aid it needs until better cared for. Many would spring to the spot with open arms. Why? 'Tis the power of that great something we call brotherly love, which moves foot to foot and with hand to back.

George Catlin, the painter and writer, once wrote: 'Unaided and unadvised, I resolved to use my art and so much of the labors of my future life as might be required, in rescuing from oblivion the books and customs of the vanishing races of native men in America, to which end I plainly saw they were hastening before the approach and certain progress of civilization."

More than six hundred pictures and valuable writings are now safely placed in the Smithsonian Institution as his monument. It was he who wanted 'A Nation's Park,' containing man and beast in all the wildness and freshness of their Nature's beauty. He wanted the Redman to have one spot he might call his own.

Thus, in another way, George Catlin felt the thrill of true brotherhood in common with an unfortunate race. "A Roosevelt and other right-minded men of our country are patiently and courageously fighting for ways and means to stop the secret, as well as the open, taking away and hoarding up of this earth and the fullness thereof, by those to whom it belongeth not.

"Men and women with bright, intelligent minds, in Russia bare their breasts and risk their lives before baronets and ballets, or risk their liberty for Siberian prison in order that an autocracy, sitting on its throne for three hundred years, shall be forced to listen to a demand for a rightful government. Why? Because all these heard the mighty cry of the common people, their brothers, and answered it.

"Lewis and Clark never could have reached the Oregon country with their small company, if all the Indians on the way had been savage and hostile. Why? Because they were spurred to their task by a sincere intent to treat the Indians as men and brothers, not to rob and deceive them.

So, they had no trouble in finding the friendly Indians, whose help gave us the splendid Northwest Territory, which shall be greater than even any kingdom Solomon ever dreamed of, in all his glory, as told in the traditions of history. "Man is but a grown-up child, and while he still hears the piercing cry of a child, or the forced shriek of an injured grownup, his brotherhood sense has passed from that beautiful keenness of his own childhood into a blunted, dull and selfish, nature, and because of this he is no longer quick to hear the far sadder, still and inmost cry from the sorely tried and distressed souls of the grown-up children about him, seeking help just as wistfully and needing it quite as much as the little child; To be able to give help in such cases, is to have within us the true brotherhood of man.

We are told the number five alludes to the five senses, and of these hearing, seeing, and feeling are Masonically considered most important. For many years, philosophers have said there is a sixth sense, and so there is—greater than all the others. When rightly tuned, it hears heart cries which fall unheeded on ears of clay that hear not; it sees the storms of life and signs of distress in a troubled heart, where dull eye of flesh is blind; it feels the thrill of desire to battle for justice to the oppressed; and it feels a boundless sympathy stretching forth to encourage the struggling fighter in life's stream, and sheds rays of light on the sorrowing; while mortal body is unmoved by any touch which will recognize a brother in the dark as well as in the light. O, greater than them all, and all in one!

Can we with the grips we now have, raise the deadened master sense to a bright and living perpendicular, or must we look for some other grip we know not and for light we have not received?

O, Masonry, let thy actions, not thy words, tell the world that thou hast light abundantly!

"Brotherhood is a mysterious inner being which moves freely as water; is man's everyday need and without which he cannot live or be happy.

Like water, always water, whether it be found in fairest flower or fruit, or in terrible poison, in foul or in rotten mass; it spreads in great or little streams throughout all mankind as one. Now sluggishly, ebbing away to lowest depths, where are the swamps or stupidity or slimy baseness with the minds of those unlearned or of gross and beastly nature.

Yet ceaselessly at work, changing those to whom it comes, purifying and lifting them up. Until at last it rises in kindly splendor, like soft and beautiful clouds in the blue sky, from whence again it gently cometh in all its purity to where mean, rank or coarse growths are found, again to where the waving grains of industry and kindly fruits of charity and truth in valley and plain are seen.

Yet again to where rare and beautiful flowers of learned and wise minds may be found, high on the mountain side of a good life, to be seen and known in all their worth,—only by the few. Whether we find brotherhood in minds like lofty mountains, joyous, rippling streams, or in oceans vast depths of wisdom.—'tis ever the same mighty life stream of brotherhood or man, which seeks its way on the level of time and flows thus unto itself again and again, it matters not where or how widely apart man from man may be on this earth, for one touch of it proves all the word is kin."

What a world this would be if all the Masons throughout this wide

Universe were to follow this same grand doctrine of Universal Brotherhood. And yet, why should they not? The book of the mysteries is open to them all.

"Why then should they not all gradually imbibe the grand truths of their outer philosophy? Theirs is the opportunity, but will they accept it?

CONCRNING THE SOUL

This is one of those subjects that we can think about. One that we can approach and endeavor to partly comprehend. One that is always interesting because it is the only reality of ultimate being that is a part of ourselves and at the same time it is not fully comprehensible to us in its entirety and in its detail on account of our own limitations. Like all psychic problems we shall be sure to lose the larger comprehension if we insist upon fine definitions and close drawn determinations, so I therefore bid you look upon it with as extended mental scope as possible, knowing that the broadening out of your conceptions will bring you an increase of understanding. In order to avoid confusion in the use of terms I shall use the words "individual" and "individuality" as associated with the idea of "Being" and I shall use the words "person" and "personality" as associated with the idea of Existence. Anterior to all life attributes, back of Intellect, Emotion, Will, back of all manifest action in the Unity of Duality, there subsists Being, Eternal Living Love, from which all manifestation proceeds and as it proceeds it takes on limitation, hence quality becomes qualities.

I shall therefore consider that Being is Eternal and Existence is the vehicle or means, whereby Individual Being is evolved and made manifest. I shall associate the idea of individual Soul with the idea of Being and shall consider the personality as the immediate environment and vehicle for the soul's manifest functions, and in the entire discussion I would have you keep in mind that we are trying to measure and define a "somewhat" that is immaterial, imponderable and infinite in material terms having a limitation measured by our physical nerve capacity.

When you consider this carefully, you will see why there must be a difference of comprehension among students and yon will also see why the subject cannot be discussed exhaustively. In the first place: The soul cannot be described as a "something" for our idea of a "thing" is inseparably connected with the idea of length, breadth and thickness and these attributes the soul does not possess. In the second place: The soul being immaterial and imponderable and we being obliged to formulate ideas and conceptions through and by means of a material body or vehicle, it becomes evident at once that the best and most correct conception of our subject will be gained by a consideration of the attributes and manifest qualities of the soul rather than by a discussion of its essential nature. This is illustrated by a study of other imponderables.

We recognize a "somewhat" that we call electricity, but we cognize it only through its manifested quality as exhibited in phenomena. We know that it possesses the ability to accomplish certain results under known conditions, but there remains very much that we do not know, owing to our limitations.

We are able to learn much by analogy and comparison with other forms of energy, for we have arrived at the point of energy in the universe, which is constant although it may be transformed into many special manifestations, all of which are correlated and therefore in harmony. We feel fully warranted in using analogy and correspondence in our research after truth because we are satisfied that "there is one law and he that worketh is one," and consequently we feel that manifestation will be filled with analogies and correspondences which we may study with great benefit.

The ancient dictum says: "If thou wouldst know, thou must interrogate that which contains the answer." Let us therefore look into ourselves and see if we can find anything to aid us in our research. Beginning at the lower, we first interrogate physical man. In this we want facts and science furnishes them. The late Professor Huxley states the position with great clearness and is therefore quoted.

In speaking of animal life in general, he says: "The physiological activities manifest by the complex whole, represent the sum, or rather the resultant, of the separate and independent physiological activities resident in each of the simple constituents." In other words, the personality of man with all his potencies and potentialities represents the resultant, or the sum of all the activities, potencies and potentialities of the units of his physical system.

The United States is a nation because each and every individual citizen has delegated certain activities, potencies and potentialities to a certain aggregation called Congress. If it be true that the physical man with all his activities is a composite resultant of individual cell potencies, and if it be true that the mental and psychic phenomena exhibited by physical man are part of these activities, it then follows: That the individual soul must have its seat in this center of activity.

"The Immanent consciousness of all the cells of a man's entity, cause, by their polarization, a central unity of consciousness, which is more than the sum total of all the consciousness, because it is on a higher plane." I am aware this view is not accepted by the Orthodox Church and for that reason I would bid you to examine it very carefully.

The untied opinion of a large body of learned men is entitled to your respectful consideration and if you are to take radical departure therefrom, you should do so only a after profound consideration. I therefore request you to make a careful study of the line of thought that I have indicated before you go further.

The fundamental principles that underlie the modes of operation in natural growth are very simple. One of these principles teaches us that "the tendency of all evolution is towards centralization and individualization." Another one of these principles teaches us that all growth, that tends towards centralization and individualization is accomplished by means of the transformation and development of the forms and potencies of "life stuff" already existing. That is to say: Beginning at the lowest form of life—the protoplasmic unit—all growth is but a modification, a differentiation and a re-adaptation of the original cell and its outgrowth, together with an accompanying development of its inherent potentialities. Man stands today, the result of this principle of growth and development; a mass of primary cells, altered, transformed, adapted. One group of cells, transformed, forming bone, another group of transformed cells forming muscle, another attending to the visceral functions and still another forming the nerve system and the recognized seat of consciousness, and man himself, the real man, not the physical vehicle ordinarily classed as man, but the imponderable Ego, the reality contained within the physical and manifested through it—the one who says of himself—I am, is the individualized entity, is the polarized centralization and individualization of the psychic lives of each and all the Living cells component in his physical organization.

The verdict of science on this point is clear and unmistakable, for seventy years the cell theory propounded by Swann, has been in the arena of discussion and it is now definitely and unanimously accepted—briefly it is, that every animal, man included, presented itself as the sum of its vital unities, that the activities of an organism are the sum of the activities of its component cells. All that man is, in his mentality, in his emotional comprehensions, in his so-called God-like attributes he owes to the developed potentialities of the cell units of structure and to their commerce with the environment. The state of consciousness of the real self, of any one man, at any given moment, is the resultant of the centralization and focalization of the combined states of consciousness of all his physical cell entities at that given moment. That phase of the "I am," the Ego that we recognize and name "the lower self," is therefore the ordinary physical consensus of these cell activities functioning on the environment according to natural tendency, moving along the line of least resistance.

That phase of the "I am," the Ego that we recognize as the "Higher Self," is therefore the consensus and polarization of these same entities recognized by the Ego upon their higher plane of potentiality. The Ego recognizes this potentiality upon the spiritual plane as an advanced step, a development of greater powers than these exhibited on the physical plane. It is a principle that, in manifestation, the higher and the lower must always exist and in the line of human progress the lower is always used as a means of attaining the higher. The lower self is the round of the "Jacob's ladder" that the Ego must always stand upon in order to prepare himself for the next step in advance. This so called "Higher Self" is the progressive soul. This is the "Prodigal Son" who recognizes "The Father" a long way off! And who says to himself, "these busies of materiality are unsatisfactory!

This companionship with the animals is unworthy of me! I will arise and go unto my father!" Mark you! The prodigal forms his own conclusions, based upon his own experience, and the determination to "go to the father" is his own act. Once his footsteps are turned towards home, once his attitude is changed to the right direction, the mighty Father-Mother Love is extended to him, supporting him and sustaining him on the pathway. This is the esoteric sense of the church doctrine called the "Persistence of the Saints." The Soul of man developed to the point of spiritual self-recognition and its relation to the Divine Father-Mother and the perception of the love that exists between the two as a bond attracting them together, and shall finally draw them together permanently.

The "Elect of God" are those who recognize this drawing relationship and who, like the prodigal son, determine that they will "arise and go to the Father." The act known as "conversion." The "Elect of God" then, are those who, of their own free will and accord, elect to conform their conduct to a harmonious accordance with the Divine Mode of Action in Manifestation.

They "elect" themselves and the great loving heart of the Father recognizes and confirms the election and adopts them into Sonship. Every cell unit of the human body shows the dual and the triune aspect of manifestation. Each cell is composed of these parts and each part has its separate function and potency.

From the outside proceeding inward, we have: First. The outside containing membrane, a modification of the protoplasm itself, whose function is to surround and protect its protoplasmic contents and also to act as a medium of communication between the cell and its environ.

Second. A semi-liquid mass of specially modified protoplasm contained within the enveloping membrane whose function is nourishing and sustaining.

Third. The nucleus, a concrete mass of more highly differentiated protoplasm in which reside all the higher potencies and functions of the unit, Correspondingly, as the outer membrane acts as a container and as a vehicle of contact between the cell contents and the environment, so the physical body of man acts pondingly as the contained protoplasmic mass of cell furnishes nourishment and is the source from which the power and the energy of accomplishment is drawn, so the physical activities of man contained within the form give life-energy and furnish the propelling power, thus holding up and sustaining the entire structure; and, correspondingly, as all these exterior and contained powers and potencies, are constantly focalizing their potentialities to the life center, the nucleus, so all the power contained in man's physical organism is constantly ministering to and furnishing sustaining power, focalizing all potentialities to its life center—the soul.

As the nucleus is the life center containing the potency of the morphological unit of structure, so the soul is the life center containing the present and future potency and potentiality of that aggregation of morphological units that we call the living man.

Now, I have not told you definitely what the soul is, but I have instituted a comparison to tell you what the soul is like. Similarly, as Congress expresses the soul of the American Nation, so the seat of reason and emotion expresses the soul of man. Similarly, as the Congressional acts and the terminations express the character of the American Nation, so the soul of man expresses the character of the man himself.

Similarly, as the American Nation makes the progress in power, wisdom and goodness, thus expressing its growth in character, so the soul of man makes progress and power, wisdom and goodness, expresses this growth by the demonstration of its character—and mind you—the progress of elevation is similar in both cases. It comes from the growth and development of the inherent potentialities of its units of structure.

It is a psychic process dealing with the psychic development of the psychic potentialities of psychic elements and as far as we definitely know there are no means of soul growth provided for in nature without contact with a material environment.

The measurement of the soul and its standing in the scale of progressive development is determined by what we call the character of the individual, and the measurement of character and its standing in the scale of progressive development is determined by the degree of harmonious conformity of the individual with the divine mode of action in manifestation.

There are three prominent theories regarding the genesis and procession of the human soul, and each theory has its own special class of adherents. These theories may be briefly stated as follows:

First.—The Materialistic Theory holds: "That the human, soul is the product of the molecular and chemical changes of the living body, and that its existence terminates when these activities cease." This theory is held by agnostic scientists, ultra-materialists, nihilists, and others of a sympathetic class.

Second.—The Christian Church Theory holds: "That God creates and furnishes a new soul for each human body born into the world. That this soul is immortal, that it has but one life experience and but one chance for eternal happiness.

This chance is given to each soul during the continuance of its earth life, and as the soul uses, accepts or rejects this chance, its eternal future condition will be determined. This theory, without essential modifications, is held by the Roman and Greek Catholic Church, the Protestant Christian Church, and in a more or less modified form, by the great majority of all those who class themselves as Christians.

Third.—The Oriental Theory, particularly predicates the repeated descent of the human soul into material human bodies for the purpose of repeated and extended experience to be gained by actual contact with a material environment. That the object to be gained by this contact is, the formation of such an individual character as will be necessarily permanent and fitted for a higher and more refined state of existence.

This theory is held by Buddhists, Brahmins, Theosophists, Occultists and Mystics generally, and is rapidly being absorbed by western thought. Probably three-fourths of the civilized world are in sympathy with this theory, and one reason why it was found included in the statement of belief adopted by the Christian Church can be based on the well-known fact that early fathers of the church proceeded upon the belief that Jesus came to declare a new gospel, one that would replace and do away with the old philosophies and particularly those not taught or foreshadowed by their special revelations contained in the old testament and other sacred Jewish writings.

They considered that their special mission was to formulate a philosophy that would be in conformity with such a view. In this way the new doctrines of "Substitution," the "Vicarious Atonement," and "Salvation by Faith," came to be inserted and while there is an aspect of truth in all these doctrines, it yet remains highly probable that they had their origin in the synthetic and philosophical brain of the Apostle Paul and were by him, impressed upon the early Christian Church; for these doctrines, as now formulated and understood, cannot be justly based upon or inferred from any of the direct teachings of Jesus as handed down to us. The scope of this inquiry covers more particularly the first two theories named and we will therefore give them our first attention. In the consideration of the materialistic theory, it must always be borne in mind, that the scientific observer is hedged in by, and his expression of opinion is limited to, the field of observed facts; therefore, a statement made by a student of science must be taken with this limitation in view.

Looking at the theory in such a light, it simply means that the scientist states: That so far as his knowledge of the related facts extends, he is obliged to come to the conclusion, that the human soul is the product of the molecular and chemical changes of the living body and that its existence terminates when these activities cease.

Many pseudo-scientists who hold to such a statement are more or less ignorant of the facts and possibly, are themselves in a state of incomplete evolution so far as their spiritual perceptions are concerned. The opinion of such should be taken with due allowance, for it remains a fact, although not fully understood, that, just as a blind man is incapacitated from forming a correct opinion of the phenomena of light, as a person of undeveloped spiritual perception is proportionately, incapacitated from form in g a correct opinion of spiritual phenomena. This is a truth that you would do well to consider very carefully.

The materialistic theory contains truth. The soul cannot be exteriorly manifested except by means of a material vehicle, (the body and its nerve system) and this material vehicle cannot be provided and sustained except "through the molecular and chemical changes of the living body;" but, to say that the existence of the human soul terminates when these activities cease, is an unwarranted assumption and its effect is to stultify the Wisdom and Love of God, and to make His work in creation objectless and, so far as we can discover, chaotic and insane. The fact of a future existence need not be argued in this day, for it has become a fact of practically universal consciousness.

The Orthodox Church Theory: As this is very important, it will be well to consider it in detail. Let us take up the first proposition: "God creates and furnishes a new soul for each human body born into the world." In the sense in which this statement is generally accepted, this is not true. In the larger sense and viewed in the light of God's mode of action in manifestation, in the light of the divine mode of evolution, it is true.

The church has been right when it has held to the nobler esoteric view, and it has been in error in its popular explanation of the truth owing largely to the spiritual ignorance of its priests, and the spiritual incapacity and ignorance of its members, and instead of elevating the people by education it has too often been the policy to attempt to materialize the truth, and thus bring it into the range of comprehension of the ignorant.

Herein can be seen as the cause of failure in the teachings of divine truth; the ignorance and limitation of the spiritual comprehension of its teachers, and the more dense ignorance and spirituality incompetence of the masses together, causing a lowering of spirituality. This was the cause of the sorrow of the Master: "He came to His own, and his own received him not." This is why he so often had to say: "He that hath ears to hear, let him hear." In all the exhibition of God's mode of manifestation, there is no "fiat" creation. Everything manifested in creation comes to our comprehension by the regular process of natural law. Everything that manifests life, manifests that life by a process of natural growth.

Professor E. Ray Lancaster, an entirely competent authority, under date of the year 1907, voices the opinion of the scientific men of the day when he says: "There is no school, or body of thinkers at the present day, who are acquainted with the facts now ascertained, which denies the orderly evolution of the Cosmos by the regular operation of a more or less completely ascertained series of properties resident in the material of which it consists," and "Man is held to be a part of nature, a product of the definite and orderly evolution which is universal."

It took millions of years for the orderly process of natural law to perfect a body that should be a fit vehicle for even a rudimentary human soul. This is what is implied when it is said, that "God made man out of the dust of the earth." Jesus understood this, when he said, that "God is able, out of these stones, to raise up children unto Abraham;" yet Jesus would not explain the occult meaning of this truth, for he knew the ignorance that held the people enchained and that the explanation was utterly beyond their comprehension. The Master well knew that the distortion and prostitution of truth caused by an inability to comprehend it, was far more fatal to spirituality than mere ignorance. It is true that "God made man out of the dust of the earth," but during the millions of years that man was in process of evolvement God never interfered with the process; the result is that as man has the prerogative of independent choice, he is practically self-made and consequently self-responsible.

If God had, in any way, interfered with the natural process of man's evolution, such an act would have destroyed, in proportionate part, man's self-responsibility. If God had created man as a "living soul" after the manner taught by the church, i.e., a "fiat" creation, the result would be that man would be a living automaton and God would become responsible for him, and it necessarily follows that if such a creature committed any act that we term a moral sin, the creature himself would not be the sinner because he obeyed the impulses of an organization in the production of which he had no part or lot.

Such a creature could not acquire a correct idea of moral responsibility. When the church promulgated such a doctrine, the operation of the processes of nature was very little understood and consequently the views now expressed were utterly impossible of comprehension at that time, but it is for us to more fully understand and comprehend that the unfoldment of truth is progressive, and that it is right and fitting for all seekers after truth to carefully and diligently examine and prove all things, and to bring forth out of the treasure house of the understanding, things "both new and old."

Viewed in the light of latter-day knowledge, this church theory is seen to be unworthy on account of the gross limitation that it puts on the justice and wisdom of God for it presupposes that God is obliged to interfere with His own creation in order to make it do its work to suit Him, and the inference naturally is drawn that God was not able to do better, that He was constrained by some sort of a necessity that obliged Him to work under certain limitations. When man constructs a large and complicated machine carefully calculated to do a certain character of work and to turn out a definite and finished product, the supervising engineer has to be constantly with it, in person or by deputy, and he has to hold himself in readiness to make proper corrections and adjustments; the hammer, wrench and oil cup are always at hand, readjustments are always expected; Why? Because man is finite and limited, and works with materials of limitation.

His work is therefore more or less imperfect. Not so with God. He is infinitely perfect and infinitely unlimited. He projects the ideal of creation and it is an accomplishment. He looks upon it and pronounces it good. He desires, wishes, wills that it shall be accomplished according to His ideal; and so it is. That is the act of creation.

The expressed wish of God before time was. Since the time that God said, "Let us make man in our own likeness and image" millions and millions of years have passed, and in all that time there has been no interference, no change in the plan, no adjustments for the reason that no change for the better was possible, the plan was and is absolutely perfect.

Further, this process of "making man" is still going on, for man—the ideal man—is to be made in the likeness and image of his maker and we are, as a body, far from realizing this expectation, but the same process of natural law, (God's Mode of Action) that has brought us so far on our journey, is fully competent to complete God's work and to present Him with His realized ideal.

God is immanent in nature and nature derives its life and power from this immanence. Listen to the word given by the disciple that Jesus loved. "Originally was the Word (logos) and the Word was with God, and the Word was God. The same was originally with God, and the Word was God. The same was originally and, without Him came into existence, not even one thing which has come into existence."

This is the only "fiat" creation, all since is but the working out of the original plan and the accomplishment of the original ideal. In a sense God is always saying: "Let us make man" and the process is continuous and still going on and the "Elder Brothers" who have won the race and are entitled to "sit down at the right hand of the Majesty on High" are, as yet, comparatively only a small proportion of those for whom our Heavenly Father has provided room.

The Christian church further holds: that the soul of man is immortal; that it has but one life experience, and but one chance of eternal happiness or eternal misery; that this one chance is given to each soul during its earth life experience and if this soul elects to accept the terms of the offer, as promulgated by the church, it will be apportioned to a condition of eternal happiness and if the soul refuses the offer or declines the same, or even if it is in ignorance of its provisions, in that alternative event, the individual soul will then be allotted to a condition of misery, suffering and punishment from which there shall be no release or abatement.

You have been already shown how it is perfectly true that in one aspect, God does create human soul, and you have also been shown that it is perfectly true, in another aspect, that man creates his own soul and that it follows, in so doing, man assumes and takes upon himself the entire responsibility for the soul's acts and choices; with this double view you will recognize the momentous fact, that during the entire time of this soul creation, man has an un-asked interference extended to him.

Man may have all the help and sympathy he will ask for, but the asking must be from a free and unfettered choice on the part of the man himself. Under these conditions, only can he take upon himself and assume for himself, the entire responsibility of his own work. The theory assumes that each soul, "ipso facto," immortal, has only one life experience on earth, and during that experience, it has thrust upon it the self-choice of eternal happiness or eternal punishment. It is very evident that this statement needs modification.

If it is true that God created a human soul, in the manner certified by the church, place it in a condition of ignorance both of its self and of its author, surrounded it with warring, adverse conditions, placed in the care of the average church member's intelligence, made it immortal by its author's fiat and not with the consent of the soul-self, required of it the performance of fealty of which it was either ignorant or misinformed, and then condemned it to eternal and miserable punishment for the non-performance of a requirement forced upon it by a superior power; then, if this is accepted as truth, it becomes evident to all thinking men that there is something wrong with our conception of God's Mode of Action; there is a jarring condition and our idea of that harmony, that self-evidently must exist. It further becomes evident that it is highly probable that the wrong conception lies within the scope of our own ignorance and that it is our imperative duty to so modify our ideas as to make the adjustment harmonious.

It seems evident that: If God created a separate soul for each separate human body that is, and has been, born into the world, and; If he created that soul eternal immortal by irrevocable edict and, likewise; If he enforced the penalty of disobedience upon it and did not give it a full and fair chance, a clear field and abundant opportunity together with an untrammeled self-hood sufficiently endowed to make an irrevocable choice, having full knowledge of its present and future importance, and a full conception of its eternal significance; if this be true it will then follow:

That the great majority of mankind will render a verdict pronouncing such a condition not only unjust, but entirely contrary to their idea of the Justice and Goodness of the Almighty One, the Loving Heavenly Father. And such a verdict will be right. This statement of the doctrine of the church is not overdrawn, exaggerated or unfair. It is a condensed statement of the actual doctrine as set forth, and any student can verify its terms.

Humanity is now sufficiently intelligent to render a substantially correct verdict and today, anyone may read that verdict in the non-acceptance of the doctrines as set forth in church standards and while the theologians lament the repudiation of their doctrine, they also recognize and realize the importance and necessity of an amended statement. This amendment and reconstruction they have attempted to make, and this attempt has given rise to numerous sects and denominations.

Their want of success has for a reason, that the entire statement must be remodeled, and that many of their articles of belief must be practically abandoned and their identity so transformed as to make them unrecognizable in order to permit their statement to conform to the knowledge of the actual facts now before us.

This demand is now confronting them but, at present, they are not willing to make the needed concessions. They still insist that God made the earth, a material creation, and that He then made man, a spiritual creation, and that law on one plane of spiritual creation may conflict with law on the plane of material creation, and that this conflict is in harmony with what they designate as "God's Plan and Purpose." When asked to explain the reason of this conflict and the reasonableness of this "fiat" creation, they are unable to do so and are very likely to recite the old and well-used formula regarding "the all-wise dispensations of an inscrutable providence."

This is not a position of honorable consideration of the All-Wise Creator, for it is now evident to all that the Father desires that all men shall know Him and knowing, give Him honor and love. When we speak of the church, we necessarily bring to our minds the idea of religion, and it should be distinctly understood and steadfastly borne in mind that we are not now considering the subject of religion but that we are considering the subject of theology, that form of philosophy that has to do with the reasonable explanation of the phenomena of religion.

Religion, like all expressions of spirituality, has the dual aspect; it has its rise in the emotional nature, and has largely to do with the emotional aspect, but with it goes the consideration of the mental aspect by which the emotions are mentally satisfied and more or less understood. We are not dealing with the emotional factor, and the reader will kindly bear in mind that when we speak of the church as wrong and inadequate, we refer only to the philosophical explanation of its emotional phenomena. We are not attacking the good that the church is accomplishing in providing spiritual satisfaction for that heart-hunger that is experienced by those who "hunger and thirst after rightness" nor are we criticizing those priests of all sects and callings—"servants of the Living God"—who, in devotion to the Voice of the Spirit are daily and hourly serving in the spiritual temple; those who, by precept and example, are "doing justly, loving mercy and walking humbly with their God."

Those who are "anointed by the spirit of devotion to preach the glad tidings to the poor; who are sent to heal the broken-hearted, to preach deliverance to the captives, recovering of sight to the blind, and to set at liberty them that are bruised;" these are God's men doing God's service and in all places, whether in or out of the church, of whatsoever creed or denomination, let all men give them honor. Lest such brethren be offended, let us say that the desire is to reform the old, to transform it to the later-day conception of the new, and provide for their use a better explanation of the holy mysteries; for it is true, that ultimately the conception of the emotional aspect must conform to, and be explained by, the mentality, and ultimately these two must be in full and loving accord.

God is Harmony and Harmony is Love. Love, "Wisdom and Justice are One." We hold this to be true, that our conceptions must he remodeled, transformed and refined, until this understanding of truth is attained.

Thus, will devoutness become sincere and thus will God's worship be perfected. Two thousand years ago, the Master taught this truth, and today we can see that the great mass of the people have made progress, for it is a fact that the great majority of all civilized souls admit the truth of the existence of a Supreme Being. If this is questioned, we have only to consider the fact that nearly all the fraternal societies make this confession a condition of membership. While it remains true that great numbers of individual souls have attained to very high degree of spiritual evolution, it also remains true that the great majority of human souls have not as yet, attained to a high degree of progress. This progress is necessarily slow, but even in our generation we can note a material advance; the advance in the unfoldment of knowledge has enabled the mass of mankind to slowly but surely rise to higher power and better conceptions, and while we would give honor to the devoted priest, we would honor Tyndall, Huxley, Darwin, Spencer and others who have nobly striven to remove the boundaries of ignorance as far from humanity as possible.

Honor to all who are endeavoring to search out and elucidate truth, no matter in what field or under what name, for such are doing God's work, no matter what their personal confession spiritually may be or how far they may be advanced in their own spiritual evolution. What mankind needs is light, more light, and each light bringer contributes to the general dissolution of darkness and to the enlightenment of mankind. Darkness is not a reality. Darkness is, because light is absent. Light appears and darkness is not; Light cometh from the Father.

In our endeavor to search out the meaning of divine truth, it is well for us to stop and candidly consider where the mass of mankind is now located in the line of progress. Too often we are disposed to locate man, not where he really is, but where he is expected to be ultimately. Ideally, it is true that man is created in the image and likeness of God, but in point of fact, man at this present day, man as a race and collectively considered, is really very far from realizing the ideal.

The explanation lies in the consideration of the evolutionary process as a continuous one and also one that is far from being completed. True, God seeing the completed end from the beginning, looks upon it and pronounces it good; but that does not imply that God is satisfied with the present incomplete development of man except as a part of the process that will end in the perfect realization of the projected ideal. The fact is that, at present, redemption is accomplished by single souls.

Individuals that in their spiritual development and progress are in advance of their race. Those who, through struggle and trial, through danger and difficulty, have chosen to hasten the consummation of that better part, the early realization of the divine inheritance. For the great mass of mankind the day of redemption is yet far in the future, and before it dawns the way must be prepared by the more universal diffusion of knowledge, for the truth remains, that the ignorance, negligence and weakness of mankind is responsible for most of the adverse conditions against which the mass of mankind are in constant rebellion.

In point of fact the restraints on the human will are very few, and provided man institutes no grave offense against his fellowman there is little interference with his doing pretty much as he pleases. Free will, the ability of the self-conscious individual to do as he pleases, the individual right of choice, is an inherent principle, and it exists in the nature and constitution of things manifested.

The reason why the Church, as a body, does not take up its genuine work and carry it through to success is, that the majority of its members have not progressed far enough in the spiritualization of their souls to enable them to accomplish the work. The Church is an assembly, an "Ecclesia," of individual souls, gathered together out of the mass of mankind for the purpose of mutual aid and assistance in attaining soul growth. When it is understood that this growth is through regular evolutionary modes and that its attainment is progressive and not instantaneous, it becomes apparent that there will be differences in growth, and that individuals will be in different states of attainment.

Observe, therefore, the wrong and injustice of classing any church member as a "hypocrite" just because he has not made rapid progress in soul growth or has not come up to idealized standards. Everyone who publicly allies himself with those who seek spiritual growth is entitled to be considered as honest in so doing; no matter how feeble the walk or how weak the profession, each one is trying in his own way and after his own manner to achieve that which is praiseworthy, and each striving soul is entitled to, and should receive consideration in so doing.

The world owes Judas Iscariot and the class he represents, an explanation and an apology. Correct judgment must be based upon the proper interpretation of the interior motive, prompting the action and not on the exterior appearance of the action itself. I speak of "the Church" as that mass of mankind who have chosen to publicly or privately avow their desire to seek for spiritual growth and its progressive unfoldment; in this vast body there will be found a diversity of creeds or statements of belief, each statement being one that seems best fitted to its special class of mankind at a certain stage of their unfoldment.

This being the case, it is evident that as any part, or as the whole progresses, it will make a change in their creeds more or less necessary. Creed is a crystallization of belief. When man outgrows it, when knowledge compels a change in belief, then creed has to be correspondingly changed in order that mankind may be free, the restraints placed upon the mind must be loosened, for as mind becomes more and more comprehensive the conception broadens.

When Lazarus came into his perception of the immortal life, the Master commanded that the grave clothes which confined him should be loosened in order that he might have freedom. To even the casual observer, it is evident that a great wave of so-called New Thought is going over the entire world today. What is it but an awakening to a realization of the practical fact of God's immanence in nature, of the actuality of the "Emanuel"—God with us?

The realization of the conception of God as Living Love—in us—about us—through us—all available for the asking. In the olden times the same truth was told, but the many did not grasp it.

Today, universal scholarship has raised the standard of mental power so much higher and makes its attainment so universal that the mass of mankind can grasp and comprehend the truth. The old creeds and forms of belief are not to be destroyed, but the misconceptions are to be transformed into a clearer understanding.

All growth is by an improving process of transformation and the "New Thought" will declare a better and purer conception of God, and it will show that God is helping us to give a clearer and more lofty view of His character in that the new conception demonstrates the special aspect of truth that Jesus declared; God is Love and God desires that man should understand and love Him.

What is mythically called "the day of woman" is dawning and the emotional quality of divinity is to be not only declared but it is to be experimentally demonstrated. God is not only infinite in power and might, but in harmony and peace, and in living, ever present and readily available love. God was declared as the Mighty King and Supreme Ruler for those who needed ruling, but in these latter days, God is declared as the Father-Mother not only powerful but compassionate, one who is a very present help in time of everyone's need. The day of dogma is passing and the day of understanding, the day when we are to know that the name "Emanuel" has for us definite and helpful meaning; that the tender, sympathetic living love of God is ever present with us and for us. It is no new truth; it is a new and massive comprehension of the old truth that the Egyptians taught in the character of Isis and that the Hebrews typified when they addressed God under the name of El Shaddai.

The Pearl of Great Price is always the spiritually developed human soul and it is always the "woman" who sweeps the house, diligently, until she finds it; for "sweeping the house" means the cleaning and purifying of the vehicle, and this is accomplished most largely by the emotions. The desire to do right and to be found in the path of rightness is from the emotional aspect of our duality, which is typified as the female, thus distinguishing if from the more positive and forceful aspect of the mentality, typified as the male. Without emotion, without desire, feeling and what we might call "wantness," there is no possible progress, either physical, mental, moral or spiritual. The mentality is an aid to progress and an essential factor, for by its use, the soul becomes acquainted with the best and wisest way.

The mentality ratifies and makes the pathway that the soul desires and, for this reason, philosophy and theology are cold, while religion is warm and impulsive. Religion is the attitude of the human soul to the living, loving life of the great Father-Mother of all. Personal, heartfelt religion is the real thing and the real attitude; theology is simply the reason for the attitude, it is not the attitude itself. The individual soul, in its partly developed state, can have a preponderance of either of these factors but the balanced union of the two is the establishment of the soul on the rock of understanding, and when this is accomplished it is compared to the structure which is founded upon a rock; the winds and the waves may attack it and all elementary force may be expended upon it, but it will not fall; for it has a sure foundation. As the divine is shown to us in triune manifestation, so the soul has need of the trinity in its growth, i.e., right desire, right understanding and right action. The correct growth of the individual emotional life necessitates active cooperation between the mental and emotional factors of individuality, supported and reinforced by the free action of the individual will. When these conditions are adopted and when they are working in harmony with the divine mode of action, then is correct individual soul growth assured. Again, the message to each one:

> "My ways shall be thy ways,
> And thy ways shall be my ways.
> Peace cometh with understanding."

ESOTERIC PROGNOSTICATIONS

Relative to the conditions now prevailing here upon earth. The confusing conditions will be eradicated only when states men learn that there are higher powers than political intrigues, motives and interests. When they learn the might that exists in truth; when they learn that the great moral and philosophical ideas which have seized on many souls are the most efficient, durable forces which are acting in the world; when they learn that the past and present are not the future, but that the changes already existing in the minds of men are only forerunners, the signs of mightier revolutions.

Politicians, absorbed in near objects, are prophets only on a small scale, and though they may foretell the outcome of the coming election, the breaking of a deep moral conviction in the mass of men is a mystery which they have little drill to interpret The future of this country is to take its shape, not from the struggles of parties or leaders for power or station, but from the great principles which are silently unfolding themselves in the minds of mankind. A far higher and more rational conception of freedom than entered the minds of those in past ages is spreading itself and is changing the face of society. Equality before the law has become the watchword of all civilized countries.

The worth of a human being is better understood. His worth as an individual, on his own account, and not at a useful tool for others progress, it found to attach a sacredness and dignity to every man because each man is immortal.

Such is the current of thought. Principles of a higher order are beginning to operate, and the dawn of these everlasting tights is a sure omen of a brighter day. In the great conflict between the oriental and western world, which was decided at Thermopylae and Marathon: in the great conflict between polytheism and Theism in the American revolution: in these grandest epochs of history, what was it that won the victory? Not political management nor self-interest, but the principles of freedom, moral power and enthusiasm, the divine aspirations of the human soul. Great thoughts and great emotions have a place in human history which no historian has ever given to them, and the future will be more determined by these than by the past.

We find, in the planetary influences, as taught by astrology, the great fundamental principles underlying these periods of progress. It is a law of that unseen, but most certain dominion, which even here among the blinding shadows which conceal His immediate workings. The Great Infinite Force of all life is administering that they, who being set anywhere to do His will neglect to do it, are replaced by other and more faithful instruments.

How its operation is, in every case, to be reconciled with the reality of man's agency and separate probations, we may be unable to perceive; how amidst the conflicting waves of man's evil wills and rebellious impulses, and the mighty tempest of this troubled world. He does yet so rule that all these separate wills, each singly and independent, do all work out together the wise purpose to His eternal council, we may be unable to conceive. That it should be so is essential to the reality of His Government.

That there is nothing repugnant to human nature in the basis of Astrology is proven by the number of great minds which have been led by it, when properly prepared by education; and the arguments now held conclusive against Astrology get their strength in the minds of the people from no other circumstance than that which formerly was the proof of considerations which were held equally decisive in favor of it. viz., the basis of education.

MYSTICAL INFLUENCE OF THE NO. 7

The Electric and Magnetic vibrations in the atmosphere, the continuous and gradual change from day to night, the ebb and flow of the tides, the seasons of the year and alterations of temperature, times of famine and plenty, epidemic of sickness and crime, the birth and death of the physical of all organized beings, the vibrations of color and sound, the different stages of life and destiny in members of the same family, important changes and discoveries in the progressive sciences,—are all due directly or indirectly to the never ending and varying ethereal vibratory forces, or astral-magnetism, which pervade the universe, operating according to its prevailing destiny and quality upon every atomic part of the earth and all that exists upon it. The fact is, there are seven primary orbs, in this our solar system; viz., the Sun, Moon, Mercury, Venus, Jupiter, Mars, and Saturn.

These assume various scales of interaction, according to the plane of manifestation on which their operations fall, as, for instance, in the seven ages of man; in the seven primary colors of the prism, naturally illustrated by the rainbow; in the seven primary sounds of the musical scale; in the seven characters of wisdom and so on. This number is one of great and mystic influence on human life, and when we stop to consider the ponderous, natural forces at work about us, from which the activity of this number upon mundane effects is derived, it is little to be wondered at The seventh day in acute disease is considered one of the most critical to the fate of the patient, and after birth the seventh hour decides whether the child will live.

In seven days, the cord falls off; in twice seven days the eyes follow a light; in thrice seven days, the child turns the head; seven months give teeth; in twice seven months, the child sits firmly; thrice seven months, it begins to talk; and in four times seven months it begins to walk strongly. After seven years, the child comes to the age of reason, and teeth of second set appear; after twice seven it the arrival of the generative power; in thrice seven, the hair of manhood it completed; In four times seven growth ceases; at thirty-five is the greatest strength; at forty-nine, the greatest discretion, and seventy is the natural length of life.

The peculiar influence of this number has, from the earliest ages, been attributed to the influx of the seven primary orbs of the solar system in their electro-magnetic actions upon the earth and all that breathes upon its surface. The seven days of the week are derived from the same source, and the successful physician selects his remedies according to astral sympathies with the necessities of his patient. The successful surgeon selects such moments for performing operations as are in astral sympathy with the life forces of his patient and the nature of the operation. The successful agriculturist selects times for preparing the soil or sowing the seed, which are in astral sympathy with the conditions. So with the successful navigator; where ever we may turn in the region of science and art, whether of an exact or progressive nature, we find a reference in the origin of required force and action to the great celestial machinery.

THE NEW THEOLOGY-DUALISM

In order that we may make a practical study of the subject of duality, let me sketch an outline for your careful study. In it, please trace the progress of development and see the working of that great mode of Divine action that we call evolution. Observe that through all changes and transformation, the one principle under consideration remains constant.

We will consider the transformation of that faculty or function of the emotional nature that we call "Desire." We will assume that "want" springs from the requirement of the exoteric condition of our dual nature and that "desire" springs from the esoteric or interior conditions.

Referring to any textbook, you will find that the lowest forms of life exhibit rudimentary phases of two primary faculties of consciousness. These are Memory and Desire. Here is a duality that is absolutely necessary to enable the organism to enter into a life of relation with its environment; memory to enable it to discriminate and profit by its experience in making choices necessary for the sustentation of life and desire to give it the motive for the attempt to continue its existence. Desire, being of the emotional nature, its effect is to impel the organism in the effort to continue its existence.

It is from the universal consciousness that the organism has differentiated and, as a unit of consciousness, it has begun its independent line of individual effort on the road upward to the Father of all. In this little unit of the Divine consciousness rests the potency of its hereafter, and the faint recognition of this potentiality by the unit itself, is the fountain head of the materialized emotion that we call desire.

Following this primary manifestation in the most rudimentary forms of organized life, we find that desire assumes a further condition of duality, i.e. First: Nutrition. The quest and absorption of that which will nourish and give life to the organism. Second: The avoidance of that which is destructive to the safety of the organism. Here we see the "pair of opposites" that our Oriental brothers accentuate in their philosophy.

PERSONALITY

Sometimes it may seem very strange that anyone should take time, labor or strength of mental energy, even the smallest fraction, to consider the single word, out of the tens of thousands set in array, over against us, for the exercise and training of our knowledge and understanding. Are not all words vibrant breath? Coming from one source, do they not all return to the place from whence they came? Will they not accomplish to the full that whereunto they were sent? Suppose all these questions are answered affirmatively, may it not be in order to ask: What is it to which they are sent? All results of the projective force must rest somewhere. The word that rouses millions of human beings to war—to the horrible slaughter of each other, is but vibrant breath, yet it leaves the deep-cut lines of sorrow and pain, not only on the souls of the generation that receives the first impact, but on the evolving entities of hundreds of millions yet to come.

Perhaps it has not occurred to our occult and mystic students that the great realm denominated "the astral" is filled with a peculiar substance, out of which souls are made. We talk of universal matter, of universal spirit, universal mind and of the great Oversoul. This last, however, is regarded by the stern students of the higher occultism, as poetically fanciful.

They desire, should be charged to words, only that which is germane to them, thus saving a waste of force in trying to comprehend lines of thought, which do not belong to them. It is a part of the Great Creator's law that all vibration must create or manifest. As there is but the one force, so there is but one vibration. To this we are introduced on five different planes: seeing, hearing, smelling, tasting and feeling. The vibration we contact with is all one. Our conception of it depends upon the organ or set of organs with which we have received our impressions of this marvelously simple method or obtaining vast results.

Every vibration then, no matter how faint, pictures itself somewhere. Where else could we reasonably look for this picture, than on the astral substance? Here it becomes indelible and ineffaceable. It constitutes a soul for each life, for all lives. It also is the sum and substance of that thing which the "Record of the Adepts" names as "the lost soul;" or that accumulation of the pictures of experience during one life, which must be thrown aside, or carried forward to be absorbed into life, the total spiritual consciousness of each life, thus constituting the ego, or assimilation of oneness, of each human being's entity making up the entirety of our individual existence as apart from the whole astral domain. It is as if a set portion of the vast astral realm was allotted, by some bound or mete, to ourselves, for our use and behoof, so long as we shall have occasion for such ownership. It is of the individual we speak, when we say: "As a man, I admire him," or "I detest him."

It seems to be a fact, hardly needing demonstration, that the individual does not of necessity become visible to the contacting conditions of the manifested either things or beings; but holds itself as far away from all the visible as the separating veil of the physical and spiritual will permit. The individual is really the reflection of the ego, from the changing web of its mazy surfaces.

Whatever activity, even of the slightest, we have at any time, during any life, imprinted upon these wonderful mirrors, remains forever impressed upon the airy gauze. The thinness of these retaining films is inconceivable to mortal mind, yet it has a habitation and a name, thus each gains for itself a point in the solidarity of the soul-building; every man's life for itself, being before God, the result of the mortal life, one and many as expressing the unfolding of an ego, which has always been responsible for the souls that it has created under the lash and scourge of un-numbered centuries. As the individuality is the reflection of the ego from the spiritual side of itself, acting through the mentality, the personality is the expression of the same ego, governed by the shaping soul of the present. To illustrate: Our Government buys silver for its Mints, from whomsoever hath it to sell. Under the charge of skilled workmen, it undergoes metallurgy processes of refining and shaping, until as a disc of silver it is presented to powerful dies which stamp the Government symbol of value on each piece.

Up to that moment, the Government, the silver, its prescribed weight and size, all were in existence; yet it was only metal. As soon as the shadow of the Government rested permanently upon it, its functions and nature changed. It henceforth carries something of its own—the intangible, ever-acting decree of potency that is personality. We hold our personality, to and of ourselves, as a mathematical repetend, which we may readily calculate, if we only have the key.

Our peculiarities are the exact counterpart of our soul force, not of the soul itself but of its influence on the astral substance. This theory readily accounts for the wide difference in the appearance of manifested unfolding under apparently similar circumstances, but whose outcome presents not the slightest alignment nor likeness, even. We often meet in stances most marked, because of the constant contact of children of one father and mother, born and trained under the same external circumstances. They are not and never will be the same. The difference is just as marked as if they were born on opposite sides of the globe. Is not this proof that the quality we name personality is a result of an earth-operating force? But where does the balance of the total expression come from? There are only two store houses from which we may gather perception or knowledge of the existent—one visible, the other invisible. In the case of personality, we find ample proof that the puzzling quality is the pressure of the invisible—the misty counterfeit of a reality becoming a trademark of our expression in manifestation.

Man's personality is the reflection on the invisible plane, of the forming soul on the visible plane, and is therefore not amenable to human measurements nor standards.

FREEDOM OF THE MIND

Next to the freedom of the body, if not first in the role of desirable things, comes the freedom of the mind—soul. Freedom of the body is held as a God-given right by practically all organized Churches in Christendom. But how does this affect their creed when applied to freedom of the soul?

Those who have climbed the pinnacle of Church greatness usually in or during the course of their life finally acknowledge the Church an unprogressive superstitious hierarchy, and because of the knowledge learned in the bitter school of experience and from a kindly desire to tell the truth, they find themselves abandoned by the Church for heresy or some other equally bad smelling charge.

The people, uneducated, except from an orthodox point of view, these awakened souls find themselves alone, abandoned and a drift on the great ocean of human progress, and because of their in ability to do little other than the work they have just been ejected from, often early find the world so bitter that self-destruction seems the only avenue of escape.

Those who have the ship of Church in charge can foretell with considerable accuracy the doom of all who bow not the knee in humble submission even at the cost of a wounded conscience, Thus, with the sword in one hand, the cross in the other, the Churches have, for many centuries, been advancing their forces of superstition, proclaiming peace upon earth, yet destroying the very God of peace amongst men.

The little child scarcely away from its mother's bosom is taught the blackening tale of an eternal hell, within its pure little mind is instilled the thought that will produce fear of an unknown nature until its death unless perchance Dame Reason shall assert her power and reclaim it to true light. I often think it is indeed a wonder that man can stop long enough to learn the simplest of education with that fear disturbing his mentality. Happily, all do not believe in the falsehood.

The harm that has been rendered the human family by these incongruous, inconsistent doctrines is past measurement and deplorable. The theologies of our Churches mostly consist in a vain attempt to reconcile the impossible with the known and immutable laws of God. Thus, much of the first history of creation interpreted by them from the Bible would have us believe God created the world; then after His creation, which was good, changed the laws so that a serpent (wisdom) could destroy His own handiwork, or in other words, could, from the start, set aside His immutable laws.

Now I cannot, with thousands of others, see how one can remain entangled in such a mess of incompresensibles, when nature about us speaks in such beautiful tones of the true object of creation on this as well as other spheres, unless this blindness is traceable to an etiology of bread and butter. But it is not the work of the societies working for Universal Brotherhood of man to quarrel with those who are old enough to see the errors of their ways.

The mystic societies working for this universal end know the attempt to show them light is worse than thrown away. On the other hand, it is our duty, in addition to our own right living, to free as many minds as come within our reach seeking light from fear, cowardice and superstition, instead teaching them the great immutable truths so strangely stamped on each product of the Divine Creator, and when qualified give unto them those things that will make them workers in the great vineyard of the Master.

It is our duty, after doing what lies in our power to free the mind, to endeavor to promote healthy thought, progressive research, into the great volumes of nature, the unfoldment of the true meaning of evolution, past as well as present and future. Thus, the proper conception of Nature's laws will lead them to see the true light and the necessity of a universal brotherhood of man.

In thus moving apace, though silently, with our otherwise disinterested organizations, we will eventually prove our true worth and turn the eyes of all to the avenues wherein truth is found pure and unadulterated.

While I have attached my life and work principally to one organization, yet there are others in which I can plainly see the ova rapidly becoming an embryo that will eventually give birth to that end. Thus, from it I can see in the horizon of the misty present a ray of pure light arising as though from the dead, the sun whose mantle of kindness, charity and protection will once more upon this earth give to man that tranquility of mind arising out of freedom from thoughts of error that now seems to cloud this intended vision. Let us, each and every mystic society that has the good of the masses at heart, strive as never before to teach poor humbled man his rightful mission upon this earth.

WHAT IS A MASTER OR ADEPT

In the September "The Word," there is an article on the subject and in which the writer states: "A man becomes an adept, master or Mahatma while his physical body is still alive. One does not become either, nor attain immortality, after death. After attaining adeptship, or becoming a master or mahatma, one may, according to his class and degree, remain away from the world or return to and act with the physical world. Adepts often work in the world, though the world does not know them as adepts. Masters are rarely present in the world; only under most important circumstances do mahatmas move among the world."

At this day, there are many masters of the secret schools working among men and those schools are working harmoniously as never before. The religion of illumination will soon be before the people, and behind this movement there are masters of the highest type. Men who care nothing for money except that which is needed for the propaganda of their grand work.

These men do not allow themselves to be known as masters, they work amongst men as do other men. They follow their trade or profession as do other men, but with all this they work day-and-night for the

New Religion. The author says further: "Everyone has the possibility of knowing adepts, masters and mahatmas: but it is a latent possibility, it is not actual ability. No one will ever be able to know an adept, master or mahatma, or to know the difference and relationships between them until he has at least apprehended these differences and relationships within his own make up.

It is possible for a man to know these differences and to distinguish between the natures and beings within and outside himself, even though he may not as yet have fully developed bodies equal to such things. Of course, this is the theosophical view of the subject but all in all it is a good one. It is impossible to prove a master to one who knows nothing concerning the deeper mysteries. It is just as impossible to prove to the profane that man is immortal. The initiate can teach humanity, but it cannot prove anything for a belief in a thing is not the proof of it.

THE SUN AND THE SOUL

The sun and the soul are both awe-inspiring and mysterious—the sun, nearly a hundred million miles away, yet our constant daily companion, and the soul, an integral part of ourselves, no space separating us from it, and, indeed, closer to us than the shadow to the object. But, notwithstanding this intimate companionship, both continue to be a riddle to the human intellect. The promptings of intuition, however, teach us that there exists a mysteriously intimate relationship between the two.

From time to time, throughout history, great scientists and religious philosophers have tried to build systems of science and religion using the sun as a central figure. For a little while, they managed to hold the attention of the world's people by means of the fundamental truth involved. Prompted from higher sources, these efforts have been repeated, so that we have good reasons not to deny the existence of a connecting link between the sun and the soul. Some Mystery Teachings maintain that this is a fact. They recognize the sun as giver and sustainer of life on this globe, and, not without reason. We can observe, how in due season all vital energy responds to his magic warmth and light, thus supplying material evidence to justify the supposition. We are concerned principally with the relationship existing between the sun and the soul.

The wise educator draws out of a child all of its latent good qualities, in order to overshadow and to subdue the evil tendencies, thus building what we call a character. Just so the sun draws out of all kingdoms, from period to period, from epoch to epoch during evolution, those finer vehicles, which are neither material nor spiritual, but which constitute in man the so-called soul. The most conclusive proof to justify this statement is found in the law of correspondences.

So let us consider the influence and the effects of the sun's rays upon mineral, vegetable, animal, and human life. The greater part of the mineral kingdom is in darkness. Minerals are, more or less, in a chaotic state. Some, more evolved than others, are crystalline and capable of reflecting sunlight. Man declares most precious those minerals that, by reason of composition and structure, are the best reflectors of the sun's rays. Chiefest among them is the diamond. Thus, we see that the influence of the celestial fire-ball upon the lowest kingdom is an established fact. In regard to plant life, science recognizes heliotropism. The general term "tropism" is used to name any uniform and characteristic reaction of an organism to its environment. Heliotropism is that reaction caused by the influence of the sun.

Heliotropic plants bend their stem towards the source of light. Because of this peculiarity, speculative minds have attributed to plants as a rudimentary mind. Others have tried to explain the phenomenon as due to physical or chemical processes. The keenest of our scientists now admit that the leaves of heliotropic plants in particular, and of all plants in general, possess rudimentary organs corresponding to the human eye. The function of such organs is to receive the sunlight in the prolongation of their axis.

These rudimentary eyes endow the plant with a limited sense of light-perception; and, in response to it, the plant leaves turn toward the sun. A certain kind of moss, which grows in rocky clefts, is provided with lenses to focus upon the green leaves, the scanty rays of the sun that reach it in its seclusion. These lenses appear like cat's eyes in the dark. Science admits that the sun has created on the immotile plant a rudimentary eye, through which his light gains a vertical ingress into the vegetable structure.

According to the Mystery Teachings, all plant growth is due to the lines of force radiating vertically from the center of the earth. Thus, both profane science and arcane philosophy tread common ground. The immotile plant grows upright from the earth, from which it takes sustenance in mineral form, transmuting it into its own specialized physical form.

But the scientifically-discovered rudimentary organs for light-perception are the sun's instruments for the development of the specific occult, etheric, or vital, body of the plant, which must draw its particles from the sun. Since we know that minerals do not possess an etheric body, we can readily understand why they have not the corresponding functional organs found in plants. But let us advance another step, and consider the class of plants that have already developed a perfect etheric body; the violet, for example. It grows in the shade, because it does not require the same volume of sunlight as does the thistle. Now, if we further admit that the eye was called forth by the light of the sun—animals living exclusively in the dark womb of the earth have no eyes—is it not a logical conclusion that, in time, the effect of the sunlight upon the eye in turn must produce a special result in the animal make up? This special result is the animal desire-body.

In contradistinction to the immotile plant, we find in animal life the quality of motility. Moreover, we find the higher animals possessing a horizontal spine, perfect eyes, and desires. The animals, which, according to the Mystery Teachings, respond to the lines of force encircling the earth in a horizontal direction, move in all quarters of the globe, in order to develop their desire-bodies by contact with a variety of experiences produced in the constant change of location. It can be readily appreciated that the motility of the animal, combined with the absence of eyes, would result in a general and continued destruction of forms. The animal, then, would have no opportunity for life expression. Without eyes or sense perception, such creatures would inevitably perish through collision with other forms. It is principally the sunlight in connection with the eye that enables the animal to develop the specific, animal desire body. Those animals still low in the order of evolution and whose motility permits, wander about from place to place, because they need all the available sunshine for the development of their finer vehicles. Note especially the birds of passage.

Some may assume that such birds migrate to warmer countries in search of food. It so happens, however strange, that most of them eat insects, thus assimilating animal desire-stuff, which is only a roundabout way of absorbing and building into the desire-body under the sun's influence. Nature always makes use of all available means to gain her ends most rapidly. We may infer from the foregoing statement that the influence of the sun upon the vital and desire-bodies is of the greatest importance in the development of individuality.

It is not by accident that the greater part of the less developed humanity lives in those divisions of the globe where they have plenty of effective sunshine. Here, their passional nature is aroused and the evolutionary process, as it were, is accelerated. In man, the solar ray is transformed into nervous fluid, which is stored up in the nerve centers. These centers supply the bodily needs in any emergency and at times when the solar source cannot be tapped. In the upright man, the positive solar force and the negative earth force establish a current, which bears a close relation to our consciousness.

If our supply of solar fluid is exhausted, and we change our position from a vertical to a horizontal one, such as when retiring for the night, consciousness changes rapidly and we fall into the state called sleep. So much for the outward manifestation of the sun. The further development of individuality would cease, were it not that, in turn an inward sun, the Ego, asserts its influence. Man possesses the uprightness of the plant in his physical form and the downrightness of the animal in his desires. He is thus nailed to the cross—the vertical beam representing all that is pure and uplifting in him, the horizontal beam symbolizing his animal nature. It is in consideration of this fact that the world's literature is burdened with epigrams such as the following: "Is not this a mad world, are not these madmen who leave so frequent battles as perpetual memorials of their madness to all succeeding ages?" "Few see their disease, all love it;" "Men will only cease to be fools, when they will cease to be;" "No great genius without a touch of madness."

Indeed, if we search history, we find much to praise, but more to blame. It is as if the wine of error had been administered by drunken teachers. The desires holding sway in the primitive races, the young unfolding concrete mind ran parallel with a sense of gratification. In time, the Ego had perfected the organ for light-perception from the spiritual sun within the abstract mind. Since man has learned to use his abstract mind, his tendency is toward the development of an upright spiritual nature.

So, in turn, the rays of the physical sun, focused in our physical eye, have kindled our inner spiritual light. The aspect of the stars has helped to make people religious. Form and color became the foundation of art. The eye, when it first learned to aim at an object, became the objective point for our technical achievements. Heavenward, sunward, has been the course of evolution. History tells us of the Stone Age and of cave dwellers, human beings living in the mineral womb of the earth, of people, whose gods were of stone. The volume of solar light received by them was in full accord with the extent of spiritual enlightenment they possessed.

Later on, history speaks of nomadic tribes that were as heliotropic as our plants are today. They learned of one God and believed in Him. But men in time returned to their eaves, they built houses and learned to use artificial light. During this period, their philosophies resembled their dwelling places: they were materialistic; their religions resembled the artificial lights; superstition reigned supreme. However, the cry for pure sunshine came again, and with it, pure spirituality in religion. Indeed, it is worthy of notice that more sunlight always kindled higher spirituality in man. At the present day, a marked change for the better is apparent.

"Back to the sun, the source of life and light!" we hear the materially-minded calling us. "Back to the Son, Jesus the Christ!" is the voice from the spiritual teachers. Beware of philosophies that do not recognize Him. Philosophers prefer to think; and thinking about life may be of great importance. But the greatest thoughts have been generated by those who lived the purest, the strongest, the fullest lives. Such as they have seen joy and sorrow, face to face; have endured the conflict of man's dual nature; have struggled and conquered.

They alone have the fullest knowledge; born of experience, and having paid the price, they enjoy the greatest freedom. Their interpretation of life must remain the standard of authority. Cold scientific thinking cannot replace the inspirational wisdom and revelation of a saint. As the sun has been and is today the great cosmic educator through his outward influence, so the Sun of Righteousness, Jesus the Christ, was and is the great spiritual educator of humanity. The imitation of Christ must become the Cosmic Goal.

LIFE AND DEATH

LIFE and death, death and life again! So live that you may be able to smile at death. "Flowers bloom and fade, the fruit begins to swell. So, when our bodies die, our Souls in glory dwell." But if our souls are to dwell in glory, we must first live a good life. That is the secret. Death laughs at life, but what is death, and why is it necessary to understand anything about it? We apply the terms life and death to things of change.

Man is not life, man is not death. But he experiences those changes described as life and death. In the new education, the philosophy of death will take, as it has taken in the long past, a great place. Man ought to learn the glorious art of dying. There is a wonderful passage in the Gita: "Who are you, man?" In the first two lines, the Lord describes man as soul. "You are not born, and so you cannot die." Then who are you positively? You are undying, eternal and ever-present.

Then what is it that frightens you? What is this fear of death? It is only the encasements, envelopes, bodies that you use from time to time for experience that come and go. There are three great systems of the Philosophy of Death: the Indian, the Tibetan and the Egyptian.

All are great and ancient, but the oldest and most completely organized is the Indian. It lays down rules for guidance from childhood up to the stage of death of the physical body, and down into life again after death. The Tibetan is based upon the same fundamentals—man as Soul, life as preparation just before the change known as death. It gives man all the necessary help to receive the change cheerfully, and also gives him a glimpse of life after death.

The Egyptian admits man as Soul, but develops the process of preservation of the house more than it does the training for the life of the Soul. The Soul in Egypt is symbolized as a bird,—a splendid symbol—soaring high, though shut up in a cage, captive. So the soul flies, soars, and tries to reach its own place. The pyramids are glorious specimens of the art of preservation of the "house" for the return of the bird, or the soul, who must find the house intact. In the Tibetan teachings, the Gurus, or teachers, give a person an intimation of the time of death, and ask him to prepare himself. Generally the process occupies a few months.

Returning to the Indian method, to understand death, and to realize the value of death as a necessary change in evolution, you must first know the value of life. There is one line in the Gita which summarizes the philosophy of life and death. "The thought that is predominant at the moment of change called death determines for man his future in the next incarnation." And therefore, the Lord says, "It is the hardest thing to remember then how to surrender yourself to His Will at the moment of death." It is so hard that you cannot do it unless your life is a school of training. It is not possible for man to concentrate his mind on God unless he has trained himself to live as a Soul. He must prepare himself gradually for the change, and consider it as a gateway into the Higher Life. To die is the glorious privilege of man.

Spirit and matter begin the work of creation, of growth, of evolution, and of consummation, only when united. The process begins when they are put together by Higher Will. It is necessary for Spirit to become separated from matter from time to time, for it to obtain a better vehicle for higher experience. If you were incased in one body for all time, you could never grow. You need the change, a better fitted instrument. Therefore, death is a useful change only for those who understand how to live. There is often the ever-turning wheel of life and death, without progress, because the simple change of body, known as death, has brought no improvement. We must use death as a gateway to a larger life, and return from it broadened by the experience. Otherwise, death fails in its purpose. We want to go from stage to stage in ever-growing consciousness of life, and so live and so die that each time the life after death is a better and higher life. Each time you put on a body and begin to live in the house of earth, utilize opportunities.

Understand that you are the indweller, and that the house is there for your experience. The Laws of Karma, Justice, Love, Fraternity, Cooperation, Harmony, Service, all make one Law of Love and Life. In fact, man can only be helped by the Law of Love and Cooperation with the higher laws of life. Through love, you make yourself a channel, a self-conscious instrument, a living person, not a mere psychological asset, a token of life. In order to understand the Philosophy of Death we must understand the life after death.

We are living all the time in many worlds. Each individual lives in a world of his own, that is, the world of personality. But he is simultaneously contacting, using, and living in a number of worlds, each world fitted to be a field of activity and experience for each of the bodies being used as instruments. The two worlds most vitally important for experience are those two immediate worlds, the physical and the super-physical. Both are worlds of matter and motion.

The same laws hold good, the same thoughts and feeling, and the same character. You even bear the same names. There is no difference in consciousness in the individual or in the habits of the individual. The sciences, especially the science of Yoga in the highest sense, are intended to help men find methods, quick processes leading to heights of Illumination and Perfection, by better cooperation with the laws. There is no royal road to perfection. There is only one method, and it is a slow up-hill process. But for strong minds, willing hearts, for those who understand the laws, there is always a path open. They must use their own effort, but they are helped by the great Guides.

Today the minds of the children and the young are filled with fear of death. Tragic! This fear must go. For fear is the greatest danger and the worst enemy of man. The goal is fearlessness, deathlessness. And unless we root out this fear by living a life of perfect harmony, unless we live a life of positive love and conscious cooperation, the psychological complex will always be dangerous. Fear of death, fear of opposition, fear of obstacles, fear of failure, these are not realities but shadows. Death is a great shadow on many thresholds, and the problem of it must be faced cheerfully. The better we do it, the more able we shall be to live a higher life. Build a better future by living a good life now, and then a nobler picture for the life to come is formed.

THE SOUL'S ETERNALITY

All philosophical research may be conducted from two different standpoints, viz., the empirical and the transcendental. By the former method, things are considered as they appear to us, as the senses present them to our minds; by the latter method, they are considered as they really are, not depending on, but transcending the senses. From the empirical standpoint, we behold the physical aspect of things which is the wrong side of which the spiritual aspect is the right side. The wrong and the right side, however, rest on truth. To investigate one side and ignore the other is misleading, leads to conclusions that are incomplete and to knowledge that waits to be achieved. Hegel, in his masterly grasp of higher principles, truly says:

"Every thought involves its contradictory; but the contradictory is not a mere negation, it is in itself positive; the conception of unity is not more positive than its contradictory, the conception of plurality. Every thought, therefore, as it involves its contradictory, adds to its own contents, and by the combination of the two contradictories, we rise to absolute knowledge." That "rising to absolute knowledge" is the aim which all philosophical researches seek to attain, more so even than the scientifical researches, for science is concerned with facts, whilst philosophy is concerned with principles back of the facts, with the subtle realities of which the facts are but the grosser manifestation. It is scientifically demonstrated that the knowledge received by the eye is not the result of radiation in the object perceived, soft arms of the atmosphere." . . . . "the soul circumscribeth all things" . . . . "the soul knows only the soul."

Why does "the soul know only the soul"? Because there is nothing else to be known, because it is the Absolute Reality, the last term back of which nothing is. The word Immortality applied to the soul, is a self-contradiction, for immortality implies mortality, which in its turn implies birth, a quality which cannot be predicated of the soul, for in looking for the soul, we are looking for the last Essence, for that which projects a shadow, but is never itself projected; for that which supports all manifestations, but is not supported by anything; for that which radiates upon, and illumines objects, but is not illumined by any, nor radiated upon. We are looking for that upon which the whole universe reposes, but which reposes on nothing, the primeval cause of all things which never can be an effect, the Absolute Reality of which the world is but the mask. How, then, can the word "immortality" be attributed to that which exists neither in time nor space, that which is infinite, pure, simple, omnipresent, omniscient, omnipotent, the One without a Second (Ekadvitya)?

The Soul is not "immortal," it is eternal, infinite, limitless. Stripped of these attributes, what remains is something which exists in time and space, which is finite, which is a creation, a form, hence perishable. But let us grant for a moment that the soul, as commonly understood, is a form, a set of limitations. Obviously, the form in itself has no existence, for when we look at a gold ring, we cannot think of the ring as distinct from the gold and the only real thing in it is the gold, for, in an instant we may destroy the form but the gold, the substance never can be destroyed, it may be resolved to its native state, but destroyed never—matter is indestructible. Similarly with the hypothetical formal soul, its form may and must, be destroyed—it is the inexorable fate of all forms,—but there remains the essence, the substratum which defies all attempt at destruction and which stands pure, self-existent, self-luminous when the form that obscured it has passed away. If we may call the formal entity soul, then the essence, the formless and infinite of which the formal entity was but a mask, what shall we call it? Emerson calls it the "Over Soul" to shield himself, I suppose, from the aggressiveness of Orthodox Churchianity. There is but one infinite soul, it has no "over" nor "under" connected with it, it fills all space and beyond space, it is the Boundless, the Unconditioned, the Absolute, the Eternal. "That by which everything is known, that which is not known by anything, realize that knower to be the Atma." (Shankara.)

A test of the imperishableness of the soul is that a man cannot think of himself as dead. Aspirations are incessantly flowing out of the breast of man, aspirations for rising up and reaching out towards the beautiful, the perfect. Many and diverse may be the roads he takes, but his face is ever turned towards the light.

"Different rivers taking their starts from different mountains, running straight or crooked, at last come into the ocean, so Shiva, all are coming into Thee!"

Intuitively, man knows that he is free and no attempt to circumscribe his freedom, however trifling it may be, remains without his emphatic protest. His true nature is freedom. Can there exist two free beings in the universe or out of it? Like the Sphinx man may say:

"I am the sum total of ancient wisdom, I am the synthesis of man. I have a brow which thinks and breasts which heave with love; I have the lion's claws for the fight, the bull's hips for labor and the eagle's wings for ascending towards the light."

These are all attributes of the soul reflecting in man, vehicles, as it were, by which he may rise to self-realization and see the soul back of the form, the Infinite back of the finite, the Eternal back of the perishable.

"The sun does not shine there, nor the moon or the stars, nor these lightening's and much less this fire. When it shines, everything shines after it; by its light, all this is lighted!"—Katha Up. ii. 5-15.

The indomitable courage that braces a man for action; the hope that flows ever new from his breast; the love that streams out of his heart; the reverence that subdues his native pride; the devotion that makes him forget all, even his own life, to rush into danger and save others; the genius that glows in his works, all these rest on a principle that is eternal, not on one that is transient. Only the Eternal, the Infinite can reflect in man's beauties which transcend the world of senses and of facts, only the Omnipotent radiancy can throw a tinge of supreme glory on the play of the elements in nature. Says Walt Whitman:

"What do you think is the grandeur of Storms and dismemberments and the deadliest battles and wrecks and the wildest fury of the elements and the power of the sea and the motion of nature and the throes of human desires and dignity and hate and love? "It is that something in the Soul which says:

"Rage on, whirl on, I tread master here and everywhere. Master of the spasms of the sky and of the shatter of the sea, Master of Nature and passion and death, and of all terrors and all pains!"

In the last talk there are several propositions worthy of your careful attention and study, among them I have selected the following as the subject for present consideration, viz., "That it is a reasonable proposition to attempt the formulation of a philosophical statement of spiritual law, having for its primary postulates a correct statement of the facts pertaining to the laws of matter and materialization."

In other words: Materialism, correctly stated, must be accepted as the basis on which to build a correct statement of spiritualism. Geology, chemistry, biology, and all the allied sciences must be accepted and their ascertained facts must be used as units in the construction of a correct system of theology. A knowledge of the laws of matter and of our material environment must be acquired as the rudimentary, basic knowledge that shall lead us to a correct knowledge of God. To quote the words of the writer published in 1886: "The laws of the great hereafter must find their antecedents in the laws of manifest nature: matter and life force; matter and intellect. Matter and morals are so closely interwoven and associated in nature that there can be no system of laws for one that will not apply to the other."

My comrades, there is one God, and there is and can be but one systematic statement of truth about God, for it must partake of the unity as well as the fullness of his nature. The Master tells us that God is the Alpha and the Omega, the beginning and the end. The likeness is unto the alphabet wherein God is the first and last expression and between the two, embraced within them, stands the symbols that pertain to God knowledge. Between the beginning and the end, there is manifestation and manifestation is in God, and we are in manifestation. The invitation is to acquire knowledge of God's alphabet, so that he who runs the race may have a "reason for the hope that is within him."

How correctly we can formulate this statement is altogether another thing. We are finite and the subject of our statement is infinite, and words are limitations of limited ideas, still we may indicate the line along which such study should be made, and it is our duty as well as our privilege to make the attempt, and honestly and earnestly strive to comprehend that grand science that embraces all other knowledge to the utmost extent of our finite ability. There is one temple of truth, but there are many worshippers in the temple, each one using formulas of expression adapted to his individual state of conscious perception. Reflect on this and see for yourself the absolute necessity for the broadest charity that each one should have for the opinion of others. Also recognize the rank folly of disputation over subjects that lay hold on infinity. The Master tells it all in one sentence: "let your light shine," i.e., let your knowledge, let your goodness, let your spirituality and your God-likeness be apparent without words, carry it in your aura.

The temple of truth must be built upon a rock and that rock will be found to be a perfect and complete understanding of the facts of material science. Paul, the initiate, says: "The invisible things of God, from the creation of the world are clearly seen, being understood by the things that are made." This you recognize as a re-statement of the ancient mystic axiom: "As in the microcosm, so in the macrocosm."

God's word in nature and God's revelation must harmonize. Nature is in God and nature is God's vehicle of manifestation and revelation. We are the ones in error because we do not fully understand the one or the other. Herein lies the beauty and necessity of humility; the reverential cognizance of the greatness of the object of our study is, indeed, the beginning of wisdom. The question will naturally present itself: Why has not such a statement been attempted before this seemingly late day? There are two forms or methods of reasoning whereby intellectual conclusions are reached. One is called the deductive and the other is called inductive method.

The deductive method has been with us from earliest history and is the system known to the vast majority of the civilized world today, while the inductive method is of later development, dating from the time of Lord Bacon and not coming into extensive use until within the last few decades. The difference between these two methods, mark the divergence between ancient and modern science. Since the adoption of the inductive method the march of science, and the progress and diffusion of knowledge has been simply wonderful and in a very large measure this has been brought about by the inductive method of reasoning and the adoption of the scientific method of investigation.

The day of argument and disputation has passed. Partisanship has ceased. Facts are the only things admitted as evidence and one adverse fact clearly proven will destroy any theory no matter how high the standing or how learned its proposer. Briefly, the scientific method is this: An investigator in some specific line of scientific inquiry, after long study and examination, arrives at conclusions that seem to him to be reasonable; he makes a statement of his views, which he calls an "hypothesis," and he formulates his reasons in its favor, which he supports with a as units in the construction of a correct system of theology.

A knowledge of the laws of matter and of our material environment must be acquired as the rudimentary, basic knowledge that shall lead us to a correct knowledge of God. To quote the words of the writer published in 1886: "The laws of the great hereafter must find their antecedents in the laws of manifest nature: matter and life force; matter and intellect. Matter and morals are so closely interwoven and associated in nature that there can be no system of laws for one that will not apply to the other." My comrades, there is one God, and there is and can be but one systematic statement of truth about God, for it must partake of the unity as well as the fullness of his nature. The Master tells us that God is the Alpha and the Omega, the beginning and the end. The likeness is unto the alphabet wherein God is the first and last expression and between the two, embraced within them, stands the symbols that pertain to God knowledge.

Between the beginning and the end, there is manifestation and manifestation is in God, and we are in manifestation. The invitation is to acquire knowledge of God's alphabet, so that he who runs the race may have a "reason for the hope that is within him." How correctly we can formulate this statement is altogether another thing. We are finite and the subject of our statement is infinite and words are limitations of limited ideas, still we may indicate the line along which such study should be made, and it is our duty as well as our privilege to make the attempt, and honestly and earnestly strive to comprehend that grand science that embraces all other knowledge to the utmost extent of our finite ability.

There is one temple of truth, but there are many worshippers in the temple, each one using formulas of expression adapted to his individual state of conscious perception. Reflect on this and see for yourself the absolute necessity for the broadest charity that each one should have for the opinion of others. Also recognize the rank folly of disputation over subjects that lay hold on infinity. The Master tells it all in one sentence: "let your light shine," i.e., let your knowledge, let your goodness, let your spirituality and your God-likeness be apparent without words, carry it in your aura.

The temple of truth must be built upon a rock and that statement of all the facts pertaining to the subject within the scope of his knowledge. This is presented to the world for criticism and consideration, and after full examination and debate, after all known facts have been presented, if the hypothesis still stands, if it is found to be supported by all the facts bearing upon it; if it satisfactorily correlates with all and antagonizes none, it is finally adopted as a true proposition of science and takes its place as a portion of the accumulated knowledge of the world. In this manner, the atomic theory; the doctrine on the conservation and correlation of force; the dogma of the indestructibility of matter, mind and energy; the doctrine of evolution; the un-dilatory theory of light and the presence and properties of the luminiferous ether, have each and every one been thrown into the arena of scientific criticism, have all survived the ordeal and are all accepted as truths of science today.

Science has found that truth has inherent life, so it is put into condition and made to fight for its own life, and if the supposed truth does not survive the ordeal, science does not accept it for her own. As you see, the inductive method collects facts and from them it builds its conclusions.

It is a system that has foundations. It is synthetic and it is safe. Gradually, all branches of learning are embracing and, as far as practicable, are adopting this method of thought.

Material science is now being reseated on this basis, and the study of that form of knowledge that pertains to the nonmaterial is coming into line, and for the first time in history, psychology has a substratum of proven facts on which to base its conclusions. In a rough way, it may be said that the deductive method begins at the top and works downward, and that the inductive method begins at the bottom and builds upward. This may be said, however, that both methods possess points of advantage, and both methods may be true and correct; the proof of this will lay in the fact that if both are correct, they will meet at the middle distance and form a solid column of truth, thus proving both methods to be what they should be; solid pillars in God's Temple of Truth. Student members of this Brotherhood use both methods, and consequently the opinions of different members are to be construed as from different view-points of a common truth.

I am aware that the hypothesis that I am now presenting will occasion criticism, and I sincerely trust that it will. The earnest desire of the writer is to contribute to the presentation of theological truth and to this end honest criticism is a thing to be courted in order that any incorrect or misleading statements may be corrected. Of all the departments of classified knowledge that we dignify by the name of "science" there are none that approach the science of theology in grandeur and importance, for it is a reasonable explanation of the relation that "religion" institutes between the individual human soul and the great source of all wisdom and all love.

II

For anyone to be right, he must be in harmony with the divine mode of action on his plane of consciousness.

1. The student should be very careful to search out the meaning of words as used in the discussion of any line of thought, and especially does this apply to studies connected with the exposition of science and philosophy, as distinctions are closely drawn and words are carefully selected to be used in their exact sense, so that they may clearly express definite ideas. The word "axiom" means, "a self-evident and necessary truth," ... "a proposition which, of necessity, must be taken for granted."

2. All systems of philosophy are predicted on certain fundamental statements of fact or supposed fact. In the construction of the system, these statements may be likened to the foundations on which a superstructure is to be erected. The student should, therefore, thoroughly and exhaustively analyze these primary statements. He should subject them to all tests within his power and should apply to them all known methods of research in order to ascertain their reliability and correctness; for it is evident that any error in the basic condition will impair the system in direct proportion to its deviation from an absolute standard of correctness. The question then at once presents itself. Is this statement axiomatic? Is it a self-evident truth? Does your mental and emotional consciousness harmoniously recognize and consent to this statement? Is it true to you now, without debate?

Your careful analysis of this question is vital to your progress in correct thinking, for there is probably nothing in all this conscious universe as important to a spiritually self-conscious entity as a correct statement of spiritual truth, for that which is true for today is of necessity true for all time and is therefore an unfailing guide to future progress. The Master says, that "a house built on solid foundations shall stand." Look well, therefore, to this statement. Ask yourself the question: Is it true to you, today, that one individual that is in harmony with the divine mode of action is, and must be, in a state of rightness?

3. Rightness must be considered in its dual aspect; that is, rightness as it "subsists" in its omniscient, infinite and divine aspect, and rightness as it "exists" in finite manifestation. It is evident that absolute rightness must be complete and entire. There can, of necessity, be no failure—no weak condition—no flaw or blemish in its operation; otherwise, there would be incompleteness and want of wisdom in the character of the All-Wise, which is unthinkable. It follows that as rightness is an attribute of the divine character, and therefore a factor in the divine mode of action, a principle and a part of the actuating power behind the action itself; the action must, of itself, be absolutely right and all correlative finite action in harmony therewith, must be relatively right. Furthermore, there cannot be two standards of rightness; one for God himself, and one for God's created and objective universe, and therefore rightness as we understand it must be in relative harmony with rightness as God understands it.

The difference being in degree and not in kind. Infinite rightness "subsists" as a factor of Omniscience; it is an eternal principle, an attribute of the divine character. In manifestation, rightness "exists" in the nature of all things manifested. All modes of divine action bear fruit in rightness; otherwise, this wonderful universe would be a chaos of mismanagement.

4. The divine mode of action being absolutely right, may we not be able to comprehend what rightness is, provided we can correctly comprehend and interpret this mode of action? And that being granted, may we not be able to come into harmony with these modes of action and thus appropriately place ourselves in a condition of rightness? And, furthermore, does it not seem to be the rational and proper way to acquire a knowledge of God's rightness by undertaking an earnest and diligent investigation of his modes of action as manifested in our environment?

5. The acquisition and tabulation of the facts connected with the study of the phenomena of the divine mode of action as realized in the manifest universe is called "science," and the acquisition and tabulation of discoveries of the spiritual ethics contained as principles in the same modes of action and the application of these principles to the spiritual evolution of the individual is called "religion," and the systematic tabulation of these spiritual principles into an orderly and rational statement is called "theology" or God-knowledge. Science, in the generally accepted understanding of the term, is "exoteric," and pertains to the knowledge and understanding of the phenomena of manifestation; while religion is

"esoteric" and pertains to that knowledge and understanding that leads to an interior and spiritual unfoldment.

Both are phases of the unfoldment of man's knowledge of rightness. EXOTERIC, FOR THE SATISFACTION OF THE UNDERSTANDING AND AS A FOUNDATION FOR A KNOWLEDGE OF INTERIOR AND HIDDEN PRINCIPLES; AND ESOTERIC FOR THE HARMONIZING OF THE INDIVIDUAL SOUL WITH THE DIVINE. In a universe of rightness, wherein harmony subsists, there can be no conflict between these two. The procession of truth is from one source and from one only. Religion and science are handmaidens and children of the one. This is no assumption. This is an inherent fact, "in the nature of things."

6. In the consideration of this topic as applied to the individual, there are two things that must be carefully borne in mind, i.e., the mental as distinguished from the emotional condition of the individual. The nature dominated by reason as distinguished from the nature dominated by feeling. Science makes its demands more particularly upon the mental consciousness. Religion appeals to both, but more particularly to the emotional. The harmony between religion and science depends upon a correct comprehension of the divine mode of action, both by the mental and the emotional consciousness; both by the head and the heart, and therefore the individual must come into a condition of harmony with his own dual nature before he can fully and correctly come into full harmony with the dual expression of the one reality.

7. There is an axiom handed down to us by the ancient mystics which reads as follows: "There is one law and He that worketh is One." This is a universe of reason, of sanity, and of harmony; a moment's pause and reflection will force the conclusion that this statement is, and must be true. The law of gravitation that Newton discovered by observing the fall of an apple pertains throughout all space. Huxley says, that "any law, or mode of action that is true today is true for all time."

The skilled astronomer can place his instrument today, and at a given time in the future he will tell you the hour, moment and second that a named star will cross its center line. There is one law!

The divine mode of action as it pertains to physical growth, does not contradict the divine mode of action as it pertains to spiritual growth. The narrative of physical growth is the allegory that contains the unfolding of the story of spiritual growth. Material science is the "container" or matrix, out of which we get the understanding that enables us to state the science of theology. The "temple not made with hands, eternal in the heavens," has for its foundation stones the hard and immutable facts of materiality.

The law that pertains to the physical plane is the same law, unfolded, developed and spiritualized, that pertains to the mental, moral and spiritual planes, or states of consciousness, and the mode, method and process of growth from the lower to the higher is correspondingly the same. If the interpretation of the law of physical growth is correctly stated by what we call the "law of evolution," then in order to correctly understand the law of spiritual growth we must observe the same law unfolded, developed and spiritualized as it works upon the higher plane; for law on one plane of consciousness does not conflict with law on any other plane of consciousness. No religion or theology can be correctly formulated that does not fully harmonize with the facts that interpret the divine modes of action on all planes of existence.

8. If it is true that rightness consists in being in a condition of harmony with the divine modes of action, it necessarily follows: That anything that is not in such a condition of harmony is not in a condition of rightness; and it also follows that this condition of un-rightness is proportional to its degree of divergence from the divine mode of action. If the first condition is one of truth, the second condition is one of error and it is self-evident that this condition of error can be eliminated or corrected by any action that will restore the harmony.

To illustrate: You can strike wrong notes upon a musical instrument and a discord will be the result, but you can correct that discord by striking the right notes and thus effect a restoration of harmony. Your mentality informs you which notes are incorrect and your emotions cooperating with your will impel you to make the correction. Thus, by your own act and choice, you place yourself in a condition of harmony.

9. Two sets of factors may be considered in this connection: Rightness as distinguished from wrongness.

HARMONY AS DISTINGUISHED FROM DISCORD. TRUTH AS DISTINGUISHED FROM ERROR.

CONCERNING THE TRINITY

In order that we may make a practical study of the subject of duality, let me sketch an outline for your careful consideration. In it, please trace the progress of development and see the working of that great mode of the Divine action that we call evolution. Observe that through all changes and transformation that one principle under consideration remains constant.

We will consider the transformation of that faculty or function of the emotional nature that we call "Desire." We will assume that "want springs from the requirements of the exoteric condition of our dual nature and that "desire" springs from the esoteric or interior condition. Referring to any textbook, you will find that the lowest forms of life exhibit rudimentary phases of two primary faculties of consciousness. These are memory and desire.

Here is a primary duality that is absolutely necessary to enable the organism to enter into a life of relation with its environment; memory to enable it to discriminate and profit by its experience in making choices necessary for the sustentation of life, and desire to give it the motive for the attempt to continue its existence. Desire, being of the emotional nature, its effects is to impel the organism in the effort to continue existence. It is from the universal consciousness that the organism has differentiated and, as a unit of consciousness, it has begun its independent line of individual effort on the road upward to the Father of all. In this little unit of the divine consciousness rests the potency of its hereafter, and the faint recognition of this potentiality by the unit itself, is the fountain head of the materialized emotion that we call desire.

Following this primary manifestation in the most rudimentary forms of organized life, we find that desire assumes a further condition of duality, i.e., 1. Nutrition. The quest and absorption of that which will nourish and give life to the organism. 2. Avoidance of that which is destructive to the safety of the organism. Here we see the "pair of opposites" that our oriental brothers accentuate in their philosophy. After a time of trial and experience, the organism makes a forward step in its evolution. The search for that which will nourish, develop a higher phase, i.e., 1. Search for pleasure. 2. Avoidance of pain. The organism finds a degree of satisfaction and comfort under certain conditions and in searching for such conditions, it learns to discriminate and avoid that which gives pain and discomfort. You see at once that the rudimentary mental (memory) and the rudimentary emotional (desire) travel side by side, and the progress of one makes conditions fit for the progress of the other, and you also see that it is the parallel progress of this duality that is a measure of the fitness of the organism in its evolutionary unfoldment.

The last pair referred to (search for pleasure and the avoidance of pain) by more or less experience and adaptation, makes the organism ready for another dual phase of its development 1. The search for knowledge. 2. The avoidance of mistakes. You recognize at once that the search for pleasure coupled with and backed by the emotion of desire puts the organism into a condition where it wants to know how pleasure and sensation can be most readily found, and pari passu how pain can be avoided. Memory being a factor in this growth, the desire for knowledge is fostered and its growth, and the growth of the necessary nerve tissue is developed. Out of this and in a higher line of progress comes the development of the organism into a condition where it can propound to itself the next higher question: 1. The search for the real. 2. The avoidance of illusion. That which is for the permanent good as opposed to that which is seemingly for the temporary good. The discernment of the future good of the organism as opposed to its present advantage. Here, you perceive, is where a great growth and development and specialization of its vehicle—the physical body—to enable it to comprehend, apprehend and assimilate the idea involved. It is the passage from the realm of illusion and appearance to the domain of that which is real and everlasting.

After the organism and its contained entity has reached the "human" stage, there is no more specialization in the way of developing more physical functions, but there is a perfecting of the higher and finer functions and a refinement of the organization—for here the start is made—in the involution or involuted evolution of the individualization of the spiritual consciousness of the entity. Spiritual knowledge becomes spiritual understanding and spiritual power becomes a leading factor in the spiritual growth of the divine man that is in the process of development. Old things are transformed into new. The spiritual alchemy has transformed the base metal into pure gold, and desire that ministered to the Avant's of the physical body has transformed itself into desire that ministers to the needs of the soul that has itself been transformed into eternal individualization. Physical want and physical hunger have been "lifted up" and the "blurred, undefined unit of consciousness" has been evolved into a spiritual entity that cries unto God as the child cries for the father. Let no one speak slightingly of evolution, for it is God's way unto righteousness. It is what the Master meant when He declared that "God is able out of these stories to raise up children unto Abraham."

There is One Law and He that worketh is One.

The orthodox theological definition concerning this subject has occasioned war and bloodshed among nations; persecutions, imprisonment, divisions of churches and State; estrangements, ostracism and gross un-charity among brothers of the Christian faith.

Why? Simply because the early fathers of the Church insisted upon making a close definition of something that, in the nature of the case, could not be closely defined All definitions are limitations, and they took upon themselves the responsibility of putting a material limitation upon that which was not material. They insisted upon reducing a question relating to infinity to definite proportions. We cannot justly blame them for their mistake.

Their zeal was to do God service and their desire was in the right direction. The demand was upon them and they had to answer to the best of their ability; their intent was for good and for the glory of God.

True, it is that there were many victims of their mistake. There were thousands and thousands that went down to judgment and to death; yet the mistake of the Church was no mistake for the victims, for the very courage that they showed in facing persecution and death has its reflex action in the strengthening of their spiritual stature. Again: If the question of the trinity had been stated in that early day in the terms in which it can be stated today it would have resulted in disaster to the Christian religion for it must be remembered that religion is of the attitude of the individual soul to the Supreme—and is largely influenced by the emotional nature of man—while theological philosophy is the reasonable explanation of that attitude and is largely of and, from the mental nature Mankind was not then in a condition to receive a more correct statement; knowledge was not sufficiently diffused.

They had to have an explanation suited to their own mental development. Knowledge always precedes understanding, and knowledge of all the factors pertaining to any given subject must be assembled before definite understanding can be arrived at Democritus, the philosopher, who lived six hundred years before the Christian era, announced the principles of the doctrine of evolution, but the world was not ready to receive it and not until the time of Wallace and Darwin, seconded by Tyndall, Spencer, Huxley and others as its exponents was it possible of fair consideration.

The new statement of theology is to contain all that Jesus taught. He attempted no philosophy he taught in parables so the common people could catch the esoteric meanings, and simple as was His teaching, it has taken the world two thousand years to begin to understand them. During this time the factors of knowledge necessary to the better understanding of divine truth have been discovered, and the duty now before the Church—the Ecclesia—is to formulate a careful restatement of its philosophy so that the esoteric truth that it has been teaching for two thousand years can be better understood.

The sacred books of all nations and all religions have aided and sustained mankind for ages, and still will continue to aid and assist, but the time has come, and man has sufficiently advanced in knowledge so that he can now begin to read the greater Bible—God's truth, written large in creation. Let no one blame the Church! Let no one cast aside the essential esoteric truth contained in her teachings, for of these truths she has been the faithful custodian; but rather let there be an honest, earnest and united endeavor to understand and to make clear the meaning of these truths so that in the light of the new knowledge, God may be glorified.

IS THE SOUL PROPHETIC?

Those internal promptings, those secret warnings, those mysterious and otherwise unaccountable impulses, are not explicable on any other principle than that the soul is prophetic. To attribute this wonderful power merely to the mind is not enough, for it would be investing a material substance with an immaterial quality. We must look for it then, in the soul—that imperishable, impalpable, indescribable something, which eludes, after death, the investigations of the living, and baffles their most searching scrutiny when still in its earthly tenement. It is, besides, difficult to conceive that the mere brain—which may be said to constitute the mind is so formed as to receive the delicate impressions which must arise from this species of external influence.

All communications with the brain must be originally transmitted by the nerves and consequently can only be susceptible to palpable and immediate impressions from within. For instance, no one, by merely thinking, can at once attain the full knowledge of algebra, or become instantaneously conversant with the most simple of sciences. There is no language which can be gained by intuition alone; all learning must be progressive. It follows, then, that in the mind, at least, there can be no predictive power. The duality of the brain, or double constitution of the intellectual faculties, is now generally admitted. But, as with two eyes, and two ears, we only see one object, and hear one sound, so, though possessed of two separate, perfect thinking machines, we are conscious only of having one mind. Should the two compartments, by accident or disease, not work simultaneously, an erroneous perception of images will arise, the false deductions of the one not being corrected by the accurate impression of the other; and this is what we understand by insanity. The brain, then, or the mind—for in this light we hold them to be convertible terms—is too dependent on the restrictions of mere matter to be conscious of anticipate events. But how different is it with the soul, that heavenly essence, which animates alike with its wondrous spiritual influence on the child and the philosopher?

Independent of all the arguments so well-known and so universally recognized, on the existence in our forms of an immortal part, which neither Time nor Death—the two great Juggernauts of the universe—can injure, or destroy, we have here a still stronger proof of the "divinity that stirs within us." All presentiments, all sudden and irresistible impulses, are the prophetic promptings of the immortal soul. The innate feeling that impels a man to pursue a life of virtue rather than of vice, is but one ordinary phase in which this secret working of the soul becomes manifest. Our creed, then, resolves itself into this—that the soul is prophetic, and that we have a silent yet ever willing monitor to lead us to future benefits, or to avert from us threatening evils. We would, therefore, exhort all to obey those mysterious impulses to which we have before averted; and from our own experience, as well as from that of others, we guarantee they can never be led astray. As true science advances, we believe that this doctrine will reveal some of the hitherto inexplicable mysteries of that extraordinary mesmeric state denominated clairvoyance, which, by throwing the merely mental powers into a trance, gives the soul greater freedom and liberty of action. The metaphysical poet, Wordsworth, must have had some conception of this influence when he felt,

"A presence that disturbs me with the joy
Of elevated thoughts—a sense sublime
Of something far more deeply interfused

Whose dwelling is the light of setting suns,
And the round ocean, and the living air,
And the blue sky, and in the mind of man,
A motion and a spirit that impels
All thinking things, all objects of all thought,
And rolls them through all things."

It cannot be denied that Denial and Assent are, in some fashion, correlators of each other. Like all other things of the earthly, physical nature, they must follow an immutable, fixed law. This law is so interrelated, that like the track of the planets in the heavens, its whole series of variations and continuous movements can be located and mapped out, for students and other seekers.

It seems to be everlastingly affirmed throughout all Nature, the most intense effects are produced by the efforts of opposites for adjustment. The degree of innate power always measures the esoteric vibration, which is and always must rest in the esoteric expression.

Taking this, then, as the statement of the law, let us see if the great universe, which is said to be the result of the word of the all-potent in naming, or as quaintly expressed: "Let there be!" The acknowledged starting point of all that is or will be in the outpouring of manifestation, Perhaps the simplest statement is: "that which is and that which is not."

Taking this for granted, we may suppose that all which responded to the awfully potent "Let there be!"—the expressed will of God, constituted the massed assent of the universe, represented by thought impulses, be they longer or shorter in duration.

On the contrary, dissent or denial represented the massed feeling of obstruction, ranging from momentary doubt and question, to the fierce conditions of opposition, ready to carry out an experience of its own beliefs through the utmost peril to the extreme limit. As the one is all, so we can only conclude, that the great oceans of denial or assent were, at the first, projected as dissent resulting from its own conscious knowledge, as the results of its seizing upon the immensity of space, it alone could fill.

It must also be true that both exist as absolute necessities, proving to us, manifestation is the result only of joint action of the positive and negative. All things existent are but the outcome of the force at once omnipotent and omnipresent. We cannot imagine a God who does not consider the work of His hands; or who does not meditate upon the immensity of the infinite interests, which are the result of the motion of its thought. Like our own thoughts, it may favor or disapprove of the assured arrangement and outcome of certain sequences. Even this attitude of the thought of God, where it only as regarded itself, would produce the sensation everywhere, or opposition, of negative action arising simply from the disapproval by the omniscient of anything but perfection.

The Apostle Paul, writing to the Romans, said: "For to be carnally (materially) minded, is death; but to be spiritually minded is life and peace. Because the carnal mind is enmity against God; for it is not subject to the law of God, neither indeed can be. So, then they that are in the flesh (physical) cannot please God." Instead of the usual explanation of the carnal mind, being enmity against God, it would seem simply, the statement intended to be made is that all enmity or opposition held by mortal thought is the reflex action of God's own disapproval; becomes the carnal mind, which thus arrays itself as the state of consciousness, we recognize as negative or in opposition to the existing conditions.

There can be no conditions of conflicting entities, which men attempt to set up as good and evil, because all things work from the embryo to the perfect, which is the plan of God. All material conditions, begin and end, and after the end a period of intermission. Then another beginning and end.

It is out of these shifting influxes and effluxes man gathers his ideas of opposition or enmity. But let us sit with ourselves, and reason how the movements of our minds resemble these of the All-Wise, Omnipotent; we have a plan of activity on some line, in which the means and end are an equation to be worked out. With our limited knowledge, we may be hours in thought travail. But the decision comes at last.

We are obliged to leave more or less to the experience to be won from the experiments we are to try. This leaves little impression on the astral currents, for we are but monads of the Monad. But when the one, alter the same fashion, plans, His varying thought vibrates the whole universe.

Evil, then, is the force of these rejected conditions and while its power to move remains, naturally assimilates with everything of like character. It is the result of denial or dissent. Does it not seem as likely, that God knowing the issues and how man's interests are to be affected thereby, may seek to avoid the things man regards negative and always to be striven against, thereby only increasing against himself the weight of inertia which he must reuse himself either to act as a barrier or a repelling force.

The effort at equilibrium which man attempts, he calls dissent or denial. He cheers and comforts himself with the idea that he is always on the side of the right and true when he takes this attitude, but it is certainly a question.

The one admission is, it is no easy job to hold the position of resistance in the restraining of an intangible crushing, whose in tangibility is something eternally favoring it. Then, as we have hinted at, its persistent constancy in the line of pressure is another puzzling element of its action.

Man, a creature of two stopping places, the end and the beginning, is always looking for a stopping or resting place, but constant force gives denial of no chance for rest; to be a successful potency must be increased to its utmost. In reality, it must be the aggressor. We have been accustomed to considering the denial or dissent must be couched in the two letters n-o. That is not true, for yes often carries more of denial potency than a no. The potency holds the positive element. Denial is and must be positive.

Now, by inference, we conclude assent is simply the concurring of the negative, an agreement to abide and act with. It does not seem to have the elements of power that inhere in the simplest obstruction presented by nature. Inertia, the awful Jennie of Earth, the first man found in his pathway, as his lungs inhaled the pure air of heaven and the last enemy or obstruction the last man will have overcome and slain, as the gates of an eternal happy peace swing wide open to his enraptured gaze. For now, Oh, Man! this Jennie is Death. Denial and not assent, is his conqueror. I believe, therefore, denial holds the most potency.

DISAPPOINTMENTS

If there is any situation which confronts us more constantly and unremittingly than another, it is "disappointment." Every effort which is put forth on our own behalf or in aid of our friends or our work seems doomed to turn out differently than we had planned, and often the results of our action are the very opposite from those we intended and desired.

Every day, in some small way, things go wrong, or what we call wrong, and some days we have to call to our assistance all the patience and all the courage of which we are master not to succumb to the conditions which issue, all uncalled for as it would seem, from that which we have done with the very best intentions. If there is any philosophy or law of life which can do away with disappointment, we would like to know and follow it.

There is such a teaching, though it is of a nature which all men will not accept, only those who are beginning to free themselves from the slavery of the lower nature. For the mass of mankind does not yet realize the bondage in which it is being held, and not many are yet ready to subdue "desire."

Up to the present stage of the growth of the race, desire has been their teacher, their highest and their best, for without it, no awakening of the soul would have been possible. Desire is the law of the soul, and the soul follows where desire leads: does man desire wealth, the powers of the soul will concentrate upon its acquisition; does he pine for love, for power, for fame, immediately his desire places at his disposal the necessary motive power to start in pursuit of the desired object.

And so, Balzac formulates the teachings of the ancients when he says: "A constant desire is a promise of fulfillment," for this is the law. Fulfillment must and will eventually come where the desire is strong and constant, but it may be long in arriving and meanwhile we are beset with disappointments, which are bitter and crushing in direct proportion to the force of our desire. It is evident that there in a close connection between desire and disappointment, even children teach us this in their play when they say: "Don't expect anything and you won't be disappointed," showing that the race has already evolved so far in understanding.

At the present moment men are called upon to take a forward step, under a new teacher "Faith" and to relegate desire to a secondary place. The result of this change when it is accomplished, will be the elimination altogether from the life of "disappointment."

Under our new teacher, we shall learn that all our life in an orderly sequence, that God is above and over all, and that His is law will provide us with all that we need and ought to have. We know that God is Wisdom and Love, therefore, if we are logical, when things go wrong, that to when they do not follow the course which we laid provided for, Faith will lend us to see His Hand in the untoward event, and will show us how to follow His design rather than our own.

Every change which the Great Power deigns to make in our plans is eagerly embraced by the disciple; to him it is not a disappointment, but an intimation from the Father of some better way to follow, and: he at once begins to search it out, he is not discouraged at the non-success of his efforts in some particular direction, but instead, he acquiesces and finds another and a better way.

Thus, innumerable mistakes are avoided, for when the disciple is willing to hear, he may receive guidance in all the affairs of his daily life in just this way. Not passive resignation, but cheerful acquiescence leading to activity in some now direction, is the work of Faith; for "Faith without works is dead." And where there is Faith, there can be no disappointments.

HOW CAN WE HOPE TO ATTAIN PERFECTION

Examining the sting of a bee, we find it without flaw. No minute part of the polished surface, from its keen, sharp point, to the strong muscles that move it at the will of the insect to which it belongs, shows flaw of any kind, nor deviation from the magnificent polish of its surface. Perhaps the nearest approach to the bee's stinger is the fine cambric needle of man's handiwork. But when this is put under the lenses of a microscope of high power, the apparent high polish of the surface is one mass of inequalities, and deadened luster. Nothing could better illustrate the difference between the works of God and of man.

The one perfect in every stage of formation and development; the other following the irregularities of the thought that designed and created. These are but single examples of the whole of nature and man's works. The one is perfect in every detail. The other imperfect and more or less disturbed. We say these matters are the design and handiwork of nature, meaning thereby, they are the productions upon the original thought model of God's designs and manifestation.

Throughout all the rounds of manifestation the same condition rules. When we come to question of the cause, the answer is near at hand. God's thoughts are perfectly finished and complete. Man's creative attempts are imperfect and unfinished. This answers fully and fairly the question: "What is perfection?"

There is no model of perfection for man save the AII-Good. It is perfect in all its acts, both of manifestation and of interest. All the wise ones, the Sol-om-ons, the Trismegistus and Magi of the far past; the experts and adepts of the present, have but one message for both the manifested and the ummanifested; the wise and the foolish of today, it is: "love God and look to Him for advancement on all lines and in all places."

As you know God and seek to be like him, so will you gain that which it is. This conclusion, then, tells us what perfection is—the perfection which some men and especially the Hermetic Brotherhood seek to attain.

Naturally, the next questions are, how shall we attain? What are the readiest and most reliable methods for this attainment? The preposition entering into the answer contains the elements. God and ourselves. Let us meditate a little while, after the Hermetic method, on each. God is all, because it is perfection. In perfection, nothing is left out, nothing can fall short of its place in totality of the harmony of the whole. Because of this completeness in the ideal, it is regarded by man as omni-potent: omni-scient; and omni-present, in all its relations to man. Can it not then be regarded as an axiomatic statement:

"THE MORE WE CONTEMPLATE GOD, PERMITTING OURSELVES TO BECOME UNITIZED IN HIS PERFECT LOVE, WHICH CASTETH OUT FEAR, THE NEARER AND NEARER SHALL WE APPROACH THAT ATTAINMENT, WHICH IS THE ACME OF ALL PERFECTION."

In the teaching of the Brotherhood, from its beginning in the present incarnation, the power of thought has always been recognized as a most potent factor, in the relations of man, to himself, his fellows and his God. Existence is in two forms: the manifested and the unmanifested—energy and resistance.

The scientists of today are investigating the changing conditions of life, as if they were, for the first time, newborn. As a sample of their work, permit me to give you a few extracts from a recent publication:

"Do we not again see our investigations have only a temporary value? Will we be content to see matter dissolving itself into multi-revolving electrodes? Such a mysterious dissolution of component atoms appears to be universal and inevitable. It occurs when a piece of glass is rubbed with silk. It is present in the sunshine, in a raindrop, in lightning, in a flame, in a waterfall, and in the roaring sea. Although the whole range of experience is too short to form a parallax, whereby foretell the disappearance of matter (manifestation) nevertheless it is possible that formless nebulae will again prevail, when the hour-glass of eternity has run out."

"The probability that science may yet find all matter disappearing in a world of pure energy is, in the highest degree, interesting to those who give any thought to primal truths. It is well known that philosophy has long since eliminated matter from the world of pure being and has expressed all material phenomena in terms of mind. Should science in its turn eliminate matter and express its manifestations in terms of formless energy (thought) we might have something like a reunion of science and philosophy on a common basis; and through that union, gain a clearer knowledge of both the universe and the soul."

When our most advanced scientists thus openly and positively declare there is no matter per se and that all that appears to mortal sense is but the manifestation of force or pure energy, they are certainly coming back, not only to the Hermetic teachings of today, but also to the doctrines and utterances of Hermes Trismegistus, the thrice-wise of the long ago.

We, the Hermetic Brotherhood, seek then to attain perfection by learning how to think, when to think, and what to think. Of one thing we are absolutely certain, the fact that pure thought is final perfection, the unmanifested it. The more we mix desires, selfish purpose or form manifestation with pure energy or thought, the farther are we from perfection. Let us always remember impure thought is the result of an attempted conglomeration, in varying proportions, of pure energy—the unmanifested, with the desires and mortal conditions of manifestations. In no other sense are the terms pure and impure thought applicable or true. It must then necessarily follow, the purer our thought the nearer the nearer are we to the attainment of perfection.

THE METAPHYSICAL ASPECT OP IMMORTALITY

I am going a step outside the line which science would recognize or which can be verified by anyone easily. I am coming now into the more difficult experiments in regard to the existence of the soul. I mean by the soul a living, self-conscious intelligence, showing forth mental attributes at will, and being able to show forth attributes higher than mental as it grows and develops and asserts itself on higher planes than the physical and the astral. The beginning, of training along this line of thought, which leads us really into what is called the practice of Yoga, is first to use your mind to control your body and your senses so as to convince yourself that the mind is something higher than the body, more powerful than the senses. Set yourself to work to check some expression of the senses to which you habitually have yielded; cease taking some article of food that is very attractive; drop some form of drink that is very pleasurable and stimulating; leave off some form of physical pleasure to which you are particularly addicted.

I do not mean give it up altogether, but give it up for a time, to show that there is something in you, to prove to yourself beyond possibility of dispute that there is something in you that can control all that part of your nature which you call the senses or the bodily expression. Make yourself do a thing against the desire of the senses, and choose a time when the sense is rampant, when it is longing for that particular gratification, eager to have it, when the thing is right in front of you, and you are just putting out your hand to grasp it.

Stop and say: "I am stronger than you; you shall not gratify that desire." The only use of the experiment is that it convinces you, as nothing else does, that you are not your senses and not your body; that you are something higher—let us say for the moment, the mind, and that you can control this body and these senses that very often run away with you. I do not mean that you can always control them; you cannot until you practice; there will be times when the senses, like unbroken horses, will, as it were, take the bit in their teeth and run away with the mind and everything else and you plunge right after them; they carry you off; but you will know even then that they are carrying you off and you feel that they are stronger than you and are having their way. In a sort of upside-down fashion, even then you will distinguish between you and the wild, headlong influences and impulses that hold you captive for the time.

Now, that is a very elementary experiment, but you had better do it so as to be sure there is something in you stronger than the senses. Let us suppose that you now are ready to take the next step. It is able to control the body; it is able to control the sense. Is it able to control itself? You take up a very difficult book and you want to master that book. A good deal depends on your mastering it. Perhaps you are going to pass an examination. Unless you can master that book in the night time you will fail and that will throw you back in your career; and you sit down and work at it; your mind wanders; when you want to concentrate on some mathematical problem you are thinking, you find of something quite different; your mind goes off and you have to bring it back; and this happens over and over again, and you put your book down and you say, "Oh, I am not in the humor; I cannot do it." What sort of a mind is that? It won't work when it is wanted, and it can't do what is its special business, because it is not in the humor. And then you begin to say, "Why shouldn't I control the mind?" And in that very phrase, you are asserting something that is higher than the mind—I. "I mean that this mind shall do what I want it to do and to be fixed on that book."

You concentrate your attention; you gather up something which is strong in you, and you fix the mind on that subject and you work at it. What is it that has done it? It can't be the mind that has done it, which has been running all over the place. It is something that is there which is able to master the mind and turn it to that point where it is wanted to work. Then you feel, "That is the thing I am going to look for now. I have found that the mind is above the senses—I know that, but here is something which is above the mind, and I must go in search of that. Perhaps that is the soul. The force that I feel, which masters my vagrant mind, this strength that I find within myself, which groups my wandering thoughts and compels their obedience, what is that? That seems to be myself. I am controlling my mind."

When that point is reached and when the habit has been made of the mind being fixed on a thing at order, there will have grown up a very definite consciousness of some¬thing which is behind that mind and masters it as the mind did the senses, and then the student may think it worthwhile to take steps to find out what that something is, and then generally he will have to ask somebody who has gone rather further in this than he has, "What is the next step that I ought to take? I find something here that is higher than, more than, the mind. How am I to find out what it is?" And in some book that he reads, or by someone whom he meets who can explain to him, he learns there are certain practices, definite practices, what is called meditation, and by following out those you can develop that consciousness which is higher than the mind.

When a person has reached this point, if no other person comes in his way, you may be sure that he will find a book; he will take up the book in the public library and read it; or some friend will say, "Have you seen that book?" and will introduce the book to him. Somehow or other, the book will come in his way. Because there are always more advanced souls watching to see when any soul evolving reaches the point where it can take help; where it is ready for further help; and if there is not available someone in the physical body who can give the help that the soul wants, then it will be directed to the finding of the book where the practical teaching will be given. It is the action of the helpers of men who come with a helping hand to that seeking soul and place within its reach the knowledge that is the next step in its experiments, and rules for meditation will be found and studied and practiced, and when those rules are studied and practiced what happens is this: That with each day's meditation the consciousness beyond the mind grows stronger and stronger, more and more asserting itself, more and more as it were revealing itself, until presently the whole center of consciousness will be shifted upwards and the man will realize that he is not at all his mind, but a great deal more than the mind, and he will then begin to sense things that the mind cannot sense, become conscious of thoughts that the mind is unable to appreciate; and now and then there will come down a great rush, as it were, of thoughts that dominate the mind and that the mind is unable to explain, although it realizes them as true when once they are presented to it. And then arises the question: "I did not argue myself up to this; I did not reach it by logic; I did not reach it by argument; I did not reach it by thinking. It came to me suddenly. Whence did it come?" And the consciousness arises slowly, "It came from myself; that higher part of myself which is beyond the mind and which in the quiet of the mind is able to assert itself." For as has often been said, just as a lake unruffled by the wind will reflect sun, or mountain, or flowers, but ruffled gives only broken images, so when the mind is quiet the higher thought is reflected in the lake of the mind, but as long as the winds of thoughts blow over it, it is ruffled and only broken images are seen. In the quiet of the mind, then, the higher thought asserts itself.

Then comes another stage, a higher stage. The student tries more and more to identify himself with the higher thought; gropes after it, as it were; tries to feel it as himself; concentrates his effort and keeps the mind absolutely still; and at some moment of that experience, without warning, without effort, without anything in which the lower mind takes part, suddenly the consciousness will be outside the body and the man will know himself as the living consciousness looking at the body that he has left. Over and over again in different scriptures, this statement is found. You may read, for instance, in one of the Hindoo scriptures, that a man should be able to separate the soul from the body as you may separate grain from the sheath that enfolds it.

Or, in another phrase, that when the man has dominated the mind, he rises out of the body in a brilliant body of light—a statement literally true, the body in which the soul arises, the soul itself, that is luminous, radiant, glorious exceedingly, a body of light. No words could better explain this appearance, no phrase more graphically describe the man rising out of the physical body in a body of light. I quote that ancient scripture in order that you may not for a moment imagine this is simply a modern investigation. All those who know the soul have passed through that experience. It is the final proof that the man is a living soul; not argument, not reasoning, not inference, not authority, not faith, not hearsay, but knowledge. I am this living consciousness, and that body I have left is only a garment that I wore. It is not me; it is not myself. That is not I; I am here; that I have thrown off; I have escaped it; I am free from it. And that experience mentioned in those ancient scriptures is mentioned in other scriptures, too; it is the invariable experience of the prophet, and the teacher, and the seer, for none can faithfully teach the things of the soul except by his own knowledge. As long as he is only repeating what intellectually he has learned, he may do the most useful work, but he has not that stamp of first-hand knowledge which carries conviction with it to those whom he teaches. Second-hand knowledge is always liable to be challenged.

Questions may be asked which it is almost impossible to answer, if you are only repeating what you have learned intellectually. A necessary stage. I am not speaking against it. All go through it who reaches the other. But if the world is still to have witnesses of the immortality of the soul; if the world of the nineteenth century is to have what the world has had in all other ages, the first-hand testimony of living souls that they know that they exist, then men in the nineteenth century must go through the same training that they have gone through in other times, for only thus is first-hand knowledge attainable and the question of the existence of the soul is put forevermore beyond possibility of doubt or of challenge. The first time there may be a sense of bewilderment, or confusion, or wondering what this strange thing is that has happened; but as it is repeated day after day, week after week, month after month, year after year, that consciousness outside the body is as real and more real than that within the body; for, coming back into the body time after time, the soul experiences that entering the body is like going into a prison house; that it is like leaving the open air and going into a cellar or a vault; that the sight is dimmed; that the hearing has grown almost deaf; that all the powers of the soul are limited and deadened, and that this body is indeed as St. Paul, the great initiate, called it, the body of death, not the body of life. We call this life; it is not life at all. We call it life; it is simply the limited, imprisoned, dull, dwarfed existence which the soul takes to itself for a short time of its experience in order to gain certain physical knowledge which otherwise it would be unable to acquire for lack of suitable instruments.

But as you become men of meditation that higher life becomes your vivid, real life, and this life becomes a sort of dream, recognized as an illusion, as duties that have to be discharged, obligations that have to be paid, where much has to be done; but the world, it is a world of prison, not the world of life; and then we realize that we ourselves are that living, active, powerful, perceiving intelligence to whom the worlds lie open and heaven is the native land, the natural and rightful dwelling place.

These are the lines along which we pass to the final proof of the existence of the soul. See how gradual the stages have been; how we began on the physical plane with physical experiments; how we passed then a little on into the region of dreams and action outside the body; how then we took up the question that we recognize of the use of the difference between the body and the senses and the mind; and then how we found the assertion of something beyond that mind, more real and more powerful than that; and then how encouraged by those lower experiments we penetrated into the higher, and paid the price which is necessary for that first-hand knowledge of the soul. Truly, it is worthwhile. I do not pretend that it can be gained without paying the price. I do not pretend that you can lay vehemently on the life of the body and the senses and the mind and at the same time carry on this evolution of the higher life, but this I tell you; that all you lose is merely the pleasure which you have outgrown, and which, therefore, no longer attracts you. You lose that in the way that you lose your toys when you grow out of childhood; you do not want them.

It is not that anyone takes them away from you or breaks them; you do not want them any longer; you have found a higher enjoyment, toys of a finer kind; but the mind is also a toy, though finer than the toy of the senses; that also is recognized as a toy in the higher regions of the life. Gradually you give up then those pleasures; they have lost their savor; but you perform your duties better than you have performed them before. Don't fall into the mistake that some people do when they begin meditating of going about the world in their waking life in a fog, in a dream, abstracted, so that everybody says, "Why, that person is losing his mind."

That is not the way to meditate. Meditation makes men more effective, not less keen, not blinder; more alert, not less alert; more observant, not less observant. The stage where people are dreaming is a very early stage of the training of the mind, when they are still so weak that they cannot manage their mind at all; and I have noticed over and over again, if I take for a moment a personal illustration, that I, who have done a good deal in this way of meditation, who have trained myself carefully along the road that I have been pointing out to you, I often notice when I am with people who have never dreamed of that at all and who call themselves quick, observant people of the world, that I see things that they miss, observe things that pass them unobserved, notice all kinds of tiny things in the streets, in the railways cars, in people, which pass by them without making the slightest impression. And I only mention that to show you that it is not necessary to lose the powers of the lower mind while you are busy evolving the higher. The fact is you have them much more at your command, and just because you do not wear them out by worry and fuss and anxiety, they are much more available when you want to use them; indeed, common sense is very marked; reason, logic, intelligence, caution, prudence, all these qualities come out strongly and brilliantly. The man becomes greater and not less on the mental plane because he works in a region beyond and above the intellect. He is given his life. He is not robbed of the lower life; he has lost it, and in losing it, he finds it. Resigning the lower he finds, the higher flowing into him fully and the lower is more brilliant than it ever was before. He asks for nothing; everything comes to him. He seeks for nothing; all things flow to him unasked. He makes no demands; nature pours out on him her treasures. He is ever pouring forth all that he possesses. He is always full, although ever emptying himself.

Those are the paradoxes of the life of the soul; those the realities proven as true when the existence of the soul is known; and if I have not tried to win you by mere skill of pen or picture, or what would be called appeals to emotion and feelings, it is because I wanted to win your reason step by step along this path, because I wanted to show you without emotion, without appeals to intuition, without making, as I might make, my appeals to that knowledge within every one of you, that you are immortal existence? And that death is not your master. Instead of appealing to that, as I have the right to appeal to it, I have led you step by step along the path of the reason; I have shown you why you should take each new step when the others behind are taken; and let me concluding say a word to those who do not need to take the lower steps of this toilsome path, who do not need to prove that the soul exists, who are filled with the consciousness that they are living souls, who, though they know it not first-hand in knowledge, yet have a deep and undying conviction that no logic can shake, no argument can alter, no scoff can vary, no jeer and no proof can change. Beaten in argument, confused by logic, bewildered by proof, they still say, "I feel, I know, I am a living soul."

To those I would say, trouble not yourselves about the lower steps; trouble not yourselves with all the arguments I am using as to proof, over and over again reiterated, intended to convince the materialist. Trust your intuitions, and act on its truth. The inner voice never misleads. It is the self-whispering its own existence and imperially commanding your belief. Yield your belief to the voice within. Take it for true, though you have not proven it as true, and act on that internal conviction as though it were true. Then begin with the processes of meditation I hastily alluded to. Take as you may take the books where these are traced out for you one by one. Begin to practice them. Do not waste any more time in reasoning out other processes that you are not ready to understand. Trust the voice within you. Follow the guidance's who thus have marked out for you, who have trodden that road and have proved it to be true. Then swiftly and easily you will gain the knowledge. Then, without long delay, you will know of your own knowledge that these things are true. If the soul speaks to you, don't wait for the confirmation of the intellect. Trust the divine voice; obey the divine impulse; follow out the road traced by sages, by prophets, by teachers, verified by disciples who in the present day have trodden it and know it to lead to the rightful goal. Then you, too, shall know; then you, too, shall share; then your intuition shall be confirmed by knowledge, and you shall feel yourselves the living, the immortal soul.

That is my message to you, then, to those who need not the proof and appeal to the intuition; and in giving you the message, I speak not of myself; in giving you the message, I bring you no new thing; I confirm to you in your own day and time what every prophet has asserted; what every disciple has taught; what every divine man has proclaimed. As a messenger of that brotherhood, I do but repeat their message. There is the weight of the evidence, and not in my poor reassertion of it. What is it that one soul should have found to be true, what all the great souls have declared? If you would have authority, take theirs. If you would rely on the word of another, rely on their word. Remember that what I speak is indeed spoken with my lips, but with their voice, and I bring to you the testimony of the ages; I bring to you the message from an innumerable company.

I, but weak and poor in my own knowledge, limited and circumscribed in my own experience, servant of that great brotherhood, holding it the proudest privilege and delight to be able to serve and to give my obedience, I speak their word. I do not dare to endorse it, as it were, though knowing it to be true. I put it on their testimony, unshakable, immovable, back to the furthest antiquity, down to the present day, an unbroken army of mighty witnesses, an innumerable company of prophets, of teachers, of saints. Their messenger, I speak their message. You can prove its truth for yourselves, if you will.

KARMA AS INFINITE PATIENCE

Sir Isaac Newton, in formulating his first Law of Movement, gave expression to one of the modes of Karma on the physical plane, when he said: "Action and Reaction are equal and opposite in direction." Science proclaims the law of Cause and Effect. Logic builds upon the principle that consequences are true to their antecedents. "Invariability of succession is found by observation to obtain between every fact in Nature and some other fact which has preceded it."

All of our common experience, indeed, teaches us to act according to our estimate of the consequences to follow; so that we work or rest, indulge ourselves or make sacrifices, scheme and plan, eat and drink, for the most part with a regard to the effects of these activities upon our life as a whole. We do not, perhaps, recognize this law of Cause and Effect by its Oriental name of Karma, but we show ourselves perfectly familiar with its working on the physical plane and in the realm of thought. The religions of Christendom, alone, form an exception to this acceptance of the law. Although all great teachers have proclaimed with one voice, "Whatsoever a man soweth, that shall he also reap," and although we find it distinctly set forth in the scriptures of all ages, still many Christians seek to find an escape for the sinner, by which his "re-action" would not be "equal and opposite in direction" to his action. Others with greater Courage and sincerity, recognize the universal presence of the law of compensation in the visible world, and are seeking the principle of eternal and universal retributive justice, which shall secure to every man the exact reward of his deeds, infallibly repairing human wrongs—ever making for readjustment tending to equilibrium in the physical, and harmony in the moral world.

This idea of justice, seen as Equity, Love, and Mercy, is far from finding any intelligible expression in the western religious teaching, but in the Orient, it is known as the Law of Karma, and is one of the fundamentals of true living. In the Occident, where the opinion prevails that we have but this one life in which to work out the salvation, each one of his own soul, there appears to be great inequality in the distribution of Nature's benefits; for some men are born poor and others rich, some are intelligent, others imbecile, some live many years, others but a few moments, nor can the justice of God be seen by those whose whole life is one long agony brought about through no fault of their own in the present life.

The heart of the "Good Man" of the Western world, who knows no other teaching, aches for these tortured souls and sometimes he turns perforce away from all religions—an atheist or an agnostic. The oriental conception of God is far from other. It shows us a God of strict and impartial justice, it is true, meting out to every man what that man himself has earned and so created in the realm of cause and effect. But it shows us also a God of love and mercy in the numberless opportunities which are given the individual of triumphing over his lower nature.

Not one life but many are seen to be necessary to accomplish so stupendous a task, and so the soul is offered a countless series of incarnations on this earth and afterwards beyond, during which he will have ample opportunity for self-knowledge and for self-mastery. These afford even the weakest son of the Great Father time and occasion to learn the same lessons as his stronger brother has perhaps mastered in a few incarnations. There is no condemnation for the one who fails, only infinite patience and a new opportunity to try again and ever again until the difficulty is surmounted and the weak place strengthened. The God of Love wills that every soul shall be saved, and it is, indeed, difficult, and almost impossible, under this dispensation of mercy, for one to go astray. If he will not learn by gentleness, he is made to learn by pain, and one single thought or aspiration towards the good, one unselfish, pure desire in the whole life is enough to give that soul another opportunity. Man comes to earth with a threefold personal Karma. There is first, his whole mass of unpaid debt accumulated from the experiences of all his past lives, and which, so far, he has not been able to work off. This is called in Sanskrit, Samhita. Second, there is the destiny of his present life upon which he is entering, or Prabodha, being that portion of his Karmic responsibilities which the Lords of Karma, or the Masters who aid in the administration of this law, have selected for him to work off in his present incarnation; and, thirdly, there is the new Karma which he is going to make, or Kriomana.

Over the first two of these aspects of the law, the man has no control at the present time. In the past, they were his own creation, since he made the causes of which they are the effect; but now the only field in which he can work is the third—that of accepting the old conditions and weaving them into a new future. This, then, must he his task henceforth, humbly and cheerfully to accept his life as he finds it, to let the pendulum of human circumstance swing as it will from side to side, but always remain himself, poised at the center—to set his affection upon those things which are above and to do good to all men.

THE PRE-EXISTENCE OF THE SOUL

The thought of Immortality is always accompanied with a retrospective as well as a forward glance, and one cannot think of futurity—endless—unaccompanied by the question: "Why an unending future any more than an endless past?"

Only those who have come to accept the truth of a future existence after having been agnostics or materialists wholly reject the thought of preexistence as associated with the soul, or immortal part of man. All forms of religious thought inculcate a spiritual antecedence for humanity as well as a material one, and there are many religions of the world that distinctly advocate a conscious preexistence. The great Philosophies of the past and present—Oriental, Platonic and Psychic—advocate without question the entirety of the spiritual existence of the ego; and even Christians accept the thought that "the spirit comes from God and will return to God," really a restatement of the "Nirvana" of the Orient. The logical statement is that there can be no "Eternity" that has a beginning; and that which has a beginning in "things" (matter) must logically end in matter, i.e., if the spirit or soul of man commenced to have a conscious existence with the human body, somewhere there must be a cessation of consciousness—as if the result of disassociation from matter—or the disintegration of matter.

All organic forms germinate, grow to maturity, and decay. If spirit (conscious existence) is the result of contact with matter, or is an emanation from matter, there must come a time when that contact, or the conditions producing that emanation will cease; that would be annihilation. From no life that is capable of mental or spiritual contemplation is this thought of preexistent soul-life wholly removed; everyone is aware of possessing grander possibilities than can be expressed.

All feel that there is a depth of knowledge within them that could be given forth in human life if there "were but time," or "another chance"; all have glimpses of this a priori state, that there is a vast inheritance of hidden possibilities to be expressed sometime, somewhere, and a vast other realm that holds former expressions or states of being. Memory, ever treacherous even concerning the common things of daily existence, holds no key to this more absolute realm. In the deeper possessions of the soul, it abides; the one certainty of the soul's estate. The Platonic System of Philosophy makes of this perception that which inheres in the uncreated ego, or essence of all life. Even in the works of the somewhat materialistic philosophers of the German schools, beginning as long ago as Kant, there is the distinct statement of "a priori mind," of the supremacy of the mind or spirit, in fact a distinct statement of knowledge not born of the senses; the rejection of the material part of man as forming any source of the knowledge he possesses. We could refer to authors innumerable who distinctly declare a pre-existent state of the soul, and also a pre-existent human life. In such works as "Portent," by George MacDonald, "The Two Destinies," by Willkie Collins, and his more than equal compeer, and the recent works of Marie Corelli.

The great poets have never taught any other system of soul-life than that which is forever and forever. "From Everlasting to Everlasting" is one of the Biblical expressions concerning the eternity of being. Doubtless all religions that have succeeded, directly or indirectly, the Vedic, or original Hindoo Faith and Philosophy, as well as the Religion of the Parsee and other Oriental nations, bear traces of the preexistence of the spirit of man either as a primal entity or one with the Infinite. Professor Ghandi informs his hearers in this country that the Jainist differs from the Buddhist in this regard: that while the latter teaches that the soul, or spirit, is from the "Eternal Good," the Jainist also declares the soul to be an immortal entity.

Our thesis is this: That the soul is an eternal entity, forever conscious of its own being and conscious of existence in outward human expression—that earth-life is but a small—possibly smallest—portion of life, which is endless: one of the steps of a never-ending succession of expressions in other lives and other worlds. That the state of being—which is the soul-state—is not exchanged for the state of existence by the soul, but the soul expresses itself in the state of existence for purposes of which the soul is fully aware. That Earthly expression being included in the eternity of life, there is, as far as the soul is concerned, no death, no birth, no change—in esse. That the soul-state abides forever and continually, even while states of expression are transpiring, and sometimes forces the perception of that state through the human consciousness. That as the only unending line is the circle—in mathematics—so in logic the only unending life is forever: a past and future eternity. In fact, no past, no future, but Eternity. That soul brings into expression on Earth or other planets—through successive lives—all that is needed of the a priori state, and ultimately all knowledge of the absolute that may be required for the complete expression in the Human life. This supernal entity, this divine ego, may not resemble—even in the smallest degree—that which is expressed; especially in the primitive conditions of expressions on Earth, but gradually the expression receives more and more of the soul's estate and suggests, as well as reveals, the realm of soul that is forever the realm of causation.

Whether this preexistent state has been connected with planetary life on this Earth, or in some other world similar to our own, must, for the purposes of this article, be left to another time to discuss; but the main proposition of absolute Immortality rests as surely on the basis of pre-existence as upon future or continued existence beyond the change called death. In the mythology of the North-lands, the fair goddess Friega, who dwells in the halls of Valhalla, has charge of souls before their mortal birth and often accompanies them to their human parents and appoints guardian genii to watch over them while in Earth-life. The poets of every age have sung of the immortal heritage of the Soul.

To know that for æons upon æons before mortal time the soul was, as for the unending ages of the future it ever will be, links us at once with the Infinite, and the terror of annihilation is lost in the eternal certainty. The attempt to fix and fasten this a priori state upon the human memory, or earthly consciousness, is as useless as to attempt to experience the Eternal future in the present; both are soul possessions, and consciousness of both must be in the realms of soul. The glimmerings of this supernal state may sometimes reach the outward mind from within as, forcing itself through the human environment, the soul finds occasion for deeper expression. There is an awareness, a brooding other consciousness that shapes itself to human needs, and forms the luminous background for the urgent human work. But for this the mortal pilgrimage would be a failure, and the oppressions of material life too difficult and stifling to be borne.

FORM

Form is the limitation of spirit. It is also, so far as we know, the Cosmos, its only reasonable expression. Only through form can spirit be made manifest to man's outer consciousness, therefore, only through form can we penetrate the hidden mysteries of spirit. The variety of its manifestation is infinite, and the balance between the "too, too solid" and ethereal, the almost formless, is continually shifting. As we see in art, the pendulum swings, from period to period, between a realistic and an impressionist school, so the same thing obtains in religions, from a dogmatic Church to a Quaker assembly, with innumerable shades of ritual and non-ritual practicing bodies between the two. The form is not the essence, on that point all agree. But the question arises, can the essence be retained for any practical purpose without the form?

Can the liquid be serviceable without a vessel to contain it? "When the lamp is shattered, the light in the dust lies dead. When the cloud is scattered, the rainbow's glory is shed."

The whole of nature is an object lesson, not in order that we may merely know and recognize the objects, but that we may reach something behind or within them. All the early years of man's life, in some instances all the years, are spent in studying objects. The infant's first lessons are lessons in form. It clasps its mother's finger, a stick, an ivory thing. As soon as it begins to crawl, it makes for one solid object after another, grasps each in turn, and becomes conscious of three dimensions. It even sometimes reaches out its hands for the moon.

At a later stage, the imitative or creative faculty comes into play, and the artist strives to throw his thought into shape on canvas, in stone, wood or measured words, and becomes a painter, sculptor or poet. Even music, the most ethereal of the arts, is form, a mode of expression of emotions and ideas. The artist does not remain satisfied with one form, but rather casts it aside as inadequate to express all the thought that burns within him, he seeks ever some new form, purer, richer, or more simple, by which to give a fuller and more perfect expression. But form he must have. Goethe, that master of manifold expression, makes the earth-spirit tell Faust in words that have been splendidly rendered by I know not what translator: "Thus at the whirring loom of time I ply, and weave for God the garment thou seest Him by". Literally, "His living dress".

These reflections have been awakened in my mind by observing the tendency of certain philosophic teachers to depreciate form, and to consider all outward things as illusion. So, they are in themselves, but the same philosophers say that nature is the best teacher. I heartily agree; and nature employs form as her instrument. Others again may say: "But nature's most powerful agents are formless." Have we not the "viewless air," steam, electricity; all formless, impalpable? Yes, but before steam becomes a motor, it must be confined within the engine it is to propel. The wind gives rise to the sail and the wind-mill, and thus becomes useful to man. My contention is, as against the form-destroyers, iconoclasts of various grades, that for practical purposes thought and spirit have no existence apart from form. Form, therefore, is the necessary corollary of spirit, or to use a seeming paradox, illusion is an essential part of truth. It does not stand in antagonism to it. If recognized in its partial expression, illusion becomes the pathway to the goal, the bridge to the ultimate. But it is a bridge we cannot do without. It is a part of the great scheme of evolution, and therefore must be right in its own place.

We have only to guard against mistaking the shadow for the substance, and to be continually correcting cur observations of the sun of truth. Not only can we not afford to give up form, even in religion, but we find its use an imperative necessity, even at the risk of sometimes over-estimating the cost of we know not what blood and sorrow, what long ages of strenuous labor and painful defense. Shall we destroy the well-tried paths which have so long and safely led men to that upper chamber where the greater mysteries are enacted, and substitute new roads which may lead us astray? Must find expression. It seems a strangely contradictory state of mind which finds it hard to believe in the historical facts of the life of Christ, because these facts contain an inner signification which transcends them in importance.

If the thing signified be true, surely that is an additional reason for holding the facts to be true also, given always the premise that all truth From the standpoint of the higher ego the events of every human life have a deeper meaning than we can discern at present: but when we come to understand them aright we shall surely not say that they never happened, nor that life in the body was unnecessary. The contemplation of the highest life ever lived on earth is to the ordinary human being the surest help, and furnishes the most inspiring hope, on the upward path.

The more he contemplates, the more does that form irradiate the divine of which it is the expression. Only the Father is the Illimitable, the Formless, the Unconditioned. The moment He takes on form. He becomes the Son; when the Son has fulfilled His mission, the irradiating Spirit is diffused into the hearts of all believers, and is the Holy Spirit of Truth. How shall His teaching be preserved? A body must be formed, which shall jealously guard the traditions, transcribe the facts, store up the teaching and transmit them to posterity. Should the body be changed, there is danger of loss, but the same facts will forever find expression in some form or other. The gates of hell cannot prevail against the rock of truth. In tuition, that sun of the soul, though often beclouded, will always finally lead us right; but forms are as sign-posts that mark the road to the sanctuary wherein dwells the Holy Grail.

A THINKER

DID IT ever occur to you whence come your thoughts, ideas and impressions—and why they come? Think you they come by accident, or aimlessly, and have no meaning and purpose? Could that be in a world of perfect order, method and system?

If you can see that not one thought is given or permitted you that has not its purpose, then you are capable of analyzing a thought and determining if you wish to accept it, to admit it in your consciousness, and thereby to affect your life. But if you can go farther, then hear that always a thought comes from someone, and that by being able to concentrate on a thought and analyze it, one can trace it back to its thinker. How can that be?

Watch the mind carefully, when thus concerting, for the impressions or other "thoughts" that come, and you may find something or someone trying to tell you what you seek to know. But cease not to analyze what comes. And note also that Someone is trying to point out the difference between good and bad, truth and error, what to accept and what to reject. Heed and learn. All is for your good.

THE OCCULT

To many-people, the words, "occult" and "occultism," possess a dark and sinister meaning; and many, through ignorance, have confounded them with black art, sorcery, hypnotism, and modern spiritualism. Because black art, sorcery, and such subjects savor of the supernatural and because occult means hidden, or secret, these terms are confused and associated together in the minds of many, and are placed on the same plane.

This is a great mistake, and people do greatly err in believing them to be the same. However, there are many who are sincere and earnest in their search for truth; but too often they make the mistake of blindly following the blind leaders of the blind, who represent the truth by vague, visionary theories and by supernatural manifestations or psychic phenomena.

Although occult means hidden, or secret, there is nothing about it that is vague or visionary or spectacular. Neither is there anything objectionable, unstable, or undesirable about true occultism.

The most material and skeptical scientists of today admit the power of thought. Marconi says that a word, or its equivalent (its equivalent is a thought), creates a ripple in the air, just the same as a pebble thrown in the water creates a ripple over the surface. Marconi has proved this to be a fact; and a man is deemed foolish and ignorant today, who doubts the possibility of wireless telegraphy. Edison claims to be in touch with a power in nature we call God. He says that, within a short time, he will be able to prove to the world that there is a mysterious and unseen force dwelling, living, existing, in all nature; and that the force will permit demonstration.

There are people who know and understand what this Force is, and who know that it is possible to prove its reality. Ages and ages ago, before this continent was in existence, men lived who understood this Force and knew the Great Secret.

These men were Occultists. They were not the riff-raff and the scum of creation, who affected oddities of dress and mysterious manners; but they were men who held the balance of worlds in their power. They watched the old earth, weighted with the oppression of abused laws, sink beneath the tides and the floods; they watched the new lands appear in their stead and the birth of new races on them.

These men were leaders; for ages they controlled the destiny of nations; they were the living, breathing essences of God-like power and nobility. They were true occultists. You ask us: "Why did they not prevent the sinking of countries and nations?" We ask you: "Why did not God prevent it?"

All laws must be obeyed; otherwise, the people must suffer the consequences. Neither God nor Masters can prevent it. Moses was the greatest occultist of his time; and he is honored and almost deified by people today who are afraid of the word occult. He possessed greater power, you say, than Egyptian Magic could equal. Yes, we know it. And it is possible for the good and the faithful in this age to know where his power came from, and how he came by it. There is as much difference between true occultism and the prevailing idea of it among certain classes in this day and time as there was in the time of Moses. There was the true and the false then as there is now. There was a misunderstanding of the true occultism then as now. People object to the occult because it is secret.

Is there a successful nation anywhere that does not follow secret laws? Why does not the United States hand over the plans of her Naval Coast defense to England, Germany, Japan, or any other nation? Why are the secrets of state guarded with close, jealous care, and why is the penalty of the traitor that betrays these secrets the penalty of death? It is the secrecy of laws that holds the power, and protects the destiny of our nation.

How long would the United States stand, if her laws were betrayed into the hands of the ignorant, the crude, the unbalanced citizen? Why do not men object to the principles of the Mosaic Law and history, on the grounds of secrecy? No man ever held the truth in closer secrecy and under more careful protection than did Moses. God called him to the top of the Mount and instructed him in the laws that were for the people. Why did not Moses teach openly and gratuitously? We read: "Moses alone shall come near the Lord: but they shall not come nigh; neither shall the people go up with him. And Moses was commanded to go up to the Mount alone, where he was given the tables of stone and a law and commandments to teach the people."

The Bible gives proof enough that he was taught apart from the people and in a different manner. He possessed greater power than any other man of his time, and was the Savior of his nation. He taught the wisdom, the truth, the secrets, the laws of the Osirian and Essenean Brotherhood of that day; for he was an Initiate of that Brotherhood. He worshipped the One God, called Osiris by the Egyptians. These same laws, wisdom, truths, are known today, and can be taught to all those that will he faithful. To all those that will leave "the golden calf" of their own selfishness, and will seek a true and unerring God, these truths may be taught. These truths concerning the One God and His invisible forces have ever been taught carefully and guardedly. Secrecy is merely protective. Nature hides her greatest works from the most learned men. Tell us why. Why is the Supreme Being unseen?

If man knew God, unless he himself was God-like, he might destroy worlds. God works silently and unseen. John, the beloved disciple, tells us that no man hath seen God at any time. Man must attain the likeness of God; and it takes ages to perfect himself so as to be like unto God. These secrets, so great and powerful, are destructive, when placed in the hands of the ignorant, the treacherous, and the unloving.

Who can tell the secret of the Sun, of the lightning's flash, and of the ponderous bolts of thunder God does not betray Himself into the hands of the foolish or of the unenlightened soul; but slowly and secretly He works His own laws, the evolution of the smallest and the most imperfect, in ways that surpass the understanding of the worldly wise. In one sense, it is true that all knowledge is free and open to all. All are welcomed to the treasure-house of truth and understanding. In one sense, it is true that God, in His ways and His laws and His works, is frank and free.

There is nothing purposely mysterious about His methods. Truth is not hidden through any arbitrary, dictatorial arrangement. The fact of secrecy and of mystery is merely one necessary feature of the law itself—the law that man comprehends truth in proportion to his hunger to know the truth and to live in harmony with the truth. Man is permitted to comprehend truth as rapidly as his own hunger of soul and his own pure and unselfish motives make it possible for him to do so.

If a man wishes to understand divine law and to direct the invisible forces for his own personal interests merely—this in itself is evidence that the truth is not safe in his hands—unless his heart is cleansed of error and selfish motives, he is liable to play havoc with the subtle, invisible forces of nature, and to bring destruction and disaster both to himself and to others. Dynamite is safe in the hands of two classes of people: those that will leave it alone and not tamper with it; and those that understand its nature and the laws of its use, but that will not make it a means of devastation on their neighbor's premises. Consequently, the deepest truths are carefully guarded by those that understand them. These occult features are beneficent in their purpose. Again, in answer to the question. Why are not occult subjects taught gratuitously, it remains to be said that God does not give man life for nothing; that the universe is not constructed on the plan of something for nothing; that both divine law and ethics demand that we give for what we receive; that, for the most valuable, we pay the highest price; that all growth is based on the principle of giving out and taking in; that, unless this law of growth is observed, stag nation follows; that fair exchange is one feature of the law of duality everywhere manifest in nature. There is one sense in which it is true that Salvation is free; but there are more aspects in which it is ours in return for a high price—indeed, the highest price—even the price of attainment.

"Something for nothing" was not the practice of the Jews. We read in Exodus how gladly the Hebrews brought their gifts to the tabernacle. The disciples contributed to the support of Jesus; and, even after the crucifixion, Joseph of Arimathea placed the body of Jesus in his own tomb—one wherein none was ever laid before. Mary Magdalene anointed Him and prepared Him against the day of His burial. The disciples were admonished to take neither scrip nor purse and were told that the laborer is worthy of his hire. When the physical body needs a physician, it seems easy enough to pay the doctor's fee; but, when the soul is sick, weary, and overburdened, why is it such an arduous task to make glad returns for knowledge concerning the care of the soul? There never was a greater mistake than that of thinking it possible or right to receive something for nothing. Every mouthful of food one takes is, in its essence, food for the soul. Is it free? Money-making is not an object with teachers of the Higher Knowledge; but money is necessary, in these days of book-making and of correspondence-instruction, in order that the spreading of the truth may be made possible. True occultism is the worship of the One God and His Laws in Conscious Unity. It is the great shadow that protects the Light of His presence from the eyes of the profane, the vulgar, and the unbelieving.

True occultism is the Inner Wisdom, "the secret place" of the Most High. "He that dwelleth in the secret place of the Most High shall abide under the shadow of the Almighty." To know, to understand, and to dwell under the Shadow, called "Occult," is to be in touch with the Divine; and untold power and knowledge are given unto him who obeys the laws and unto him who dwells Within, on the Right Hand of the Truth of God.

It is to be admitted that an outcry needs to be made against phenomena, trickery, spiritualism, and hallucinations—things that are sometimes erroneously associated with the occult. Such things are no evidence of power or of wisdom. The true occultist shuns such manifestations, as one shuns poisons. In regard to supernatural manifestations that attract attention and wonder, the true occultist sounds a clear note of warning: "Beware." The true of cultist strives to live a good, upright, quiet, modest life, and makes no display of his knowledge and of his power, other than in the simplicity of kind deeds and helpful words.

THE CAUSES OF SUFFERING

Man suffers. There can be no gainsaying of that fact. There are many reasons for his suffering; but all the reasons can be grouped in three classes: the suffering that is caused by acts of his own, committed in this life; the suffering that is caused by his own acts, committed in a former life; the suffering that is caused by the acts and the thoughts of others, for which the sufferer in no way is responsible.

Suffering that comes under the first group of causes is due to the Law of Consequences, or the Law of Cause and Effect. This includes suffering that is the natural result, or inevitable consequence, of one's own thoughts and acts. An abstract statement of the principle may be formulated thus: thoughts and deeds, by the unerring operation of an impartial law, set into motion forces that return, in a reactionary influence, to the one that entertained the thoughts and committed the deeds. The law was taught by Jesus and other Masters. By Jesus it was formulated thus: "As a man soweth, so shall he reap."

Suffering that comes under the second group of causes is due also to the Law of Consequences; but it refers to suffering in this life that results from thoughts and deeds of a former existence. This is known as the Law of Karma, which means the law of cause and effect extending from one incarnation to another. Suffering that comes under the third group has no connection with the Law of Consequences. In order to understand the Law of Consequences in its bearing on the first two groups of causes of suffering, one needs to know how the record of deeds is kept and how the law works. Every thought that man thinks, every act that he commits, is recorded in the "Book of Life." This book of life is nothing other than his own soul. The keeper of this book is the conscience. Conscience is the one that transcribes therein all that man thinks, desires, and does. Man's conscience is the judge, it is that which punishes us and rewards us. In one of its aspects, it may be called memory. However, our thoughts, desires, and acts do more than make a record: they build the soul, that part of us which is to attain individual immortality. The soul-atom, or this spark of Divinity, given to us for culture and development, is a part of God.

As a soul-atom, it is immortal when we receive it from God; but it is not yet individualized: the individuality of the soul is existent in the soul-atom only in a potential state. It requires arousing and nourishing and careful guarding in order to unfold its inherent potential qualities and to become self-existent, or individualized. When we think good thoughts, when our desires are good, and when we do good, this spark from the Divine is aroused to a certain extent. If other good thoughts, desires, and deeds follow, this tiny spark of Divinity, this Fire, is aroused still more. But, when evil thoughts, desires, or deeds are encouraged, to that extent is the fire deadened thereby. If the deeds of man are more good than evil, there is a slow, but steady, growth of the soul-atom. This is one manifestation of the working of the Law of Consequences.

If man's deeds are more evil than good, there is no growth at all: the soul-atom remains in an inert, unaroused, and non-individual condition, until death of the body; then this spark goes back to the storehouse of God, and man is dead unto destruction, or is denied individual immortality. Although the soul-atom may have been aroused to some extent and may have begun to grow and to expand, yet, if the man persists in wrong thinking and in wrong doing, the evil, being a disintegrating force, causes dissolution and diffusion of the soul-forces. This, again, is a manifestation of the operation of the Law of Consequences. Thus far, we have considered the Law of Consequences, abstractly and in a general way, in its action on the soul. We will now consider it more specifically in its working in daily life.

Doing evil is like giving a note to the bank: when the note is due, we must pay it; and, moreover, we must pay interest on the amount of it. When we wrong another, even though he is not aware of it, a record is made by the Divine Law and, in some way, we must make it right or suffer the consequences, that is, pay the debt. "As we do unto others, so will we be done by," is a law under which we receive exactly what we give, with interest in addition. For this reason, if, in any way, we cause suffering or misery to another, someone—not necessarily the same person—in some way, will cause us suffering and misery. There are many ways in which we may cause suffering to another: by holding grudges against him; by being jealous; by bitterness of thought toward him; or, even, by lack of responsiveness to his kindness—these are ways in which we may cause suffering to another by our attitude of mind. Then, there are manifold ways in which we may be unjust to another by our words: by saying unkind things; by spreading evil reports; by insinuations and by subtle suggestions of discredit. Again, we may injure another by the injustice of our deeds in business transactions and in the various other means that come in the category of wrong doing. Much of our suffering comes from the reactionary influence of just such things as these; for there are few of us who have not done much and said much to cause suffering to others. Especially did we before we understood the Law. Financial losses may be traced to this breaking of law.

In some way, at some time, we did not give full value for what we received; or, in doing some work for which we received pay, we did not render the full equivalent of service. This may have continued for a long time, all of which was placed against us by the divine law, and, through meeting a loss, we are simply paying that debt with the added interest. We are called on not to pay it to the person injured, but to the law of righteousness; and this same law will see that the one whom we wronged, is recompensed according to his deserts. As taught by Jesus and the other Masters, man is here for a purpose: to gain experience; to gain understanding so that he may know good from evil; in other words, to learn that he is a creator and that he may become conscious of being the Son of God. His duty here is to learn to know the Law, his duty is to fulfil the Law. To fulfil the Law means to do those things which God would have him do; that is, to live according to the Divine Law.

No man can become free from the earth plane unless he accepts the Christ. To accept the Christ means to live in obedience to the laws that will lead him to Illumination of Soul, or to Christhood. When he reaches this Illumination, or Christhood. he has become the Son of God. If he does evil acts, he must free himself from those acts, he must pay all debts. If he does not do this before he passes to the Beyond, he must return to the earth plane and live again the earth life, until such time as he will have freed himself from this evil Karma.

When man reaches Illumination, or Sonship, no longer will he commit acts that create evil Karma. After Illumination is established, all that he does, is with the thought and the desire of good to others; and, in this way, he frees himself from evil Karma. Thus, it is not necessary for him to return to the earth plane. Reincarnation, or suffering under the Law of Karma, is only for those who refuse to live according to the Divine Law. It is true that, at times, even those who have become Illuminated, and who are, therefore, the sons of God, do again return to earth; but it is because they "so love the world," as did the Christ, that they desire to return and to suffer in order to help humanity.

For suffering that comes to us under the third group of causes, in no way are we responsible. This suffering is brought about through the malice and the hatred of others. While the suffering is as great as if brought about by our own acts, it is to be regarded as an investment rather than as punishment, or as paying a debt. This can be clearly illustrated by the life of Jesus. Although He came to earth as a pure soul. He suffered as much as any other being. This was brought about not through His own acts, but through the hatred, through the malice, and through the acts of those whom He came to serve.

In His case, it was an investment rather than payment of a debt, because He accepted it with patience. Thus, it helped Him to greater soul growth, to greater power, to greater wisdom and to more sublime Illumination. When we are made to suffer undeservedly through the acts, thoughts, and desires of others, it will help us mightily, if we will accept it and suffer in patience. It is like accepting a note from one who desired to borrow money from us: we have the note; he has the cash; but, in time, he must pay the amount of the note to us together with interest. Those who make us suffer when we are not guilty, must pay the penalty. That which they pay, must come to us for the suffering undergone. However, our suffering is changed, or transmuted, into knowledge and wisdom, which lead to higher and more sublime Illumination. Yet we must remember that there is no reward for suffering when we accept it with impatience or with a curse.

Take Jesus as an example: no matter what He had to suffer, He always bore it with patience, without a word of complaint, as though He was meeting something that was His due; and, for every agony through which He went, He received greater power to do good, and greater strength to undergo. It is not for us to know whether a given suffering is due to our own misdeeds in this life or in another or whether it is something for which in no way we are responsible; but it is for us to know that it is wise to accept it in harmony with the law of love. We see from the life of Jesus that no one is exempt from suffering so long as he is on the earth plane.

The Master oftentimes suffers as much as does the most unenlightened of God's children. Probably He suffers more than the un-enlightened, because His sensibilities are more refined and more tender. The earth plane is a training school. If we refuse to learn our lesson during school hours, we must remain after school.

To sum up the three classes of suffering that we have considered: suffering for things which we did in a past in carnation and for which we are here to make payment, with the knowledge that we can pay them all and that, if we live according to the Law, we can arouse the Divine Spark to Illumination and therefore to Immortality; suffering for thoughts, desires, and acts of the present life, also with knowledge that will lead us to Sonship with the Father; suffering for thoughts, desires, and acts of others, for which in no way we are responsible and through which, if we accept them and bear them with patience, we will receive strength and power and greater Illumination of Soul.

SOUL SCIENCE

As the name, Soul Science, indicates, the teaching is, primarily, the science of soul illumination: it unfolds and interprets the laws and the principles underlying the growth, the culture, and the training of soul powers. Every science implies its corresponding art. These instructions, when applied, become the finest of fine arts—the art of the interpretation of truth; the art of the application of truth to human needs; the art of cultivating and of encouraging the most delicate graces of heart, the most subtle uses of thought power, the most refined touches and imaging of consciousness; the art of "righteous judgment"; the art of putting a kind interpretation on the deeds of others; in short, the art of the Christ-life. They become an art that constantly lures one on to perfection—a perfection, however, that as constantly evades and escapes one's grasp; yet, with every escape, it lures the more enticingly.

The science and the art of illumination must go hand in hand: the one giving a clear understanding of the laws of truth, the other making practical application of these laws to life's needs. The title, Soul Science and Success, emphasizes the principle that soul culture leads to success. It is based on the conviction that success is secured through the intelligent direction of well-trained thought powers. True success is a practical application of the law: "Seek ye first the kingdom of God and his righteousness, and all these things will be added unto you." In this, it is to be understood that the kingdom of God means the establishment of love, truth, and justice in the thought-kingdom of man's consciousness. In proportion as these divine qualities have become the actuating principle of a man's thought-life, in that proportion has he reached the vibrations of true success. Acceptable, worthy service attracts its corresponding reward. The inculcation, in a person's nature, of the qualities of love, truth, and justice, and the intelligent direction of well-trained thought powers, will increase his efficiency in whatever profession he may serve; thus, through the study and the practice of Illuminati principles, an ever-increasing success is assured him.

Again, the designation, Soul Science and Immortality, is given to this system of instructions. The significance of this name is due to the fact that soul is the only immortal part of man's nature, and that illumination of soul leads to immortality. At the transition period known as death, the body returns to the great storehouse of elements whence it came; the spirit, or life-principle, returns to the universal storehouse of spirit, or universal life, whence it came; the mind does not continue as an individual entity; whereas the soul is that part of man's being which continues to exist. Its existence may be of various stages: as it may exist in a chaotic state, little more than a crude mingling of good and evil; or, it may be in the primitive stages of a nucleus, in which the good is beginning to take more or less definite shape and to act as a transmuting influence over the evil; or, it may have reached an advanced stage of purification such that it is a well-formed center of light, pure and radiant.

Thus, the light that lighteth all the world has become individualized and self-existent. When the soul has become a nucleus of light it has become an immortal entity. This is the true illumination; this is immortality of soul. From this, it is seen that immortality of soul is not something thrust upon mankind, whether he will or no, that it is not an inevitable fate which man is destined to meet, regardless of his own choice; but rather is it true that immortality of soul is something to be attained, something in the attainment of which man may have conscious part and free choice.

The stage of development known as immortality is a goal aimed at by Illuminati instructions. Soul Science claims to be a philosophy, a science, and a religion. As a religion, it is free from iron-clad dogmas and fettering creeds; it aims at unity and true brotherhood; it encourages freedom of individual conscience and freedom of investigation.

It bases its claim as a religion on these facts: that it interprets God and truth to human nature; that it speaks to the needs of the human heart; that it dispenses a reasonable comfort for the ills and the vicissitudes of human experience, by interpreting them in the light of Reason, Love, and Justice; that, by bringing God into the consciousness, it satisfies the nameless and indescribable longings of the human soul; that it is built on the foundation-rock of prayer—prayer the answer to which is determined not by favoritism, but by an intelligent appropriation of the divine law of supply and demand.

It bases its claim as a science on the fact that it is built on the orderly arrangement of fundamental knowledge; concerning the laws of cause and effect in human experience; knowledge concerning the creative power of thought; knowledge concerning the laws of attainment, the conditions of accomplishment, the methods of realization and fulfilment; knowledge concerning the principles that underlie the transmutation of undesirable thought-environment into desirable; knowledge that seeks practical application, not only explaining the existing conditions of life but also indicating the laws that make possible the improvement of such conditions. As a philosophy, it endeavors to trace first principles in the realms of mind and soul, and to lift the veil that hides from the untrained eye the vital connection between a given effect and its necessitating cause.

It clears one's vision regarding what is worth striving after in life. It gives satisfaction in regard to what is the ultimate end and aim of existence. Not to comprehend all knowledge is the criterion of a philosopher; but to love wisdom and to seek wisdom in regard to the vital interests of human experience. Such wisdom constitutes a practical philosophy. When the individual has established in his understanding a reasonably satisfactory philosophy of life, he is free to give all his energy in service to others; for his energies are not distracted and scattered by doubts, fears, and annoyances; his interests and his attention are not divided between this, that, and the other; his strength and vital forces are not depleted by unnecessary vexation of spirit. A philosophy that satisfies, gives to him that holds it peace and poise of mind; thereby he is enabled to give undivided attention to service for others. To sum up: Soul Science instruction is a philosophy in that it yields a satisfying conviction in regard to what constitutes the summum bonum—"the highest good" of existence; a science in that it satisfies the just and inexorable demands of reason; a religion in that it satisfies the hunger of the human heart for solace and for comfort.

In order to understand fundamental principles, it is necessary to explain the meaning of certain terms, and to indicate clearly the content of certain expressions as they are generally used in Illuminati literature. In current writings on religious, psychologic, and philosophic subjects, there is more or less confusion in the use of certain words, such as mind, soul, and spirit. Again, there is a dearth of expressions and a need of coining words to express necessary ideas. There is no adjective or noun to denote the attributes of the individualized soul, corresponding to the words spiritual and spirituality; while the words, spiritual and spirituality, are confusing; for, by their derivation, they ought to signify one thing, whereas, in common usage, they are employed to signify something else, far removed from their derivative significance. It has been suggested to use the words, soulual and souluality, to designate the attributes of the illumined soul.

The words, mind, soul, and spirit, are often used loosely; sometimes even interchangeably. General usage has established for each one many different shades of meaning. This affords variety and wealth of expression; but, by this freedom of usage, one who is striving to form a satisfactory correlation of ideas is led to confusion of thought and to in accuracy of concept. A fine and careful distinction between these words has never become universally established. Different writers and different schools of thought place their own interpretation on these terms.

A good way to determine a writer's concept of words is to read all available literature from his pen, and to note by the context their significance; thus, in time, one reaches a satisfactory comprehension of their content as used by that particular writer; also, one gains a sensitive grasp of their significance—a grasp that transcends the niceties of definition. However, it is possible to formulate some important distinctions in regard to this class of words as used in Soul Science literature. The word, spirit, as herein employed, refers to the breath of life, or to life itself, or to the life-principle. It is common to man, animals, and all animate things. It is a generic term, rather than a specific, or individual; and, as such, it emphasizes the fact that the spirit of man, at the transition state called death, returns to the universal storehouse of spirit, or life, and does not continue its existence as an individuality.

Thus, the spirit of man is mortal—mortal in the sense that it is not eternal as an individualization. To be sure, it is eternal in the sense that its particled elements return to the great universal garner of vital essences ready to be used in other manifestations; it is eternal in the sense that, although all is subject to change and renewal of form, according to the divine economy, nothing really perishes, nothing is lost. The distinction between mind and soul can best be made by pointing out their relation to each other.

To understand this relationship at the beginning of one's study is exceedingly important; for it is fundamental not only in grasping ideas, but particularly in learning to apply these ideas to practical methods of growth. These distinctions are not to be thought of as hard and fast definitions of terms, but rather as various ways of making clear the essential content of terms as used by this school of thought. The purpose is not to define the nomenclature of a science for the mere sake of doing so or for the sake of satisfying a cold, exacting, scientific type of mind, but to make clear to the earnest, sincere seeker the content of essential terms, that one may be able to apply the teachings to one's own personal needs.

The first distinction to be made is that mind is mortal, while soul is immortal. Mind is mortal in the sense that it is not eternal as an individualization. Mind is not an entity; it is a fusion of bodily and spiritual elements. It is the connecting link between body and spirit. It is not wholly of the body, nor is it wholly of the spirit. It is the link between them, the silver cord that binds the two together and makes manifestation possible. Again, mind is the creative principle of man's nature, while soul is the receptive principle.

Man uses mind as a creating implement, or a creating agency. Through the power of mind, man becomes a creator. He stands alone in this. The animal is a creator in regard to its own species, but in no other sense. Man is a creator not only in respect to his own species but in respect to other things as well. He creates character; he creates thought-environment; in large measure, he has created the conditions by which his life is surrounded. In large measure, he has the ability to change conditions, the ability to improve them if he will. This ability to alter, to transform, to improve, is one aspect of his creative tendencies.

The soul, being the receptive principle of man's nature, is the storehouse, or the receptacle, or the resultant, of that which his mind creates. When man realizes that the soul is the result of his own creation, and that it partakes of the nature of his own creative thoughts, he will learn to be careful in regard to what thoughts and moods he allows in his life. More than this, he will see that it is necessary to put forth conscious effort and to give himself effective training, in order that the creations of his mind may be pure, holy, and worthy. In time, he will come to be actuated by one desire, namely: the desire to create no thought-image and to mold no thought-form except that which is in harmony with the love, truth, and justice of the Christ-ideal. Another way of expressing the relation between mind and soul is to regard mind as the realm of causation; while soul is the result of causation, or the accumulation of that which mind has caused. Man's thought-kingdom is his cause world. His thoughts have power to produce changes, to bring about results, to affect conditions, to create environment. The Wise Man voiced this law when he said: "A merry heart doeth good like a medicine." Each one knows in his own experience how true it is that one accomplishes more when one's mind—one's cause-world—is tempered by the atmosphere of peace, poise, and composure. When man realizes that the soul is the result of his own causation and that its character corresponds to the type of influences he allows in his own thought-kingdom, he will become active and earnest in securing masterful control in this realm of causes.

To be able to take his place on the throne of the cause-world and to issue and to establish such decrees as are in harmony with the love, truth, and justice of the Christ-character—to be able to do this, will become his highest ambition. To this end he will put forth every effort; he will give to his will-power a rigorous course of training; to his desire-nature he will apply all plausible means of cleansing and of refining; his understanding he will subject to patient instruction in the principles of love, truth, and justice. Sacred literature is replete with figures which illustrate from different points of view, the creative, or active, principle of mind, and the receptive, or passive, principle of soul.

A favorite figure among all nations represents mind as the builder, or the architect, and soul as the Temple of character built by the power of mind. In this building process, mind takes the initiative; mind executes choices, selects material, rejects material, according to its own judgment; mind makes decisions and exercises will-power. The builder may pass away, or return whence it came; but the temple stands as a living testimony to the desires, the choices, the decisions, the imaginations, the thoughts that the architect permitted to enter as building-material into his structure. When man realizes that the soul is the result of his own building, that the edifice of character is the result of the mind's selecting, rejecting, and executing, he will spare no pains in giving himself such training as a Master Architect needs.

The refiner's fire, the fuller's soap, the potter's hand, the pruner's knife, the salter's salt, the alchemist's crucible,—all are figurative expressions of sacred record which illustrate some aspect of the cleansing, purifying, training, molding, and shaping of the soul. While, in this figurative language, the initiative principle may seem to be represented as a power exterior to the individual, yet, in reality, it is a vivid portrayal of the mind's active measures in cleansing, refining, shaping, directing, or training the soul.

The processes hereby indicated, symbolize the law of transmutation. To understand this law, to be able to apply it to life's needs, is an achievement worthy of much effort to attain. Transmutation of the grosser elements of one's nature into the pure gold of love, truth, and justice is the ideal placed before the student. Methods for accomplishing this end are taught in the advanced courses of training. Again, in religious annals, the soul is compared to a matchless treasure, a precious gem or a pearl of "greatest price." In this case, the mind, the conscious self, is the finder, or the seeker. These narratives are consistent in emphasizing the initiative, active nature of the finder, and the priceless, immortal value of that which is found. Such an idea as this is the basis of the oft-recurring injunction in Soul Science literature: "Find the Soul."

Once more, in mythic literature, the soul is pictured as a "sleeping beauty" that must be awakened. The sleep of the soul, however, is the sleep of latency, the sleep of potentiality, awaiting the dawn of dynamic existence. The awakening of this sleeping beauty is not a specific act, but a process—a process so long in its duration, so tedious in its steps, that many, even some who are near the morning's dawn, are unconscious of being in the stage of awakening. When the soul is referred to as a germ, or a seed, of the divine, it is spoken of as unfolding, or as being in the process of unfoldment.

This, again, is the growth, or the unfoldment, of latency and of potentiality into a state of dynamic, vital expression. After a person has reached a certain stage of unfoldment, he is responsible for making such conditions that this precious Christ-germ may properly develop. Last to be mentioned in the list of expressions indicating the relation between mind and soul, as found in religious literature, is reference to soul as a light, and to mind as the beeper of the light. In its incipient stages, the soul is a mere speck of fire and may be smothering in the ashes of a selfish personality. In this state, it needs the attention of an awakened understanding to fan and to feed it into a flame. The mind may consciously exert its activities in taking care that this flame is kept constantly fanned and fed and burning on the altar of the heart.

Thus, the mind, the self, is the Vestal Virgin, who makes it her duty to see that the temple's fire never goes out nor burns low. When this spark has become a well-formed center of pure, white light; when it has become a dynamic nucleus of fire—the Fire of Love, the Light of Truth—then the soul has reached the state called Illumination. This is the Light Within; this is the Inner Light that lighteth all the world of man's consciousness; this is the Awakened Soul; this is the Christ; this is the pearl of greatest price. When the individual has seen this light and has found its center and has become cognizant of its warming rays of love and its illuminating light of understanding, he has attained in mortality of Soul, or Soul Consciousness, or the Christ consciousness. That the light which lighteth all the world may become the Individualized Center of Light, the Immortal Soul, the Christ, of one's consciousness; that the spark of divinity may become a perfect pyramidal flame, warming the desire of nature with love and "good-will to men" and illuminating the understanding with truth—this is the aim of Soul Science instructions and systems of training.

But, lest the reader gathers from this an erroneous impression, let this thought be made clear, and receive due emphasis: Illumination of soul does not mean perfection; it is not the climax of growth; it is not the final goal of achievement; nor is it the ultimate of attainment, nor the finale of ambition, nor a pretext for cessation of effort. Rather is it the vision of what constitutes perfection: namely, an ideal that constantly recedes and enlarges, and an attainment that constantly approaches, but never transcends, its limit, and that never wearies of hastening its step toward the ever receding and ever enlarging ideal. Rather is it the beginning of growth on a higher scale of consciousness; it is the Christ in the manger, the infant, by no means competent to walk the shores of Galilee as a Master of the law nor to teach by Samaria's fount. It is an illumination that makes clear to the individual what things in life are worthy of attainment and what things are worth striving after. It directs his ambition into carefully selected channels, and condenses his desires into a distinct, well-formed purpose, and concentrates his knowledge into one satisfying conviction.

When the field for one's ambition has been conscientiously chosen; when one's desires have ceased their wanderings and have forsaken their tendency to diffusion; when one's knowledge has become systematized in harmony with the teachings of Jesus and other great Masters—one has found peace, poise, and composure of mind; and, by this attitude of mind, one is set free to do the work one is called to do. By the various statements thus far made concerning the relation of mind and soul to each other, the intention has been, to make the distinctions of practical benefit, and to convince the reader of the importance of taking active, conscious part in making such conditions in his thought world that illumination of soul may result. To be sure, it is possible for illumination to take place and the individual to be largely unconscious of it. In fact, from one point of view, it is true that unconscious, spontaneous growth is the most desirable. Yet, as one claims that it is well for the housewife to have knowledge of hygiene, sanitation, and dietetics, in order that she may provide for her household in harmony with the laws of health, so one legitimately reasons that it is well to understand the principles of soul illumination in order that this illumination may be promoted and made more orderly. As previously stated, these teachings pertain to the complete man, body, mind, and soul. The three lines of physical, mental, and soulual culture should be carried on simultaneously; yet, in the Illuminati instructions, particular attention is given to control of thought, or training of mind.

On the mental plane, culture falls in three departments, which are so vitally connected, however, that they cannot be separated, namely: purifying the desires and the motives; directing the understanding into channels of true interpretation; and training the will to act in harmony with the purified desires and the clarified understanding. The writer of this article makes no greater claim for it than that of giving the reader a "glimpse" into the purpose and the teachings of the Temple of the Illuminati. It is hoped that this glimpse will prove satisfying, and will be convincing in its effect. This article serves as an introduction merely, to the exhaustless field of interpretation that the Fraternity recognizes as its rightful heritage.

REFLECTIONS

WHO am I? What am I? From whence came I? Whither am I bound? What is it that calling me to feel, to move to sense and to actually experience the recognition of "I" as myself-the faculty of seeing myself in all things and feeling that all things are in me? Why and how do I know that down deep in my soul I have that something to which all must turn for recognition and upon which the Cosmos depends for its very existence? In moments of quiescence, abstraction, relaxation, flashes of harmonious relationship with the infinite-what is it that causes me to result in the fact that everything that moves and acts serves me in so doing; that everything done is done for me; that all that is exists in and through me? How do I know that I am here? That the place in which I now am is that from which I came and, furthermore, is that to which I am bound? These questions and many more do I ask of me and in all probability have asked since Eternity and ever have found the answer awaiting me in the Infinite Knowingness of Self, in the depth of Infinite Mind, which is Myself. This being so, and I know that it is so-who is it that asks since the Infinite Knowledge is I?

Simply that so-called relative self-seeking enlightenment and I turn to that self-gladly giving the necessary answers that the sense of duality may be erased and the relative or finite seeming may be completely absorbed in the Infinite Reality. Who am I? I am that I am. All things exist in me... All that I know, sense, feel, recognize and encompass in my mind are pans of me and exist because I admit and consent that it be so-hence I am the pivotal point or center of the universe.

Of this I am positive as I only know from or in my power of knowing or to use the vernacular, I only know from where I sit. I have heard it said that there are other personalities in existence, and this must be so because I turn to myself for evidence of that fact and find that they exist in me. I see, feel, hear and communicate with them and invariably they react to me as larder, constructively or destructively. They are parts of me. Is it not absurdly foolish of me to treat any part of myself in such a manner that I bring about a destructive result? The opposite, then is constructive; evidence of the fact that I am and also that the Infinite Intelligence and I are one. Were it possible that I, the real self, that which I know to be I, could be destroyed-chaos reign in my stead; then everything that exists in me is ended with me. The Universe would instantly become a blank-nothing instead of something-chaos not Cosmos-because all existed in me.

But Cosmos still remains even though I pass from the ken of finite or relative sense. Man still is. Personalities and individuals still go on and on. So called Matter remains, therefore I cannot be destroyed, for as all others existed in me, I also existed in them and am still co-existent with Now which is the complete definition of Eternity. From whence do I come? I come from where I now am. Whither am I bound? I am heading directly for the Whence from which I came, THE ETERNAL NOW.

THE RELATION OF THE INDIVIDUAL TO THE UNIVERSAL MIND

OH' that I might find Him, is the age-old cry that has gone up from the heart of man. This irresistible urge which is ever welling forth is nothing more nor less than Divine Mind within man himself. The fundamental concepts of Truth are best proved by the fact that civilized races of all ages have recognized and applied their conception of Deity meager, though the application may have been. It is a common experience that man often feels within himself an intelligence which is not the result of education and indeed is scarcely explainable except when considered as an intuition, a talent or a faint perception of Truth which is nevertheless something upon which he can and often does rely.

It would seem that the greatest problem of life is the attainment of some tangible, definite understanding of God or First Cause. If this can be done surely something of the Law of God can be fathomed. Once this Law is understood even in a small degree, its application becomes possible. Our criterion as to the correctness of our knowledge is indicated by Jesus' own words "by their fruits shall ye know them."

The crux of all metaphysical teaching lies in the understanding of the unity of man with the three-fold nature of Mind, or God, viz., Father, Son and Holy Ghost-spirit, soul and body-Objective Mind. Subjective Mind, and the Objectification-the Thing, the Way It Works, and the Result-all of which are in reality synonymous terms.

The Objective, or Conscious, Mind has always been known as masculine in its nature, hence the term God the Father. It is that quality of Mind which projects its thought or will. It might be said that its distinctive quality in thought. It is also termed the Absolute and reasons deductively only.

The Subconscious Mind has always been recognized as a feminine quality, receiving the thought and is the Doer or Law of God. It also reasons deductively and has power only to perform that which is suggested or commanded. This results ultimately in the third aspect of Mind which is the Objectification of the Word.

One must realize that while there is in reality but one Mind, there is another aspect of this Universal Mind, which is our own point of contact with this Mind. This is the particularization of Mind itself through man. In other words, "man comes to a point in the Universal Mind, and is the Idea of God as man." A realization of this fact will eliminate much confusion in the further contemplation of the qualities of Mind which constitute themselves into a certain definite Law by which a workable premise may be obtained.

Man, therefore, at his point of contact with the Divine, makes use of this knowledge of the Objective and Subjective Mind. This conscious mind of man reasons both inductively and deductively. This he must do at his present state of evolution or development. While now he must use his power of inductive reasoning (a finite quality which serves as a crutch, as it were) one can conceive that at some future time he will find this unnecessary and by deductive powers the ultimate shall have been attained.

The subconscious mind is, first of all entirely dependent upon the conscious mind for all its information and education except those certain fixed laws which govern all. Furthermore, it is at all times amenable to the power of suggestion by the conscious mind. It takes cognizance of its environment by means entirely independent of the physical senses or evidence and therefore perceives by intuition. It is the scat of memory and is the mind's great storehouse of all its experiences. It is thus logical to assume that man is the result of the sum total of his subconscious experience.

The operation of the subconscious mind is the Law of God, and if we can come to a realization of the fact that this Law is Infinite, we shall become cognizant of a basis for the application of this Law and we shall see in it a solution of all of life's problems. While man appears to be infinite, his experience is an everlasting evolution and as his understanding increases, his use of the Law will enhance in direct ratio.

Since there is but one Subjective or Subconscious Mind in the universe, and since this Mind is receptive, plastic, neutral, impersonal, and creative, we can get any result we desire by the impression upon It of any thought or realization, for this Mind is the Actor or Doer. The proper use of this Law constitutes a mental treatment and since this Law is absolutely impersonal, it damns as well as heals. It may be as destructive as it is constructive. Since this Mind is universal, it is obvious that absent treatment is as efficacious as present treatment, and in some respects far more potent.

The conscious mind speaks the word...... it is in fact the thing involved-and its evolution is absolutely inevitable, for the Law: is absolute and nothing can hinder or oppose its action.

To bring our contemplation to a practical conclusion, one might say that the application of whatever knowledge we possess of the Objective (or Conscious) and Subjective Mind is best consummated in a mental treatment, either of oneself or of others. The process in either case is identical, since after all it is nothing more or less than a process of self-realization of the Truth about the case involved. A good treatment consists, first, of a realization of the fact of being, which is our unity with the Universal Mind which surrounds us and of which we are an inseparable part, "in which we live and move and have our being."

Secondly, as a result of this realization of omnipotence, the word, the thing or condition desired is fearlessly spoken with conviction and the final consummation or objectification is as certain and natural as is the action of any law of nature. With the result or process, we have nothing whatever to do, since God Himself knows nothing of time or process. When we fully grasp the meaning of these facts, argumentative work in healing will no longer be necessary, for we shall but speak the word and the day of instantaneous healing shall have dawned.

SEED THOUGHTS

"By Mysticism we mean, not the extravagance of an erring fancy, but the concentration of reason in feeling, the enthusiastic love of the Good, the True, the One, the sense of the infinity of knowledge and of the marvel of the human faculties. When feeding upon such thoughts, the 'wing of the soul' is renewed and gains strength; she is raised above 'the manikins of earth' and their opinions, waiting in wonder to know, and working with reverence to find out what God in this or another life may reveal to her."

"Even if we were to suppose no more men of genius to be produced, the great writers of ancient or of modem times will remain to furnish abundant materials of education to the coming generation. Now that every nation holds communication with each other, we may truly say in a fuller sense than formerly that 'the thoughts of men are widened with the process of the suns.' They will not be 'cribbed, cabined, and confined' within a province or an island. The East will provide elements of culture to the West as well as the West to the East. The religions and literatures of the world will be open books, which he who wills may read .... In the coming age we shall carry with us the recollection of the past, in which are necessarily contained many seeds of revival and renaissance in the future."

"Good intentions, and even benevolent actions, when they are not prompted by wisdom, are of no value. We believe something to be for our good, which we afterwards find out not to be for our good. The consequences may be inevitable, for they follow an invariable law, yet they may often be the very opposite of what is expected by us . . . All actions of which the consequences are not weighed and foreseen are of this impotent and paralytic sort, and the author of them has 'the least possible power' while seeming to have the greatest. For he is actually bringing about the reverse of what he intended."

"We cannot, with implicit confidence, leap to the conclusion that every instance of so-called mystical experience furnishes us with a sure clue to the God whom our eager souls seek. To the mystic himself, the experience is evidence enough. It lights his lamp and girds his loins for action; it floods him with new power; it banishes doubt and despair as the sunrise banishes darkness. He no more wants arguments now to prove God's existence than the artist wants arguments to prove the reality of beauty, or the lover does to prove the worth of love. But it is useless to claim that mystical experiences have such ontological bearing that they will settle for everybody else the reality of God."

"There have been religious geniuses in all ages and in all countries, who have had experiences of spiritual expansion. They have been made aware of a Realm of Reality on a higher level than that revealed through the senses. They have sometimes felt invaded by the inrush of a larger Life; sometimes they have seemed to push a door inward into a larger range of being, with vastly heightened energy. The experience is always one of joy and rapture; in fact, it is probably the highest joy a mortal ever feels. But the significant fact is not the sense of expansion, or of freedom, or of joy. It is that such experiences minister to life, and conduce to the increased power of the race—energy to live by actually does come to them from somewhere. The universe backs the experience."

"Those who are finely sensitive to wider spheres of Reality impinging on their inner realm, and who correspond and cooperate with that More which seems continuous and conterminous with their lives, gain not only in capacity to correspond and cooperate, but also in power to overcome difficulties, and to put their lives into constructive service."

ONE OF THE NINE INESTIMABLES

"The last two generations have seen a marked revival of interest in the speculative thought of later antiquity. As a consequence, the opinion of the learned world on the historical development and significance of Neoplatonism has undergone drastic revision" thus writes Professor E. R. Dodds, of University College.

"The Soul is bound to the body in so far as she is directed towards the feelings which proceed from the body. She is loosed therefrom in so far as she is impassible to corporeal promptings. What Nature has bound, Nature loses. What the Soul has bound, the Soul loses. It was Nature that bound body in Soul; but the Soul bound herself in body. Accordingly, it is Nature that loses body from Soul; but Soul is loosed from body by Soul herself. There are thus two kinds of death; that known to all, when the body is loosed from the Soul: that known to philosophers, when the Soul is loosed from the body. And the one death does not always accompany the other."

Or, again, these extracts on Piety, from "Porphyry's Ad Marcellam," a little manual of devotion composed for the use of his wife:—Of all thy doings and of thine every deed and word, let God be the present witness and examiner. Whatsoever good thing we do, we must esteem God to be its author: but of evil things, "the guilt lies with ourselves who made the choice, and God is guiltless" (Plato). Wherefore we must pray to God for such things only as are worthy of Him: and ask those gifts which we can receive from none but Him.

What comes not without toil and virtue, we must pray to attain it after toil: the prayer of the indolent is but vain speech. "That which, when gotten, thou shalt not keep, ask not of God; for all that is of God's gift is inalienable, and what thou mayest not keep He will not give." (A Pythagorean proverb.)

What thou shalt no more need when thou art quit of the body, that contemn: what shall be needful to thee hereafter, toward that direct thy discipline, and bid God be thy helper.

Chose things, then, which Fortune gives and often times again retracts, thou wilt not ask for. Neither wilt thou make petition for anything before the fit season, but only when God makes plain to thee the right desire implanted in thee by Nature. God prizes not the words of the wise man, but his deeds. The wise adore God even when their lips are silent. Man by his proper doing wins God's acceptance, and through assimilation of his own nature to the Blessedness which is beyond corruption, he makes himself divine. I would have thee entertain no supposition concerning God that is unworthy of His blessed and incorruptible state. It is the chiefest fruit of piety to honor God according to the custom of the country, yet not dreaming that His perfection needs anything from thee, but only because by His most awful and blessed sanctity He challenges thy worship.

THE SPIRITUAL WORLD

WE have said many times that the spirit world is the realm of fulfillment. If we have not said this in so many words, we have certainly implied it in the statements which have been made concerning the world beyond the grave. There is no question as to the final at-one-ment of the human soul with the Great Eternal, and, in order that this condition of unity shall be produced, it becomes absolutely necessary that some of those things which have their inception in material life shall be consummated in the world of spirit.

One of the strange anomalies is to be found in the fact that so many people who are so earnestly enthusiastic in declaring their allegiance to an All-wise Providence are so terrified over the possibility of being called to face results in the spiritual world. It would naturally seem that those who have a superabundance of faith, those who have so large a measure of allegiance to the power that men call God, would be the very last to either fear or find fault with that which lies beyond the borderline of material death. It does seem that most of the people who declare themselves to be followers of the meek and lowly Sage of Galilee have somehow a perverted idea concerning the spiritual world, else they would not be as bitterly disappointed when they find themselves on the verge of transition, nor would they find their souls so full of anguish over the thought of passing from the material world into the home which had been prepared for them. Perchance one of the reasons these people have so little faith is to be found in this additional fact, that they have based all of their premises upon supposition, that they have based all of their argument upon belief rather than knowledge, that their whole tendency has been toward an inverted vision, that mental consciousness which dwells upon the things that were rather than upon those things that are plus those things that shall be. Never a man, no matter how wise the man may be, has allowed himself to dwell entirely upon the past, entertaining the view that all good was in the past, but that man has soon or late found himself enveloped by a doubt so profound and so all-consuming that he has lost the rarest beauties out of life.

The pictures which have been painted of the spiritual world have been disconcerting, to say the least. They have given mankind only two kinds of pictures—one which told or described, told of or described a place where every possible and conceivable joy was to be experienced by those who had subscribed to certain formulae which were current in the land, the denomination or the location in which they dwelt—the other told the story of an eternity of punishment bestowed upon man not because the man was necessarily either immoral or bad in any sense whatsoever, but more especially because the man had failed to subscribe to someone of the required dogmas of the various creedalistic organizations. The picture has not been one to inspire good men to be better. We are saying this because very rarely do those who tell the story of that superlative happiness which men are to receive, very rarely, we say, do those who tell that story emphasize the value, the importance and the absolute necessity of character. Invariably, the thing that they emphasize is belief, the tacit allegiance to certain of the formulae adopted by mankind. It is not strange that you are sending into the spirit world so many who are spiritually decrepit, who have reached a spiritual senility. It is the thing that was to be expected as the logical sequence of the fact that heaven was declared to be so easily attained and that the place of eternal torment was to be the sole compensation of character. We are not saying too much when we state it thus because every one of you who have had experience with certain types of theologues have this knowledge that the thing that was emphasized was not character, was not the high standard of living but, rather, the open declaration that one had accepted the particular religio-philosophical system which was prevalent by or through the acceptance of one or the other of its branches. When the man or woman who stands as the mouthpiece of those masters who have gone into the beyond, when the man or woman who stands as the exponent of the idealistic teachings of the Man of Galilee, attain the wisdom which will inspire them to emphasize the importance of integrity of character in every branch of its activity, then, and not until then, will you send into the spirit world men and women who are not spiritual weaklings, and then, and not until then, shall those recruits from your plane of life find it no longer necessary that they endure some of the conditions of which we have made mention in previous lessons.

We have said to you that all mankind finds itself on its entrance into the spirit world in the precise condition earned by the life that was led on the material plane. We have told you that they must make restitution for all of the mistakes they have made, that is, that they must outgrow the ignorance which has given rise to those mistakes. Tonight, we want to emphasize the fact that those who come into the spirit world with a large spiritual endowment find themselves most happily situated because they do not find the arduous tasks ahead of them, nor do they encounter the bitter remorse, nor yet are they under the necessity of paying so large a debt of restitution to their fellowmen. Therefore, they are most happily situated because these are the ones for whom a condition of the most delightful spiritual enfranchisement has been prepared, that is, these are the ones who find that vast opportunities open unto them immediately upon their entrance into the spirit world.

If we were to be asked, what particular word we should seek to emphasize more than any other as depicting the state of soul and mind of those who were to reach the finer things immediately upon their entrance to the spirit world, we should select the word "character," and then we would supplement that by declaring that spiritual integrity is the open sesame to every great joy and privilege to be found in the spirit world. There is no illumination save that of the mind. There is no emancipation save that of the mind. When the mind is burdened by the consciousness of a debt which it owes to the eternal laws, it suffers, it is not free any more than is the man or woman who is hopelessly involved in indebtedness on the material plane. So, we say that the spiritual integrity of those who enter the spirit world is the key which unlocks the door to every joy and every opportunity, to every happiness in the world of spirit.

This naturally suggests the necessity of every representative of a religious system emphasizing the importance of character, the importance of that spiritual integrity, because, mark you, if that spiritual integrity has not been woven in the very web of character before the individual enters the spirit world, there is a long task ahead, there is labor ahead, there is arduous schooling to be faced, there are very subtle laws to be reconciled and conformed to, there are very startling experiences to be encountered in order that the soul shall be properly awakened. But those people who come with a large spiritual endowment, those who have been spiritually equipped by virtue of their aspirations, their kindly acts, their gentle words, these are indeed fortunate in having prepared for themselves a reception which means an inspiration, and which provides a source of joy which beggars description, and it is this work that you are responsible for in a measure. Your allegiance to this institution, this class, means virtually a tacit, if not a conscious objective agreement between yourselves and us that you will emphasize the constructive side of life rather than the negative and destructive. The very verbiage of your pledge puts you on record every time you repeat it as having agreed to see the beauty and emphasize the nobility and aspire to the truth of life, and it matters not that you, perhaps, some of you, do not actually articulate the words—the thought runs through your mind. The very fact that you are here is evidence that you have subscribed to the sentiment expressed in that formula. So it means that you are evangels for this message which we are giving to humanity, that ye are evangels not only for the expression of the message by word of mouth, but that you are struggling to reach the point at which, by force of example, by dint of precept, you are giving to the world the concrete aspect of the message we desire them to have, the message we desire mankind to have, we should say. And by so doing this, do you realize that you are paving the way for an entirely different concept of life as it is here and life as it is beyond the sunset slope of material experience?

There are many souls who have been ushered into the world of spirit happier and richer, more fully spiritually endowed, because someone situated as you are situated has spoken the word which gave them hope and brought them into light. Mark you this, that when we say—"have given them hope and brought them into light—we do not have in mind the mere hope of blind belief, but rather that sturdy, vigorous, virile hope which comes as the result of wide-eyed and absolutely untrammeled knowledge of the law which obtains in the material and spiritual life. You are each and every one of you on the threshold of the world of spirit—and this by no means is calculated to suggest that any of you are near to the hour of passing out of the body—but by virtue of your consciousness of these fundamental truths, you dwell on the threshold, you are in that position wherefrom you may push the door either way—you may receive it as it is opened toward you in order to make the access of those who shall come into your presence more easy of attainment, or thrust it the other way in order that those who are traveling forward may find fewer impediments in the way of their progress.

You are the possessor, as it were, of a spiritual Jacob's Ladder which, in the last analysis, means the spiritual development which renders possible intercourse with that spiritual world of such a character as to clarify the relationship between the material and the spiritual. Out there in that spiritual world there are master souls watching, watching the advent of those who graduate from material experience. They scrutinize every person who comes, just as they analyze them before they enter, even before they depart from the material life, and this scrutiny is for the specific purpose of ascertaining whether it is possible for them to reach down and lend a hand and say unto those who enter: "Come higher because thou art ready," or whether it becomes necessary for them to meet these individuals more than halfway and lend assistance in the arousing of their mentality so that they may be inspired to continue making an effort to unfold.

They are not idle, those who have gone far in spiritual development, and just here let us correct an error which has been expressed many times by those who do not understand the law, that is that error expressed by those who have said that the exalted souls, the master souls, the Christlike souls cannot enter the earth's atmosphere. No greater mistake has ever been uttered. You will discover as you make progress that you can always traverse the trail that you have traveled before. There is no restriction which prevents any soul retracing his steps if that return is for a specific and benevolent purpose. The restrictions in the spirit world are such as to prevent souls traveling beyond a certain number of degrees from the condition in which they are before they have grown up to those higher altitudes. Men who have never been in the heights, who have never gone to the mountains, find the first traveling arduous and they are restricted by virtue of the altitude to which they must become gradually accustomed if they would not suffer dire results. Trace the analogy for yourselves. Souls who have gone into the spirit world find heights beyond which, and sometimes upon which, they are not permitted to travel. They must first grow to the point at which they are spiritually in tune with the altitude they would attain. So, when anyone says that a Jesus of Nazareth, a Socrates, a Plato, a Demosthenes, a Buddha, a Zoroaster or any one of the master souls who have lived in the past cannot return into the earth's atmosphere, be assured that such a person has made a mistake. Had they said that it was not to be expected that these great souls would spend all of their time in the earth's atmosphere, it would be a different proposition, but, know you. Good Friends, that you may always travel back over the road you have already traversed, but always you must look forward to the heights beyond as achievements that come only as the human soul has grown up to their altitude. That is why it is that there are so many people coming back in circles and classes of a certain kind, bemoaning the fact that they have not done the thing that they should have done. They discover that, notwithstanding their mere belief, they are not able to traverse the eternal highways; they are not able to penetrate the various spheres of spiritual activity immediately upon entering the spirit world.

A wonderful world it is, where the scales of justice are balanced so nicely and, we say with all deference, where the scales of a clear-eyed and perfectly seeing justice are operated in order that real justice be dispensed—not a blind goddess with unseeing eyes called upon to pass judgment, bitter judgment as is sometimes the case on the material plane. Nay, justice in the spirit world is not blind. We would that thought be emblazoned far and wide—JUSTICE IN THE SPIRIT WORLD IS NOT BLIND. They cannot mock at justice in that spirit world. They cannot appease justice by the perpetration of a second crime in order to expiate the first one. They cannot bribe justice by paying a stipend to the State in the spiritual world, as is so often done on the material plane, nor can they persuade justice against the actual and practical expression of real unadulterated justice which measures out to every human soul accordingly as that soul deserves. That is why in the spirit world there is weeping and wailing and gnashing of teeth, that is why in the spirit world you will find human beings sore afraid of what lies ahead, that is why in the spirit world you will find those who are caroling their paeans of praise and gratitude and singing songs of gladness, that is why it is that in the spirit world the vaunted philanthropists of the material realm are sometimes regarded as moneychangers in the temple of the Most High, whereas some of those who were regarded in material life as among the less desirable, less cultured, less orthodox individuals, find themselves radiantly situated, find themselves in environs, in circumstances where everything scintillates with that spiritual effulgence which sheds a beauty so rarely beautiful and exquisite as to be beyond the power of words to describe. You do not describe the big things; you feel them, and subtly you transmit your feeling to those who are in tune. So you do not describe the rarest beauties of the spirit world because you have no analogies which will fit, you have no similes which may be applied; you have no symbolism in your speech that can be employed to depict that which is to be found in the spirit world by those who bring spiritual integrity as their stock in trade.

All of this is of import to you because you are knocking at the door, because you are reaching out for that which is the bread of life, because your souls are being attuned in order that you may catch the voice which carols the music of spiritual spheres and which brings paeans of praise to your soul and which sings the everlasting glory of life, a life dominated by an eternally just deific power. Well said has it been that the failure of mankind lies in the fact that man deifies the individual who may be the mouthpiece of the religious system and becomes so enamored of the figure which they have raised upon a fictitious pedestal that they lose sight of the message of truth which the individual sought to bring. They nailed Jesus of Nazareth on the cross and then so deified the cross upon which his body was said to have hung that they have only seen the cross without sensing the symbolism. They have seen only the body, limp and lifeless, without recognizing the spirit back of it; they have visualized the crown of thorns in the pierced flesh without in the least degree understanding or appreciating the spirit of the message which the man brought to mankind. Fetish worship is what it has been, idolatry is what it has been, the building of whited sepulchers, so to speak, is what has taken place, the worship of form, of symbolism, or ritual and ceremonialism rather than the recognition of the spirit of the living Christ which has been extant in the world from the beginning of time. But a new dawn is at hand. The day approaches when men will understand the spirit world and will know it to be what it really is, a continuation of this world, this life, a world of results, of effects, of opportunities, of unfoldment, of final joy for all humanity.

Let these words sink into your souls. Carry away the message which we are giving to you tonight. Tell yourself repeatedly that there is one coin, one key that opens every door worthwhile in the world of spirit—spiritual integrity. Why, you spend countless numbers of dollars in the purchase of an ounce, perhaps, or a few ounces of attar of roses, the richest fragrance of the Orient you desire in order that it may tickle your fancy and appeal exquisitely to the olfactory nerves,—merchandise that may be brought from across a Sahara, that may be garnered in desert places, in oases in those deserts, and brought before the people who fancy that their social and religious standing depends upon the acquisition of these things that are so difficult to acquire. If one tithe of the money which is now spent for the specific purpose of adornment of bodies and the fullness of ritualism and ceremonials and the idling away of time which is frittered for mere baubles which can be crushed between the fingers like a bubble, if a tithe of that money were spent for the kind of instruction and information and leading that would assist in distilling the attar of roses which comes as a result of the proper cultivation of the qualities of humanity, why life would be as redolent of kindly deeds as the rosebud is redolent of fragrance. Kindliness, gentleness, justice, loving service, these are the things of greater value than the attar of an Omar, valuable and rare as that may be.

Why cannot the Occidental mind understand that after all is said and done those Oriental masters who speak of distilling the attar of roses and filling therewith a tiny vial that will be an open sesame to every kingdom there is, are symbolizing and suggesting the evolution and development of character, the distilling, if you please, from the rose of life that attar of spiritual-mindedness that would be the open sesame anywhere, under every circumstance, to every clime, to every kingdom, to every treasure house there is in God's Universe. Learn this on this plane of life wherein you are and be enriched greatly. Wait until you pass out of the physical body to learn this lesson and, like Shaipur, like the ancient sheik, stranded on the desert, led into the garden of Omar, compelled to labor many, many moons, in order to learn how—yea, as that ancient character crossed his Sahara, so shall the soul who has not learned his lesson find the Sahara of the soul in the world of spirit. Shall you enter the world of spirit and find a desert over which you must travel in order to reach the heights or shall you enter the world of spirit and find yourself traveling from one oasis to another, traveling where fronded palms wave and where the sun never sets upon the glories of God Almighty?

Take the message, be sure that the spiritual world is a spiritual Kimberley for those who mine the right, where every scintillant and brilliant joy is theirs, or the spiritual world is a trackless desert to those who have not learned to live.

THE NEW BIRTH

People may live near a volcano, breathe its atmosphere, hear its smothered mutterings and not know what it is. Others may live over a mine of diamonds and never find out what wealth is beneath them. All the forces of nature are hidden and most of them silent.

All the treasures of earth are buried deep out of sight and must be searched for. There are many kingdoms in the natural world, of which nearly everyone knows something. Long ago it was said, "My mind to me a kingdom is," and that has been repeated by numbers of men and through ages of years. And how true it is that the human mind is a powerful kingdom to those who recognize it so to be. How prolific it has been and how through that kingdom mankind has been elevated from ignorance and superstition.

But there is still another kingdom nearer to us than the volcano or the mine, nearer than the mineral or vegetable, than the animal, yes nearer than even man can be to man. We breathe its airs, we hear its music, we feel its nearness and yet we know it not. It is an unknown, unexplored region, and the only way to know anything of it is to be "born again" as Jesus said. According to Spiritual doctrine, there never was a birth into the flesh at all. The one and only birth is that of Spirit, so that to be born again is simply to awake to a consciousness of the real birth. In this new kingdom there is no matter or flesh, for Jesus distinctly said "flesh profiteth nothing."

We must wake from the dream existence of mortality to the life of Spirit in order to know of this kingdom, for it is one wholly of Spirit. How do we wake, or how can we be born again? By holding to the true and letting go the untrue. No one can study Principle and not know that the only reality is Spirit, and that all that the senses tell us is absolutely nothing. When we do know this, we become dead to old beliefs and thoughts and find ourselves in an entirely new world. The first glimmering of the light of truth is just like being born again, and we are quite like infants. But before these light dawns upon us, we exclaim like Nicodemus, "How can these things be?"

It is a great mystery to us when we hear that all we see with the outward eye is not real at all, is nothing. But "enter, into thy closet," which means retire within to commune with thyself, or, as the Athenians put it, "know thyself," and you will surely find that it is a true saying, flesh (matter) is nothing, is nowhere—does not exist. Nicodemus, though a man in high position could not understand the mystery of a spiritual birth. Probably he had no desire to do so, but wanted to find out what occult wisdom worked those miracles, and imagined Jesus would gladly tell a ruler whose influence was great. But if he had been puzzled by the miracles, he was still more mystified by the answer of Jesus.

Neither flattery nor praise could affect Jesus, any more than enmity and persecution. He was intent upon and absorbed in His mission and taught spiritual truths to the poorest as freely as to a ruler. He told Nieodemus plainly that a man must be born of Spirit and yet he comprehended Him not, for though he was learned in Jewish law he was materially minded. He had not denied or ignored the realm of matter or the pleasures of the senses in order to find Truth. He had not obeyed the new commandment, Love God and your neighbor as yourself. He knew nothing about living by the warm love of charity. No, he belonged to those who were ready to crucify any who differed from these tenets, to apply the rigor of the cold law to every word and even to forbidding healing on the Sabbath day or plucking corn to eat, and the cruelty of a law which said an eye for an eye, a tooth for a tooth.

How should he understand spiritual truth? And yet it seems so plain today, that we feel as if their spiritual eyes must have been holden that they might not see.

But, then as now, people refused to accept new teachings if they interfered with traditional ones even though those who lived in accordance therewith could heal the sick and raise the dead. If they had understood the words of Jesus, and had they allowed Him to teach in peace, the world would have had a different history, and today His teachings would not need reviving. The regeneration he preached would have brought the new Jerusalem Long ages ago had it been understood. But he compared the kingdom of heaven to seed, and his words have been smoldering beneath the externalities that have covered them for nineteen hundred years, till now they are springing up and bearing fruit through true spiritual teaching, in every direction, with a true understanding of their meaning which is regenerating all who really listen. All that Jesus promised is coming to pass, for we "see the kingdom of God," which is harmony, peace, rest, health and happiness.

Do you understand this regeneration taught by Jesus? If you do or if you do not, do you know any about you who do need it? Are you well and strong as Jesus was, through knowing that he and his Father were one? There is no other health and strength that is enduring. If you do not understand God to be the source of your health, it will not remain and you are not regenerated.

This regeneration brings what appear like new powers; powers to heal the sick, rescue the dying, cheer the sorrowful, and carry peace and love wherever we go.

Would you like to do all this? If you are not able to do these things, you are not regenerated, no matter how strong a creed you subscribe to or how much of an experience you can relate or how long your list of charities may be. This new birth is not the so-called conversion that makes a man live in outward morality, while his thoughts are like raving waters, or turn from his wicked ways to gain influence by appearing religious, or appear upright for fear of losing caste, or become correct in his living when his body is too worn and depleted to longer indulge in dissipation. All that is cleansing the outside of the platter from selfish motives.

Your regeneration is spiritual, or the awakening and stirring of the Spirit which has been hidden by mortality's desires and sensations, it can be compared to a new birth because it seems so wonderful, like being ushered into a new world, or being re-made, for the desires, thoughts and beliefs so change as to seem indeed new. One who is thus born again of the Spirit is so, filled with a love for all men that is God-like with the peace that passeth understanding, with gentleness, patience and a calm, born only of Spirit, that his face shines with an immortal beauty— the beauty of holiness. His presence radiates health and strength and the touch of such a one healeth all our infirmities.

ROOM FOR THE SOUL

What shall a man give in exchange for his soul? The human soul is a vastly greater, more subtle, and at the same time more substantial thing than we commonly think.

The part of it that can be put into words or deeds is but the smallest fraction of that elusive, incomprehensible being which is the real man. The world is only beginning to discover the soul, and to see how great and vital a thing it was when Jesus spoke of the losing and saving of the soul. Many of the things we are wont to dismiss as mere sentiment, emotion, imagination, as if they were but the froth upon the surface, are really not of the surface at all but of the depths. It has been truly said that the prose of the world becomes obsolete, while the poetry abides forever. The reason is that the one is dealing with external facts which are constantly changing, while the other deals with the inner reality, which is changeless and eternal. The poem, the picture, the music, which really succeeds in expressing the soul today, expresses it for all time.

There are two lines of attack against which the human soul must maintain its integrity and its paramount importance today.

The first is from the so-called practical man, who cheapens everything that cannot be coined into dollars. He sets at naught the man of feeling and sentiment and ideals, calls him a dreamer, rates him lower than yonder hard headed trader who has shut up his soul and salted away his thousands. Yet the real aristocracy of earth is to be found among these dreamers. Few of them achieve worldly success, and even those who do sustain a certain loss of simplicity and fineness of nature, which seems inseparable from the business of marketing the products of one's soul. Most of them are making a humble living by the sweat of hand or brain. There may be men working for you at a mere pittance who are far greater souls than you. But their real life is not in what you are paying them for. Their real life is in the soul, its loves, its joys, its sympathies, its ideals, its hopes.

The laws by which they live are the great laws of the soul, the laws of sincerity and faith and love, the laws of joy and of growth. These are the people who are getting the richest and most satisfying returns out of this life, and I am sure they are also the ones who are best preparing themselves for the life that is to come.

The other attack is from the rationalist, who in his pride of intellect makes light of that world of feeling which we call the soul. To him, nothing's knowledge that cannot be reduced to the language of the logical mind. This overvaluation of argument is one of the fallacies of our time. Some of the smallest minds are among the acutest logicians. We need to learn that there are more sources of knowledge than the five senses, and more kinds of knowledge than can be put into words. The soul also has its senses. There are indefinable ways in which, as it were, it puts forth its spiritual antennae and tries the quality of other souls.

The great ideals of life, the moral intuitions that are the same in all, the sense of truth and justice and spiritual worth—no one has been able to explain how these things come to us. Who shall say that the soul does not, by processes of its own, reach out and dimly but truly apprehend the world of spiritual reality in which we live and have our being? And is it not the essence of religion thus to apprehend God, feeling after him if haply we may find him?

Let us then make room for the soul! Room for its rich and beautiful inner life in the midst of that battle for gain whose uproar fills our streets. Room for its intuitions of things unseen, in the midst of that battle of human creeds which fills the outer court of the temple of true religion.

THE FIRE MYSTERY

We freely admit our Oriental character and modes of thought, and challenge the showing of any grand human idea that did not originate in the Eastern lands. We claim to know the GRAND SECRET, and to be able to teach mankind many things concerning the body, soul, will, prolongation of existence, and concentration of mental energy, never dreamed of by the thinkers of colder latitudes, and the assertion that any of our hooks contain matter opposite to the pure Chistic faith, we utterly and flatly deny. True, these hooks contain startling and extraordinary statements and beliefs; yet we boldly challenge any human being to point to one doctrine at all subversive of correct human morals, in whole or in part; or any doctrine which has the slightest tendency to draw the soul one inch away from God.

On the contrary, hosts have been saved from despair, suicide, and irremediable ruin, by perusing these works. It is urged against us that we "Believe in, and Practice Magic;" we admit the fact: we certainly do,— the pure white, bright, effulgent, radiantly glorious Magic of the human Will,—through and by which alone, human passions are made to correct themselves, and by which alone, otherwise defenseless Woman is fully armed against the coarse brutalism's of thousands of misnamed "men and husbands" and this is a purely Chistic power too, an integrant of the early Chistic faith,—dead here, and buried nearly everywhere else, beneath mountains of gabble-dust, deserts of error.

It is further charged that we have "certain quite extraordinary esoteric, or secret doctrines." We admit the fact, and the animus is apparent from that other fact, namely, "That these secret doctrines are only divulged to the pure, virtuous, and worthy."

Our assailants failed in all their schemes to penetrate these mysteries, and the inference is plain, nor can even the disaffected fail to see "the reason why." Now, however, we herewith present some of these "secret doctrines," with holding only such a concern the domestics, celestic, magnetic, and volential interests and life and power of mankind, which we only reveal to Initiates of the Higher Degrees: and be it known that there is nothing in even these secrets to soil the fabrics of the fairest and purest female mind on the whole vast earth, much less that of any man who ever lived.

We publish these things now, for the first time in our LONG history, or since the world began,—a brief and partial compend of what we believe and know, concerning methods whereby the human being can penetrate the domains of the Shadow, and glimpse the ineffable effulgence of the gorgeous light, and learn immeasurably more of the Dynamic or Mechanical, the Chemical, Sensory, Emotional, Electric, Æthic, Ethereal, Physical, Magnetic, and Intellectual Universes, or realms and grades of Being, than is possible to man not possessing our data, and, therefore, ignorant of the laws or via.

We claim to stand in the door of the dawn, within the cryptic portals of the luminous worlds, and that the lamp that lights us is Love supreme. Unlike others, we do not recognize God as the Light, for this can be seen and known, but as the UNFATHOMABLE SHADOW, the unreachable CENTER, the impenetrable MYSTERY, the unimaginable MAJESTE,— UTTERLY past discovery,—and who, as we approach, ever recedes, alluring us thus through illimitable ages and epochs, up the steep mountains of achievement,—the whole end of achievement being—in which opinion we, of course, differ from all philosophies in Christendom.

We hold that no power ever comes to man through the intellect. We say that the adage "Knowledge is Power" is false; but that Goodness alone is Power, and that pertains to the heart only, hence that Power comes only to the Soul through Love (not lust, mind you), but love, the underlying, Primal Fire life, subtending the basis of being,—the formative flowing floor of the worlds—the true sensing of which is the beginning of the road to personal power. Love lieth at the foundation, and is the synonym of life and strength and clingingness. Thus, it happens that a Loving couple grow youthful in soul, because, in their union, they strike this divine spark, replenish themselves with the essence of life, grow stronger and less brutal, and draw down to them the divine Are from the aerial spaces. (This now is by accident.)

Couples not loving, exhaust each other, and wear their souls to shreds, so that after death they enter the ethereal realms in a state of Immortal scrawniness, requiring a long lapse to reach celestial plumptitude. We claim methods of averting all this, and how?

Holding, as we do that Deity dwells within the Shadow, beyond the everlasting Flame,—the amazing glories of which minds have confounded with the very God.—we declare all things, especially the human soul, to be a form of Fire: that man is NOT the only intelligence in nature, but that there are, and the aerial spaces abound with, multi form intelligences, having their conscious origin in Æth, as man has his in matter;

and that there are GRADES of these, towering away in infinite series of hierarchies, human, and ultra-human, to an unimaginable Eterne.

We hold that the soul is a polar world of white fire within the human body; that its NEGATIVE only resides within the brain as a general dwelling; that in dreamless sleep it goes to the solar plexus to impart stores of life-fire to the body in dreams it visits (by sight and rapport) other scenery and that all dreams have a determinate meaning and purpose. We hold that the other pole of the soul is situated within the genital system; that in true marriage, the entire Soul officiates at the celebration; that both positive and negative of each parent assist at the incarnation of the new souls that genuine marriage calls into the world; that where no mutual love inspires the parents, only one of the two forces of their souls officiate, and the consequence is that the world is full of half-men, half-women, and weaklings: and thus it is seen why illegitimate children are generally the smartest,—it is because Love was the inspiration. Apply the principles laid down by us, and it is seen how wherefrom it happens that inferior-BRAINED, but strong-Loving women become mothers of mento-moral millionaires; while brainy mothers give us children born to intellectual penury; inferior brained, but large, love-natured men usually become fathers to their mental superiors; while we all know that genius generally, nay, notoriously, produces mental weaklings. We are quite aware of the extraordinary novelty of our beliefs, but we intend to revolutionize the world with them.

Nevertheless, and notwithstanding.

Now, the superior pole of the soul is in direct magnetic and ethereal contact with the Soul of Being; the foundation-fire of the universe; with all that vast domain underlying increase, growth, emotion, beauty, heat, energy; the SOLE and base of being; the subtending Love, or Fire-floor of Existence. Hence, through Love man seizes directly on all that is, and is in actual contact and rapport with all and singular every being that FEELS and LOVES within the confines of God's habitable universe. But any amount of brain or learning he may have affiliates him to a very few at most because all God's creatures love and feel, while comparatively few can think and know. Love forever against the World. The positive element or part of the soul, in the male, is in, near, and about, the prostatic gland, with three radii extending to the connected viscera, whence it happens that emasculation injures the very soul itself.

In the female, the major force of the soul resides in the uterus, with three radii extending to the right and left ovaria and the connecting viscera, whence it happens that illness or injuries THERE have the most baneful and debilitating effect upon all other departments of her nature. "A fine specimen of a man" is never spoken of any mere bundle of brains and learning, but always of one with fine physical presence and magnetic fullness, indicating love, well cultured. So also, of woman. Thus, the world unconsciously acknowledges that much of the truth enunciated now by us. Declaring that true manhood is more or lessen rapport with one or more of the upper hierarchies of Intelligent Potentialities, earth-born and not earth-born, we believe there are means whereby a person may become associated with, and receive instructions from, them.

More than that, we believe in talismans; that it is possible to construct and wear them, and that they emit a peculiar light, discernible across the gulfs of Space by these intelligent powers, just as we discern a diamond across a play house; that such are signals to the beholders, and that they will, and do, cross the chasmal steeps to save, succor, and assist the wearers, just as a good brother here flies to the relief of him who shall give the grand hailing-signs of distress. This is provable. This Asiatic mystery of the will, properly cultivated, is the highest aid to man, for it is a divine Energos, white, pure, magic; the miracle-working potentiality which cometh only to the free and wholly unshackled human soul: while to woman it is the only salvation from marital vampirism; the shield and buckler of her power, and the groundwork upon which must be builded the real rule of her influence in the world and at home.

We say that the field of its action is over the natural elements of Physical Being (1). Over the Ætherics of Space (2) Over succession of duration of events,—Time (3). But that these Powers and Energies are not to be had for the mere asking. They are obtainable only through a triumphant abnegation of mental littleness, small selftitude, and reasonless egotism; and by victorious performance of the tasks willed by IT; the very basis of the law of psychical evolution,—tasks of mind essential to the rapid growth, beneath the outer, and above the seen, of all who seek to become knowing (1), Magnetic (2), Powerful (3). For a regal, thus-trained WILL, in man or woman is the ONLY road to Vigor (1), Perpetuity of Specific Energy (2), Increment of youth-life in all, at any lapse of terrestrial time (3), Attainment of Specific Energy (4), beyond the lot of ordinary human beings—"Accidents" aside. In a word, we claim that IT is the only means of mastery over the sublimer Secrets and Forces of the Natural, Ethereal, and Celestial universes, and of the first as more concerning embodied man, because it leads directly to the key wherewith can be unlocked the Seven Gates,—Money (1), Love (2), Clairvoyance (3), Special Mental Power (4), General Power (5), Magnetic Presence (6), and Ubique, or far sight (7), Of these, the writer of this manifesto chose the second, third, and fourth, with what results, the wide world well knows.

Many are called, but few are chosen, to abide with us in absolute, full fellowship, for three reasons: First, haste, impatience. Second, grab-bleism. Because Silence is Strength; and the silent lip and steady head alone are worthy. Third, because we do not believe in the, to us, absurd dogma of human equality; it is the demonstrable negation of all human reason and experience; is a hypocritical, cruel, and delusive falsehood; puts people out of their element, and into wrong positions; it never was, will, nor can be, true; for "aristocracy" of some kind always rules, is always a unit in interests, while "democracy" always is RULED, and is eternally at war with itself, and clashing about its own interests which interests it perpetually injures and destroys But it is true that some souls are nobler, better, higher, finer, richer, riper, rounder,—these seven,—than some other souls, and are worth immeasurably more, whether weighed or plumbed in God's scales or Man's. For some souls are young, green, acid, acrid, imperfect, and non-poised, these seven,—and such stand for æons of ages gaping, on the highways, as regal souls rush in g across the deeps toward achievement; here, there, now then, up the streets of the worlds, and down the corridors of heaven,—splendid, "aristocratic" souls, who will circumnavigate eternity while the others are wondering.—"What next?" and "Did you ever?"—new souls, just created, requiring a thousand or two of ages to get their eternal sea-legs on, before being able to steadily walk the decks of the eternal ship of centuries and power, or compete with those who, living now, yet have passed their ordeals long before this civilization had taken root in the moldy soil of scores that had preceded it,—men who make and govern circumstances instead of allowing circumstances to govern them—men of absolute individuality of character, born kings of will, and majestic of purpose.

The reason why will be readily seen by recurring to the basic propositions of the divine Sciences, which declare that God, the SOUL of the universe, is positive heat, celestial fire; that the aura of Deity (God) is LOVE, the prime element of all power, the external fire-sphere, the informing and formative pulse of matter. The Induction is crystalline; for it follows that who so hath most love,—whether its expression be coarse or fine, cultured or rude—hath, therefore, most of God in him or her; the element of time being competent to the perfecting of all refining influences over the ocean, if not upon the hither side. Conversely put, the statement stands thus: who so most resembles God therefore hath most of love, goodness, and the elements of power. God is not a libertine. Now, these latent energies we claim that we alone have the true knowledge of; that we understand the laws of love, will, and ethereal force, and the principles and modes of their evolution, and crystallization in the homes, the result aimed at being the elimination of the gross, and their orderly consolidation into personal power. We hold that Love is ever, was, and eternally will be, absolutely pure. Paste is not diamond, though they resemble somewhat, nor is Love ever anything but its own transcendent self; yet normal passion is divine, because through it alone God gives true men to the great man-wanting world. There can be no small thing as unholy love; nor good badness, nor bad goodness.

True PASSION is but one, and a minor mode, of Love's expression; its officers are triplicate, and when people understand that one grand secret, farewell to social, domestic, and all other ills; and it is this grand secret we have, for long years, been teaching, somewhat, not fully, in our books, on both shores of the oceans that girdle the world. We know that brains and intellects differ, but hearts and affection are ever the same; that through these last, man can attain unto Goodness, and woman reign queen and equal, where she now serves as drudge, toy, and legal and illegal,—SOMETHING WORSE; that woman, as such, has most of love crystallized within her; and for that reason is entitled to stand the peer of the best man breathing God's free air; not by reason of her beauty, accomplishments, wealth, or any other accident, but because she hath the womb;—the perfected laboratory wherein she fashioneth, and alone completes, what it took God, Nature, and Man, singly and combined, to only begin; and that, too, so badly, that the wonder is that swarming hordes of murderers do not throng the world's highways where civilized man now walks. But so infinitely great an artiste is she, that from the worst of seed she has raised many a splendid human tree; redeemed the race from savagery; fostered and cultured art, science, religion, and all that renders earth habitable, and that, too, under all sorts of repressions and bad conditions; assuredly entitling her now to a chance of trying what SHE can do, under favorable circumstances, who did so well under the bad; and we hold this to be the strongest argument for the real "Rights of Woman" ever made since the world began; and we advance it only as one of the external reasons we entertain, holding in reserve others as much stronger and more cogent than these, as a chain cable is superior to a child's slender whipcord.

We, the Brotherhood, further hold that there are Æthereal (spacial) centers of Love, Power, Force, Energy, Goodness, and for, and of, every kind, grade, species, and order of knowledge known to man, and whereof he knows not anything; and that it is not only POSSIBLE to reach those centers, and obtain those knowledges, but that it is achievable by a vast number who now drone and doze away life, die half ripe, and wake up, when too late, to find out what fools they have been, necessitating what it is not our present purpose to reveal. In the present instance, it only remains for the purpose of this Declaration of Principles, to draw a brief comparison between our system and the very best that can possibly, truthfully be said of the very best of all other systems now extant anywhere. They are divided into two parts, one of which proceeds to totally ignore the body, mortifies the flesh, and renders life truly a semi-graveyard operation from birth to baptism, from that to death. The other allows the utmost limit to lust and license to the elect, and roundly berates all others outside. VIDE Mormonism, Perfectionism, and Islamism, and contrast them with their opposites in belief, as the Shakers. But current systems, as a general thing, bend all their energies toward the salvation of Men's souls, and, in spending their time in trying to get souls into heaven, lose sight of the bodies, which, practically may go to the other place, of so little account are they. They believe in crucifying the flesh altogether, and generally effect THAT VERY THING for the soul. They wholly lose sight of a fundamental principle of human nature, which is to take delight in doing the very thing it is sternly forbidden to.

The people of a town might not, if let alone, leave its boundaries once in ten years; but you just make a law that they SHALL NOT leave it, and that town will be empty in less than a single day. Human nature is strongly perverse, and this suggests the query that were churches and marriages based upon consent and attraction, instead of what they are based on, there wouldn't be a hell on earth or anywhere else, in less than one hundred brief years,—brief to God, and to immortal man.

Churches and marriages exist as repressions,—our system in expansion. They drive people to heaven cross-lots, over steep-down gulfs of hell, we teach them to avoid all such. They drive mankind by everlasting gabble on the horrors of deformity; we draw them by appeals to the good, the true, and the beautiful. They concern themselves about mourning; we about joy; they about making the best of a bad bargain, bearing life's crosses, abiding patiently till the end, and all that; while we teach people how to neutralize hells by wholesale,—and the worst of them, too, married ones,—and all through the White Magic of Love, Will, and Ætheriea. What teachers besides ourselves can give men and women all the information on the following list of practical points? or where are they who even pretend to know how to instruct the people? The fact is, they know nothing of what they call Magnetics, and which we call Ætherics; of what they call Will, which we call Volontiae; of what they call by a thousand names, we by the one right title, LOVE. There are certain aims, qualities, forces, ends, energies, powers, and abilities longed for, vainly, by untold millions of people, men and women, in English speaking lands, which we know the road to, and are able to so direct the wayfarer in the Paths, that, though he or she be a mere weakling, they cannot err therein. Of course, we do not propose herein to state even a quarter part of our doctrines, nor of the powers derivable, for that were to transcend our present intention; besides which, many of them have already been given to the world through the works already published. Still, it is deemed advisable to name a few, omitting such as are of a strictly domestic, social, magnetic, and ultra-recondite character. In the course of human life, millions sigh for the Power of irresistibly affecting an applosion; to draw or bring others to them, for good ends, others when afar off, actually or sympathetically. Frustrating bad plans of others, when such will prove a benefit. The precisely opposite,—to assist others, by exertion of the Æthic force of the Soul. Moral and other changes, effected by will-influence, through health changes. Increasing the dynamic life-force through the three principles. Prolonging specific energy through the single breath-force. Tirau-clairism,—ability to think clearly to a point, and know it. Relating to money dealings, losses, gains, and to forecast them? The grand secret of domestic happiness,—the law of marital discord-discovered, and its effectual antidotes, and enormously powerful ones besides,—among which is one not discovered) by us, but of incalculable value to every wedded couple whose health or finances may not warrant too frequent family additions, and thus we strike a blow directly against the monster crime of the age,—murder, red-handed, atrocious murder,—the awful crime of abortion. This is "The Golden Secret." What a vast throng of husbands and married women notoriously find home a hell for want of reciprocation, mutuality, sympathy and domesticity,—longing for death, or anything else, to mitigate or change the current horror. Now, none of these know, as we do, that: (1) power comes to the man through woman, who in turn imparts it to man; that (2) man can wholly modify woman's character, and KINDLE the ice to a gentle flame; and (3) that it lies in every unhappy woman's power to make or mar the best man living;, that she is very often responsible for her own misery, arid has the power to resist the depleting effects of Vampirism, disease thus engendered, and to wholly transform the nature of almost any man, no matter how brutal, inconsiderate, or careless. In this respect, we victoriously plant the white banner over the ram parts of the social world. We admit, and triumphantly, that we believe in the ELIXIR OF LIFE; and that the human stay on earth can be prolonged a great deal beyond the storied three score and ten. Finally, having been forced to lift the veil, we are content to abide the issue, and leave the event with God, well knowing that victory is ours.

> *"These are the great old Masters;*
> *These, the men sublime,*
> *Whose DISTINCT footsteps echo down*
> *The corridors of time."*

THE ELIXIR OF YOUTH

Is there such a thing as an Elixir of Youth? Alchemists of all ages have made the claim that there is, and that they have discovered, that which may be called the Elixir of Youth.

They claim that, by the use of it, youth can be retained many years beyond the time supposed to be allotted to man for a sojourn on earth. Medical men of all schools have been plain-spoken in their condemnation of such a doctrine, going as far as to say that it is impossible to accomplish such a thing. What is youth?

To be youthful, simply means to have the greatest possible number of new cells in the constitution of the body. The body of man is an aggregation of cells. Some of these must be new if there is to be life, although many of them may be old and worn out.

To a great extent, these cells renew themselves without effort. If not, then, every child would die as soon as all of the cells had been used up, which would be within about nine months from the time that it is born. But, in the majority of cases, these new cells do not renew themselves as rapidly as they should; and the consequence is that old age is gradually creeping upon man.

A man's thoughts have as much to do with the creation of cells as anything else, although diet, environment, work, and other things help either to destroy or to build cells. The idea of age has come to be a part of us. And the idea that all men must grow old has established an age limit, and men take it for granted that, when they reach a certain age, they must become old and feeble. The first thing for us to do, if we wish to avoid the appearance of old age, is to get rid of this "aging-idea," and to come to recognize the fact that man is a creator.

When we recognize that we are really "awake," and able to become creative in our own organism, we will search farther; and we will soon learn that, if we root out the idea of becoming aged, we have accomplished the greater part of the work in the attainment of many years with the appearance of but a few.

We stop short the destructive work in our organisms by refusing to believe that man must be aged, feeble, and decrepit at the age of eighty years. With the recognition that man is a creator, not only of his kind, but of himself as well, will come recognition of another fact—just as he thinks, so will he create.

Thus, he will polarize his mind toward the retention of youth. With this principle established in his mind, he will no longer think of age, but of youth; in all his work, he will hold the thought of youth and the power to accomplish; and these thoughts will magnetize, or polarize, the new cells that are being continually created, and will give them greater life.

Gradually, through this process of polarization, all the old cells will be destroyed, and the new cells will take their place, and an appearance of youth will be the result. Now, this process cannot be accomplished in a year, because the body is reconstructed only about every nine months. The first body after this change of life and thought takes place will be better than the former one. The next body will be better still; and, thus, the process continues until man is an entirely new being—one that recognizes nothing except that he is a creator and "the master of his own being." Now, as before stated, the diet has much to do with this subject; for, unless we gain the proper food values, we cannot create new cells that are full of vitality.

From the food, we gain the material wherewith to build the cells. Even the brain cannot be at its best if the food lacks nutritive value. It is not the amount a man eats that counts in the construction of new cells, but the value of the foods. Besides the food, there are other things to be considered; such as, bathing the body, which frees the skin from particles of dust and other foreign matter, and allows the cells to absorb magnetism and vitality from the air. Breathing also has much to do with the art of retaining youth; for the air we breathe contains all the elements that are required to give life to the cells.

These new cells, it is true, are created from the food that we take into the body, just as the body was created from the earth; but, before the body of man had life, God had to breathe into it the Breath of Life. Now this is just what we must do in order to give life to the cells. The cells are created from the food we eat, and they are then given life by the air that we breathe in.

Naturally, the more of the Law we understand, and the more we obey of it, the greater will be the life we give to the cells; and, if we know all of the Law and deliberately breathe according to the Law, then, every breath will give more and more life to the cells. Only within a short time, the newspapers have been devoting columns to the discovery made by a physician, who claims to have made from the pituitary and other glands a serum that will add many years to man's life.

A discovery of this nature is only of negative value; for, while it shows that there is life in the gland, yet, to take the serum from that gland, is to add only the principle together with much dead matter to the system of man, and will result in other conditions in the body which tend to offset the value of the years that are added.

The Mystics of old, even Paracelsus, taught that, through a system of living, or rather a system of practice, man could draw the life from the pituitary gland and transfuse it throughout the system, giving vitality to the cells, and adding many years to his life.

In the book, The Exalted Life, the author has hinted at this mystery; but it is impossible to give openly the method whereby the fluids from this gland may be drawn into the circulation of the blood, thereby to give greater life to the cells, and, through this greater life, to add many years to man's earthly existence. However, the true seeker will find the way; and, if he follows it, the results will be greatly to his benefit.

All serums—that is, all serums taken from a dead body, and then again introduced into the system of the living—may bring benefits in one way; but, as they carry dead matter with the life-giving matter, naturally a destructive agent is being introduced at the same time. No man can take dead material of another into his system without losing a part of his own identity; and, if this material be concentrated, as is the case with serum, this destruction is so much the greater.

Man has within himself all that is. He can be the master of his being; but, in order to be master, he must first come to understand the Law, and, when he does understand, he must live according to the Law.

And this not only in one department of life, but in every department. He must learn to recognize the value of the food he eats, and must give up those which may taste good, but have no food value. Bathing must have his attention. He must have natural sleep; and, above all, his thoughts must be turned into normal and natural channels.

When he has learned these lessons, he can truly begin to live, and to become a man, the image of his Creator, and a fellow creator with Him. Moreover, this new life, which the author of the book referred to above has called the Exalted Life, will in no way interfere with his duty to himself or to his family or to his fellow man: he simply exchanges his unnatural system of living for a natural one. Instead of being the slave of destiny, he becomes the master.

STORMS

As a rule, mankind trembles with fear and holds in unpleasant remembrance all storms and their accompaniment. To some, the lightning and its thunder are the jarring vibrations; to some, the high-pitched note of the irresistible, reckless wind is many octaves beyond the key of their physical, and again, to others the rushing sweep of the tornado-impelled torrents of water bring hours of timidity—a steady agony in their totality.

Again, others are on the verge of dissolution, when the rocking earthquake makes our ancient and revered mother insecure footing. To those acquainted along the ways of the mystic realm, each of these classes only refers themselves to the domains of the Four Great Angels of Fire, Air, Water and Earth. The servants of these Angels are the Salamanders, the Sylphs, the Undines and the Gnomes. There is no war between the different realms, but, instead, the closest harmony. Man talks of the war of the elements, meaning the Elemental; but there is none. They work as allies. The roar of the wind in its tempestuous rust tests to their utmost the strength of the works of men's hands; the weak; the unfinished; the too prominently placed are all at its mercy. Poor, puny man's efforts for lodgment on the earth's surface, avail but little in the strong grasp of the Wind and its attendant Sylphs, who are the power and potency of the Air.

There is another view of even the most terrific tornadoes, as the lifting force, of the most noxious gases and poisonous effluvia out of their birthplaces in the swamps of the forests and the overflown banks of tardily moving rivers; from the haunts of the vile and poverty-stricken— the noisome dens of crowded cities, which man has ever conceived and manifested to his own detriment.

All these destructive conditions, the blessed wind sweeps out into innocuous dissolution, leaving the space beneath, above and around us, free from the awful, soul dissolving touch. Fire follows the behests of the wind, and the electrical flash disintegrates what the wind cannot release. To all this is added the power of the water, the universal solvent. The collection of the idle, the inert, the detrimental, the destructive remains of what man names wastage is hunted out of its holes, where if time permitted, the earth would find means to reabsorb and deprive it of its nialific qualities. But in all hour, the inherent urge of the mobile elements of Fire, Air and Water accomplish what might consume months of the Earth's time to overcome. The Earth and the Sea give up their dead. But the Fire and the Air have no dead to give up.

They are the spirit and the life of all things, and therefore can hold no dead things in their embrace. It is the Fire that quickened! and the breath that renews the physical body and all other forms of manifestation. The Earth and the Sea are vast charnel houses, in which the lifeless bodies are stored. But we find the Four Builders are over against each other in equipoise and a just balancing. They hold their potency and dominance under the Universal Law of polarity—negative against positive. The increase or accumulation of power at any one pole, upsets equilibrium, and a storm becomes absolutely essential.

No one of the Builders can go out on a storm all by itself. The winds blow the water in some form as it rises and falls; the lightning plays its part; while the Earth receives and reacts. Vibration and motion yield the sounds of Chaos being marshaled into order. An evenly adjusted peace is the result.

Storms are the safety-valve for the preservation of life upon the Earth. They are blessings, and they never come in disguise, either. Force is produced and stored up for the continuation of atomic polarity. The stormy outburst is the result of concentration uncontrolled, sweeping on to Accomplishment, Silence and Rest. If storms were not, focused potency might destroy manifestation. Storms are like the governor of a steam-engine, which moves obediently to the changing rapidity of the motion, and in turn, regulates the flow of the motor force.

A storm does the same thing on a broader scale. The destruction of life and accumulation is often deplored, as waste. Can there be any waste? Do not all things move in cycles, going forth and returning to the starting point, crossing and re-crossing constantly?

But all storms are not on the purely physical plane. All of us know of the tornadoes, cyclones and destructive outbursts that man has permitted to overcome him. The difference between an earth storm and a body storm is that the former is not "personally conducted," but sweeps on at its own free will, for the fructification of undeveloped good.

But the ego has the body given in charge of itself, and should so control the sweeping maelstrom as to add reserve force and potency for use. "Be ye angry and sin not," is the injunction of one of the Masters. That is, allow yourself to feel the fire of the unflagging Will; the manifesting of the never dying creative force, which is our birthright.

It is not necessary to vent the feeling of some trifling thing or person. But we must control and reserve the force. Emotional storms are of minor importance, but the same impulse of Will lies at the gateway of their appearance. Anger is a God-given impulse, and is the cyclone of the soul. Blessed is he who can hold his own storm force for his own use and potential energy.

THE ORIGIN AND THE SEAT OF EVIL

"All things were made by him; and without him was not anything made that was made." This statement, one of the most positive in the Scriptures, has been accepted by many as evidence that there is no evil. Those who believe in the non-existence of evil reason thus: Since God has created all things, and since He, being good, can create nothing but good, it follows that there can be no such thing as evil; consequently, that which seems to be evil is nothing more than an illusion of sense.

It is to be admitted that God—being all good, all loving, and all wise—did not, and indeed cannot, Himself create evil as such. Therefore, in so far as He and His works are concerned, it is correct to say there is no evil.

However, the problem of evil, as seen in its manifestations and in its effects on human life, cannot be thus easily disposed of. To consider one statement of truth by itself is not sufficient.

Two fundamental factors enter into man's creation; and each factor must receive its full share of attention in solving the difficulties that have arisen through his creation.

First is the fact that man is endowed with divide powers and divine possibilities. This is indicated in the scriptural record thus: "So God created man in his own image, in the image of God created be him; . . . and breathed into his nostrils the breath of life." To be made in His own image—after His own likeness—means to be endowed with all the faculties and all the creative powers that God himself possesses. In this sense, man is an epitome of God; he is like Him in all things, except that the powers of man are limited in degree and restricted in territory.

Second is the fact of free-will and individual responsibility with which man is divinely endowed. Although given second place in order of presentation, the characteristic of free-will can, by no means, be regarded as secondary in importance. The fact of man's being made in the divine image constitutes one wing in the twofold purpose of man's creation; the fact of his being honored with power of choice and decision, of his being invested with individual responsibility in regard to his own thoughts and his own acts, of his being the recipient of the divine decree: "Choose ye whom ye will serve,"—this fact constitutes the other wing in the purpose of his creation.

As each pinion is of equal importance in the flight of the bird, so, in man's nature, each of these qualities is equally essential in order that he may realize his divine possibilities. In these two branches, or features, of truth; in these two wings, or characteristics, of man's nature, we have the key to the solution of the problem of evil—whether there is evil, what constitutes evil, who is its author, and what determines the principle of its eradication. A few self-evident conclusions are to be deduced from this twofold proposition:

First, God is responsible for evil only on the grounds of giving man freedom in the use of power.

Second, wrong use of a good faculty, wrong direction of a good power, energies and forces used for other than good purposes—these things constitute evil.

Third, man alone is responsible for evil, man alone is the author of evil. Again, almost by way of parenthesis, this proposition may be viewed from another angle, and a few simple reflections of a negative nature may be emphasized—reflections that scarcely need be given the space of a sentence for those that are free from the entanglements of the commonly accepted religious faith:

First, there are not two distinct powers in the universe—one good, the other evil.

Second, there are not in the universe two distinct divinities, one the author of good, the other the author of evil—God and Satan.

Third, the conflict of life is not between gods and demons, between divine and satanic forces; the only conflict there is, is in man's own heart, between the dual inclinations of his own nature.

These three expressed in one positive statement become: There is one Power in the universe—and only one; the use made of this one Power determines its character, whether good or evil. To restate the basic proposition of the argument, giving emphasis to the fact of "creative" ability: Since God is creative Being or Energy, man, made in His image, is endowed with creative power, creative energy, and the creative instinct; likewise, he is invested with the right of choice in directing his creative faculties and in using the creative energy.

A general truth may be formulated thus: evil is the result of the wrong use of man's creative powers. It must be explained that creative power, as used here, means much more than the ability to give life to one's own species. It means infinitely more than the creation of new beings. It includes the ability to create conditions; to effect changes in environment; the ability to visualize ideals, whether in the fine arts—music, painting, sculpture, poetry—whether in the practical arts of every description—mechanics, architecture, home-making—whether in the culture and the development of a Christly character, which is to be regarded as "the finest of fine arts" as well as the most practical of practical arts; the ability not only to visualize, but to execute such ideals and to bring them into manifestation; the ability to create a Soul according to the Divine Standard, to nurture and to develop the soulual nature and to bring it into the state of Individual Consciousness on the plane of souluality; the ability to live a life of unselfish service—such possibilities as these are included in the expression, "creative power." Creative energy is the greatest attribute of the Divine nature.

Likewise, the creative power and the creative instinct, interpreted in their fullest meaning, are the greatest and the most sublime attributes of man's nature. There is one thing, however, that man possesses and must use in his creative function, with which God is not encumbered, that is, the physical body. True, we may think of the universe as the body, or the physical expression, of the Infinite; yet, in the universe, the Divine Will is supreme, and the universe is to Him in no wise a hindrance. Since the universe is in itself non-sense-desiring, the Creative Energy is thus free from desires of sense and of flesh. Whereas, man, in that he possesses a physical organism with its demands, its appetites, and its needs, is overwhelmed by a multiplicity of desires and tendencies, which naturally become his master, unless, through careful training, the divine nature has regained its rightful supremacy in his life. Creative power God uses only for good and noble purposes—in the creation of new beings and in the creation of new conditions for the universal good. Being impersonal energy, in Him, there can be no selfish, no personal, no partial motives to prompt the use of the divine creative function.

Man, forgetful of the Divine Ideal in whose likeness he is fashioned, uses his manifold faculties and powers for selfish purposes. He uses them to create conditions that seem good for himself and for those in his immediate circle, but conditions that often are secured at the expense of others and through the pain and the suffering of others. Herein lies the evil.

To create conditions for the benefit of self, regardless of their effect on the general welfare—this constitutes evil. Again, man uses his creative faculties for the pleasure of the flesh, and at the call of the carnal self this, likewise, constitutes evil. The flesh is not in itself harmful, nor are fleshly desires in themselves evil; but to allow the flesh and fleshly desires to dictate and to control this is evil. In this connection it bears repeating that God has created no evil thing and has endowed man with no harmful faculty, but that man, through wrong use of powers innately good and noble, may bring about evil and destruction; man, through the use he makes of things in themselves good, which God has created, may cause evil. But it is asked, Wherein is man accountable for evil? What department of his being is to be held responsible for it?

In order to answer this question, it is necessary to give attention to the four departments of man's nature body, spirit, mind, and soul. Man possesses a body the gift of mother earth, through his parents. This body, being of the earth, is naturally earthly in its appetites; being of the flesh, it is naturally fleshly in its tendencies; being on the plane of sense, it is naturally sensual in its desires. The body recognizes nothing that is like its creator except the generative principle; but, in this, the physical man sees nothing except desires that belong to the flesh. Here, again, it bears repeating: the body and its demands are not in themselves evil. But to let their dictates rule the life is evil. Man possesses a Spirit, the Spirit of Life which God breathed into him at birth. This Spirit is divine, because it comes from God. Yet it is not something peculiar to man.

Every animate thing, every living creature, in fact, all that exists—not only sentient beings, but even vegetable and mineral forms—in like manner, according to its own degree, breathes in this same Divine Spirit. For it is the Life Principle, that which animates, but does not control, every living thing. Moreover, Spirit is neither personal nor individual. It is principle; it is essence, it simply is. It is neither good nor evil.

As long as man lives, he uses this life principle. At the transition called death, the Spirit leaves his inert body, and goes back to its original store house the Life Center in God whence all life comes. It is to be emphasized that this Life Principle, called Spirit in the Scriptures, is not the same thing as the soul. Besides body and spirit, man has a mind. Herein is the source and the origin of evil. Herein, likewise, must begin the eradication of evil. The mind of man is the creator of evil. The mind of man is to be held responsible for all evil that originates in his fourfold being. In what sense mind is creator of evil cannot be made clear until consideration is given to the nature of mind in itself, to the nature of the soul, to the relation that exists between mind and soul. It is to be emphasized that mind is not an entity; it is not eternal; it is not immortal as an individualization. To be sure, it is eternal in the sense that nothing is really destroyed.

Yet things that are subject to change; things the elements of which, through a process of disintegration, return to the universal storehouse of elements whence they came; things the substance of which enters into other formations and becomes essential factors in other combinations, such things as these are not to be regarded as immortal. Although they continue to live, in so far as their essences are concerned, yet they live only through change of form.

The vegetation that today stands in the field may be asked tomorrow to give its life to man. Refuse and decay, the unsightly and even the poisonous, through chemic processes, contribute to richness of soil, and live again in health-giving plant forms. Yet such things are not to be classed as entities, nor are they in any wise, conscious individual beings or creations. In this class of non-individualized beings is the mind of man to be placed. Mind is that which results from the combination of body and spirit.

When the spirit of life is breathed into the body, there results in the brain of that to which life is given, a formation, or a combination, which men call mind. Thus, animals, even the lowest forms of animate beings, possess mind in crude degree. In all forms of life, mind is mortal and not an entity. Body, spirit, and mind are all to be thought of as mortal, changeable, transitory, and evanescent.

The soul is the only part of man's being that is eternal, or immortal. To express the idea more accurately, even the soul is not immortal as an individualization until it has been so created, or developed. The soul is the divine spark, or germ of the Infinite, which is incorporated into man's nature at birth. In its simple form, it is a mere atom of potentiality, unconscious, undeveloped, un-individualized. But it possesses in latency all the capacities and all the attributes of the Divine Ideal. In this inert state, as an unaroused spark of fire, it awaits the fanning and the feeding and the careful attention of a Vestal Virgin, in order that it may become the Christ-flame of Love, ever burning on the altar within. In this inert state, as the mere image of an ideal organic structure, it awaits the hand of the architect to shape and to fashion it into the Temple of the Soul. As such, it demands creative skill. In this latent condition, as a seed, it awaits nurturing influences and conditions that promote normal growth, that it may become a vitalized organic Center of Consciousness and of activity on the plane of Being. As such, it demands creative agencies and creative forces. Now, according to the divine economy, each department of man's fourfold being has been given its particular function, or office, to fill.

To the mind, has been delegated the function of cultivating the soulual nature, and of bringing it to the state of Soul Consciousness, or Immortality. Thus, the mind is the Vestal Virgin, the mind is the architect, the mind is the creator of the soul. The mind must become the creative agency, and must wisely direct the creative forces, and must manifest creative skill. Thus, through its manifold faculties and powers, through its varied methods of activity and of execution, the mind of man is the seat and the center of responsibility in the use of creative energy. The soul of man, being an atom, or germ, of the Infinite, is designed to reproduce the distinctive attributes of the Infinite. God, as creative Being, or Energy, possesses as His chief characteristic a combination of wisdom and love that insures that creative energy shall be directed only in channels of usefulness. Thus, He is an impersonal expression of the Divine Law of Love, or an unerring Standard of Infinite Goodness.

Therefore, man, or the soul of man, being made in His image, embodies potentially an expression of wisdom and love; in other words, the soul of man, created after the divine likeness, is an embryonic embodiment of the Divine Law of Love.

IT is the growth of personality that makes life useful. "Stand aside!" says the Teacher, "and observe thy personality as though it were an object of experiment. Study thy wandering thoughts and desires." Be not attached to things of the earth. Take refuge in meditation. The value of any experience or experiment lies in its capacity to make character. Think of this.

Men of the world give most of their time and attention to their body. They naturally perish with perishable thoughts and things. They create new fetters for themselves and try to enslave others.

Cultivate the habit of seeing faults in yourself and do not criticize them in others. Restrain your tongue and your thought. There can be no real spiritual progress without good moral character. Be occupied with the thoughts of improving and perfecting yourself in every way, this will kill vanity and leave you no time to find faults in others. Obey and be grateful. Live like a child in simplicity and purity of thought, word, and deed. You must first be a good servant and a disciple before you can be a master. Discipline yourself.

Endurance of pain and willingness to sacrifice and suffer are the two great keys to the development of the power of the soul. Love the immortal and eternal, crucify the mortal and personal in yourself. Your first duty is to purify and perfect yourself. You have no right to preach and teach. A large part of the world misery is due to conceit and selfishness. Much of what goes under the name of unselfishness and impersonal work and service is born of egotism.

Turn to your own mind and train it carefully. The Guru, or Teacher, has love that knows no bounds. His unselfish and unbounded love is proof of his Divinity. Teacher, true and pure, is one who has realized his true nature and is therefore perfectly Divine. He is higher than personality. He is Brahma—the creator; Vishnu—the preserver, and Shiva—the destroyer. Abstract gods, or personification, are realities because of the teacher's perfect self-realization. Even the gods venerate a perfect Guru.

It is only through the expansion and perfection of the personality that the highest impersonal is realized. It is through the ideal of the Guru or Master that God and man are made one. Man must recognize Divinity in man before he can see it in God. The Divine man or Master leads the disciple step by step to the threshold of the Temple of Immortality.

First comes the physical presence of the Teacher as a source of inspiration. Through contact with the personality of the Teacher, the disciple learns the greatness and love of his personality. This is the second step. The dignity of character and unselfish love teach him new ideas of greatness and unselfishness. The living example of great lives and lofty ideals transforms his being. He tries to imitate them, and in doing honor to the personality of his Teacher he naturally tries to think of himself. He looks within to find where he has to begin the work of reformation, so as to be worthy of his position as disciple. This leads him to think of the principle that rules the conduct and character of his Guru. It is the third step, from personality to idea or principle. He learns from the teacher the beautiful lessons of unity of souls and purity of life. He then tries to follow them and translate them into his own life. Now he finds his soul in more harmony with that of his teacher and thus nearer God and Truth.

The fourth and last step is the recognition on the part of the disciple of the impersonal nature of the Teacher and his own divinity. Through meditation and constant practice of the golden rules laid down for his guidance, he finds that all life is one and the Teacher as well as he is drop in one ocean of Eternal Life. The Teacher now becomes an elder Brother on the same Path and God announces the highest form of an Eternal Principle animating and vitalizing all visible and invisible universe.

He now has found the God within, and he no longer reaches for Him in the outside world. Yet, he recognizes His own presence and omnipotence and continues to love and honor his Teacher as best guide and benefactor.

GOD IN MAN

MEN who are whole serve the whole. Being free, no blood ties have power over them. They walk the earth over, as Servants, as Knights, as Messengers. What do they tell in their long wanderings? Look within. You are whole. Hear within. Tone sings in you. Touch within. God is you. God is you; but you know it not, because you are only part human. You have not yet integrated the many forces of Soul which are to make in one time the Body of God. You are the builder of the Body of God.

Just as the elemental and cosmic forces of life were the builders of this human body in the mother's womb. There are many Soul forces drawn to you, forces which have worked through and have been refined by many men of the past, who you may consider your past reincarnations. These forces are the many "you's" which often surprise and baffle you, as they unexpectedly sing their song of existence. Some are very strong, some are very weak. Yet, none of them is the real You—the God that is you.

The God that is creating Itself out of the co-merging of all parts. God is the dissonant harmony of all the Soul-forces which, in a sense, are your past. Each of them pulls apart in its will for self-expression. But God is not self-expression, but harmonization. It is the synthesis of wills which you see usually as enemies fighting for the control of you, but which God sees as complements uniting to give birth to your own living God. The conscious you is the Mother of this living body of God. He builds it cell by cell, deed by deed, meditation by meditation. He is sacrificing himself to bear the living shrine, the glorious temple where all Soul Rays merge in the nine-gated sanctuaries and become Silence—the No-thing that is God.

How cruelly do we need mothers, mothers of the living God! The modern world is tragic and mad from lack of true mothers. It cries for Mothers of God, to harmonize the warring forces of Soul into the great chord of the Companions, into the wholeness of Man. It cries for seeds, for the time has come for germination. Spring's breezes are stirring the pubescent earth that longs for fulfillment. Sun-rays are stretching through the ether waiting to dart love-rays into the soil.

But where are the seed-men, men who are wholes, men whose hearts are mothers' hearts, bearers of Living substance? Sun-rays want to become roots, to push life earthward for the regeneration of the crude salts of the soil, of these salts that yesteryear were incorporated in leaves and flowers, that now are humus, dark and moist.

Men that are whole, men that are Mothers of God, men that are sacrifices to the New Life—where are they, where can they be found?

They are the true nobility of man, the Redeemers and Lovers. They are ready to break open for the new roots to push through and perform their work in the darkness. They are ready for endless crucifixions. "This is my body—eat ye all of it, that you may become whole." This is the chant of seeds—"Eat my body, that you may become whole." It's the Christ-song, and the song of wheat. The mystic plant exiled from its Venus home to the green fields of the earth. What greater Knighthood? What more sublime crusade? Fields of wheat to help the multitudes to give birth to the living God—for wheat is the sacred food of generation. It is the substance that makes whole, that above all else sustains the mating of the opposites, that brings fertility.

Fields of Mother-love stretched across vast, endless plains of time—for it is mother-love at its highest that makes possible the harmonization of the many Soul-forces into a spiritual Body in whom God may manifest. Mother-love sings to the unborn, and to the new-born. It is tone, because it is "whole" and tone is the power of wholeness, the emanation of wholeness from the heart of that which is integrated and full.

The noble Man chants his mother-love to his charges. These chants stir the heart-power in the unborn; they slowly arouse in the embryo the rhythmical motions of life, of this power of active love which is the power of blood circulation keeping the body whole. And soon the mothers feel the touch of the quickened One.

The Christ baby stirs in the womb of the Soul which has become harmonic and vibrant. His little pulse brings joy to the Mother that gladdens because the living God is to be born. Birth of the Living God! Pain and joy, strain and release, fear and supreme love—then complete dedication, all-absorbing service to the little Ones.

Is this not the supreme knighthood? The knighthood of the mothers of God. They love, they struggle, they serve and sacrifice. Their bodies are the offering: their Souls are the crucible. Their love is the strong sword that protects the new life.

Men who are whole are wombs of God. They are the messengers of eternity. They are knights of harmony, which means fullness and freedom. They are servants of the sun. They wander over the earth, holding in their consciousness the seeds of the Living God. Sowers of Seed, feeders of the hungry ones, mothers of the unborn—they are the true nobility of Man.

GOD AND MAN

THE mystery of life has puzzled thinkers for all ages. Whence have we come? Whither are we going? Why so much pain of mind, heart and body? The puzzle is indeed almost beyond man's solution.

"Truth is this to me, and that to thee; and truth or clothed or naked let it be." Again, we ask with jesting Pilate, "What is Truth?" and pause for an answer. What indeed? Some have called it Beauty, others Love—to all it means the Eternal-veiled in sooth to our feeble vision. So marvelous is the answer and so imperfect our humanity that we must see now "thru a glass darkly."

"Never the spirit was born, the spirit shall cease to be never."

Out of the bosom of the great First Cause we come—myriad sparks of divine possibilities, a part of God. Clothed in physical matter, we work our way slowly and painfully, going deeper and deeper into the material world. Stifled by sense experience, beaten on and upward by pain, the soul begins to climb the upward path back to the bosom of the Father.

On the upward road hands of older brothers in evolution are stretched out to help in proportion as the struggling soul has carried its burdens bravely, done its duty cheerfully and aided younger brothers below it on the path. A mighty chain of development links man to God, a chain of cause and effect.

But let us not think only of the God without. The Force in which we live and move and have our being is within as well, in all living things. Separated, we seem to the eyes of sense, but in truth all one—all sparks of the One mighty flame.

Whence do we come then? The answer is plain. Why the pain, grief, despair? That the soul, through suffering, may see the vision beyond the stars, and by struggle, grow strong.

Whither do we go? Therein lies the marvelous beauty and justice of the plan. Life after life, incarnation after incarnation, the steady growth continues until all the lessons have been learned and the perfect soul, unless drawn by the great renunciation to help his weaker brothers, need go no more out. "Him will I make a pillar in the temple of my God."

It is easy to say that we grow strong through suffering, but when the real tests come, we find our wills weakened and are often unable to resist the attacks that rob our souls of peace. It is then that the disciple must wear the armor of faith and know that whatever comes is for the strengthening of his will. Through Will, we rise from form to spirit in the sense that we learn to overcome or rise above the relatively unimportant affairs of a material world and center our consciousness on a plane where all is peace and permanence. Nothing lasts in the material expression of life. All is in a constant flux and flow. The only thing unchangeable is the law of change. Well, is it that this should be so, for it is through change of forms that evolution works. Constant progress should be the experience of every soul. From the lower to the higher, from the weaker to the stronger—this is the purpose of expression on the physical plane.

If then we do not learn to transmute suffering into joy, we miss the fruits of the experience. In all lives come bitter disappointments, disillusions so that the soul may be aroused to seek that which is beyond and above—the unfailing Peace, the Love that never disappoints and will not let us go until we rest our weary souls in Him.

In this way we learn to rise in the plan and thru our own experience can become the more sympathetic and compassionate to those who are still struggling in the dark and know not why they struggle.

The great plan needs the help of every human being. It is through those on earth that the forces on the higher planes must work. We here count it a joyous privilege to serve. May you know, too, the beauty of such service.

Without it, life is futile, and suffering is meaningless. With it the whole upward urge of evolution is quickened, and the race made ready for a higher development in which pain shall be no more, for God shall have wiped away all tears from the eyes of those who through struggle have become strong and through suffering tender and compassionate toward all that lives.

PROPHECY INTELLIGIBLE

The desire of extending our knowledge by acquainting ourselves with the future as well as the past, is one of the strongest instincts of the human bosom. From the conviction that such knowledge is often unattainable, reason may moderate and restrain the impulse, but it can never eradicate it. It is immovably fixed among the elementary promptings and appetencies of our mental constitution, and to disown or to disregard it is virtually to cast a reflection on the wisdom that shines forth in the high endowments of our nature.

But this is seldom done. The value of the principle is acknowledged, and it may justly be questioned whether a considerable portion of mankind, if it had been left to them to choose between the possession of foreknowledge and of Memory, would not at once have decided in favor of the former. Considering the ends for which we are made, and the vast importance of being able to adapt our plans and operations to the wants of the future, it might appear upon a superficial view that the power of Prescience would conduce far more to the leading objects of existence than the faculty of Memory. But a little reflection will serve to show the fallacy of such a conclusion, and, in the comparative estimate of the two endowments, to throw the balance altogether on the side of Memory.

In the first place, it is to be remarked, that the objects or materials of Memory are constantly increasing, while those of foreknowledge, if we possessed it, would be constantly decreasing. As the term of our existence in this world is limited, so we must set some limits to the extent of our attainments.

Vast as our intelligence is, we cannot know everything. Suppose then that a definite knowable by us in this world, is it not evident that the more an individual knows today, the less remains to be known tomorrow?—and so the stock of information before him is incessantly growing less as he advances in life, just as the remaining distance of a journey is diminished by the every day's progress of the traveler. But with Memory the case is directly the reverse. Here is no diminution, but constant accumulation; and the peculiar manner in which we are enriched by this wonderful faculty may be made more evident by an illustration.

If the mariner in navigating the ocean on a dark and stormy night, and on a course that was fraught with danger, whether from icebergs or breakers, were to affix his lamp to the stern of his vessel instead of the prow, it would not require the slightest nautical experience to prompt the exclamation that the man was bereft of his senses. In common circumstances such would be the spontaneous impression, and it would be a reasonable impression.

But suppose that the lamp was possessed of such peculiar properties, that when placed in that position its light would be continually acquiring a greater intensity and shedding abroad a wider and brighter irradiation; whereas if placed in front of the vessel, it would be continually growing dimmer and dimmer, shedding but little light before and none behind. It is obvious that in the former position it would gradually increase to such an intensity of glow, as to illuminate the watery waste before as well as behind, and finally envelope the ship's way with a flood of splendor. So, with the faculty of memory. Although more immediately and legitimately conversant with the past, yet its issues and effects reach forward to the future.

Such is the constitution of things in this world under the providence of God—such the uniform relations of cause and effect—such the established order of antecedents and consequents—that the more we know of the past the more accurately we can judge of the future. We all know that the decisions of an enlightened experience are well-nigh oracular. But what is experience, but the accumulated results of the information of Memory? He who has lived longest, seen most, and remembered most of the ways of God and of Man has the largest stock of experience, and is best qualified to pronounce judgments pertaining to the future. The lamp of his barque shines before.

To such a man, for all the practical purposes of life, experience serves in the place of prophecy, and thus is approved the verity of the couplet of Milton:

That old experience doth attain
To something of prophetic strain.

This view of the subject will appear still more obvious, if it be borne in mind, that we are enabled to avail ourselves of the memories of others as well as our own, and thus may in effect increase the amount of our own experience, and render the judgments founded upon it still more unerring in their prophetic scope.

From these considerations it will doubtless appear that beings blessed, like man, with the faculty of treasuring up the lessons of the past, are far more highly gifted of the Creator than if crowned only with the more imposing but less useful endowment of foreseeing or foretelling the future. As it is, he has the virtual advantages of the one in the exercise of the other; and if we were to denominate the divine faculty of Memory by its most appropriate epithet, we should term it the prophetico-reminiscent faculty, and should say that it was to the power of prescience as the full vintage of Abiezer to the scanty gleaning of the grapes of Ephraim.

But while we speak thus highly of Memory, it is no part of our object to undervalue or disparage the innate desire for the knowledge of the future,—the instinctive prompting to lift the curtain that shrouds that unknown world from our gaze. While we freely concede that in respect to the great mass of human affairs it is by reasoning from the past that we are to anticipate what is to come, at the same time we feel equally assured that this is not the only source upon which we are to draw for light. We are not absolutely shut up to the revelations of experience.

The desire of penetrating the hidden recesses of futurity is one of the native impulses of our being, and doubtless ordained by the Creator, when properly regulated, not only as a source of lawful but of dignified enjoyment. This is inferred by the most legitimate a priori deductions of reason, and confirmed by the unquestionable fact, that the wisdom of Jehovah has made express provision in his word for the gratification of this implanted longing in the human soul.

A multiplicity of leading facts in the history of the past goes to convince us, that there exists in the bosom of God an inherent willingness and a definite purpose to impart to his devoted servants a knowledge of future events—not perhaps to the extent that our short-sighted or prurient hankerings might desire, but so far as in finite wisdom sees would redound to our best good, and to the soundest interests of his kingdom on earth.

We advert to this truth in order to remove, if possible, the vague impression of idle yearning, of presumption, of impiety, of sacrilegious intrusion upon forbidden ground, that is so apt to connect itself with every attempt to unravel the mysteries of revelation, and to honor God by ascertaining the sense of what he has himself spoken. For nothing is more certain than that the opprobrium, which is due only to the most marked and contemptuous neglect of the divine oracles has, from many quarters, fallen upon the humble and reverential study of their entire contents.

Our position is, that God is willing that man should come to the possession of the knowledge of futurity, not indeed in unlimited measure, but to such extent as will be for his good; and what more unquestionable evidence can we adduce of this than his own express declaration? Hear then his voice in respect to the Father of the faithful:—Shall I hide from Abraham that thing which I do? Can language be more unambiguous?

Now the value of this averment depends upon its being an expression, not of his purpose in reference to a particular individual or a particular event only, but of a general principle in the conduct of his providence. Does any latent doubt linger in the mind of the reader, whether this is a principle of the divine administration?—let us then make assurance doubly sure by citing the same declaration in more general terms as uttered by the mouth of the prophet Amos:—'Surely the Lord God will do nothing, but he revealeth his secrets unto his servants the prophets.'

"With this testimony before us, we presume we hazard nothing in saying, that from the primeval epochs of his church all along through the whole line of her annals, the Most High has never projected any great and important movement without making some portion of our race privy to his counsels. It may be said of the petty potentates of the earth, that it is the glory of a king to conceal a matter," but the Universal Sovereign, who has no enemies that can take advantage of a premature disclosure, can afford to adopt a more liberal, or if you please, a less cautious policy. He can consistently bring his servants into his cabinet, and freely advise them of those intended measures which he originates for their good, and carries into execution by their agency.

But it will be asked, is there not some exclusiveness—some favoritism—in regard to these disclosures? Are they free and open to all are they not restricted to a chosen few? Is it not inti mated that prophecy is for prophets, while the great mass of men are debarred from this kind of information? We answer, prophecy is for prophets, just as holy things are for holy men.

'The secret of the Lord is with them that fear him.' It is to a certain form of character—to spirits of a certain mold—that he unveils the arcana of his bosom. It is mainly the good man—he whose soul is in sympathy with the will of his Maker—that he deigns to make the depositary of his designs. And yet at the present day, under the existing dispensation, there is no other interdict standing in the way of any man's attainment of a knowledge of his prophetic purposes, then there is as to the attainment of a true knowledge of the mercies of the Gospel. There is no other than a moral impediment existing in either case. The record of eternal life—the charter of immortal hope—is not a sealed book to anyone who is desirous to have its precious purport laid open for the rejoicing of his heart. He need not utter the invocation.

"Angels, roll the rock away,"

In order to look into the Savior's vacated sepulcher, and see there the pledge and assurance of his own resurrection in bliss and triumph. The humble, the yielding, the believing mind is the great requisite, and yet the apostle's words make it clear that there is a mystery in the believer's salvation, which can never be understood but by a certain state of heart.

And so we repeat there are certain moral prerequisites which we believe God has always insisted on in those whom he would make the 'men of his counsel.' This will appear plainer as we proceed.

We have spoken of the attainment of prophetic knowledge under the present dispensation, and we may further remark upon the distinct characteristics of the Jewish and Christian economies in regard to prophecy, that the disclosures made by God to his ancient people were immediate; i.e. they were made without the intervention of a written revelation.

The Scriptures were not yet indited. In fact, it was the embodying of these very disclosures that constituted a large part of the Scriptures themselves. But at present, when the canon is complete, we have no evidence, we believe, that any original and independent prediction is ever imparted to men.

Whatever supernatural influence is now exercised upon the human faculties in regard to future events, it is not with a view to impart to them new revelations, but simply to enable them to understand what is already revealed. And in this we suppose there is nothing any more miraculous than there would have been or was in God's hearing and answering David's prayer when he said, 'Open thou mine eyes that I may behold wondrous things out of thy law.' These things were actually in the law, and the whole drift of the Psalmist's prayer was that he might be enabled to see them. So, in looking upon a far distant landscape with a telescope, the objects of vision are not created by the telescope. They were there before, and the telescope only enables us to discern them. In like manner in regard to divine revelations, no new and original facts are communicated to any man, but supernatural influence may put the telescope to the mental eye, and enable it to behold things that would not otherwise come within its most extended range of vision.

This influence, however, we supposed to be no more miraculous than any other spiritual illumination granted to the humble and teachable mind in answer to prayer, and as a blessing upon its own diligent and sedulous use of all appointed means. For the language of prophecy is a distinct study, as much so as the language of mathematics or astronomy, and without the most assiduous investigation of the peculiar dialect of prophecy—without earnest endeavors to put ourselves in possession of the key to the sacred cipher—it will be the height of presumption to hope to be initiated into the scriptural disclosures of future things. Imagine the case of an individual utterly unable to read, whose heart was yet touched with the love of God, and who earnestly longed to be made acquainted with the contents of the word of life. Should we expect, however ardent might be the aspirations of the soul for a knowledge of the Scriptures, that person would be taught the contents of the Bible by a miracle?

Would he not be under the necessity of submitting to the same process with the youngest child, and of first learning to read before he could fully understand the word of inspired truth? And yet you will not hesitate to admit that there may be a special divine influence quickening the faculties of such an individual, and enabling him more readily to seize the rudiments of learning and compass the object of his pursuit. Just so in the attainment of prophetical science.

God does not enlighten the student of prophecy by a miracle, but he simply puts his blessing upon the use of the appropriate means. He aids his faculties in the attempt to make himself master of the key of prophecy, precisely as he might have aided Sir Isaac Newton in the attainment of those mathematical media which were necessary to the solution of the problem of the universe. This cuts off all claims to any direct supernatural illumination, and strikes at the root of all extravagance of pretension in un-riddling the hallowed mysteries of revelation. And to charge such efforts, when humbly conducted, with fanaticism, enthusiasm, folly or presumption, is in a high degree unreasonable and unjust.

METAPHYSICAL LAWS

Those who are living in undesirable environments are not usually willing to accept the idea presented in this law; it is more agreeable to place the blame elsewhere; but the fact that your surroundings are ordinary does not necessarily prove that you are an inferior person. But it does prove that you have not brought forth into full action the superior qualities that you may possess. Remember, it is the active nature that determines the surroundings in which you are to be placed; and the active nature in most persons is a mixture of conflicting forces, constantly neutralizing each other, or disturbing each other.

A disturbed nature always attracts inferiority, or is drawn into the disagreeable. When the active forces in your nature conflict and neutralize each other, your nature becomes like a leaf in the whirlwind, and you will become a victim of all the unpleasant things that you may meet.

There are a great many people with high and strong powers who never meet anything else but the dark side of things. The reason is that their active forces conflict; one desire goes this way, and another that way. Some intentions are constructive, while others go at random.

Their objects in life are constantly being changed; and what they build up one day is taken down the next. Let the average mind look closely at his own active nature and ask himself if all the forces of his being are moving constructively and harmoniously towards one great goal.

He will find that they are not. He will discover far more conflict in his own mind and consciousness than he suspected, and he will have to admit that his surroundings are exact counterparts of his own active self. There is one exception, however, that had better be considered before we proceed further; and it is nothing else but the result of misdirected sympathy.

We frequently find people in environments where we know they do not belong, but fail to discover the why, and in failing to do this, we conclude that there is nothing in the idea that people attract their own environments. But when we examine these cases, we find it necessary to reverse our hasty conclusions.

There are many people who remain where they are, not because they belong there, but because their sympathy keeps them there. They do not wish to break away, for fear others may suffer. We all know of such cases, and when we look into this subject closely, we find that misdirected sympathy is one of the greatest of obstacles to the proper adjustment of persons with their true surroundings.

If it were not for misdirected sympathy, several million people would today be living in different environments—environments far better suited to their present natures and needs. To break loose from old associations and accept new opportunities may at times seem unkind; but we must remember that we are living for the whole race, and not only for a few friends. And again, we can render the best services to the race, including our present friends, by being perfectly true to ourselves. Sentimentalism and abnormal feelings have kept down thousands of fine minds, and compelled many a human flower to wither away among weeds.

But it is not right; the entire race is kept back whenever a single person is held down; and we must seek to avoid it whenever we can.

Each individual must be permitted to be true to himself; and it is wrong for us to shed tears when a friend finds it necessary to go elsewhere to promote his progress.

You may be living today in uncongenial and unpleasant environments, or your work may call you where you know you do not belong; but what is the cause?

There are several causes. You may be held where you are on account of misdirected sympathy. If so, give reason a chance to prove to you that you are wronging everybody by staying where you are. You are not doing the right thing by yourself, nor by anybody else, unless you are at your best. You may be held where you are because you have no definite purpose in life. Then decide upon a purpose, and train all the forces of your being to work for that purpose, and that alone. Gradually, you will work away from your present surroundings, and doors will open through which you may pass to better things.

There is nothing that will take you into better environments more quickly than to have a fixed and high purpose, and to marshal all the powers of mind and soul to work for that purpose. And since this is something that everyone can do, there is now no reason whatever, why a single person should be held down.

Or, possibly you may be held where you are because your good qualities are merely negative. There are plenty of people in this condition. They mean well, and have only the best intentions, but there is no power whatever in these intentions.

If the better side of you is negative, and the "old Adam" side of you is positive and active, you are making for yourself a world that is anything but ideal. It is the "old Adam" in this case that determines what kind of surroundings you are to receive; and that all will not be glorious goes without saying.

When your better side becomes strong and positive; when you're good intentions are full of living power, and when you turn all the forces of your being into the promotion of larger and higher aims, there is going to be a change. You will soon begin to gravitate towards better environments and more congenial exterior conditions.

One of the greatest essentials in this connection, however, is that all the forces of your better nature must be in harmony, and must work together for the better environments that you have in view.

It is not what you are, negatively, inherently or potentially, that determines your present conditions in life; it is what you use and how that something is used.

There are people with small minds and insignificant abilities that have found the most desirable environments, simply because the active forces of their nature worked together with a definite object constantly in view.

Others with prodigious minds and remarkable talents have found nothing but failure and distress, simply because they did not use constructively the powers they possessed.

The quiet, steady, orderly and constant forward movement will bring you to the goal in view every time, even though your forces are so weak that you can move but slowly. But when you are endowed with extraordinary capabilities, you will rise rapidly and attain practically everything you may desire.

A certain man may not be strictly honest nor moral; nevertheless, if he has ability and employs his faculties constructively and harmoniously, he will create a superior environment. And through his power to achieve the greater things, he will be attracted towards opportunities that wall promote still further, the improvement of his environment. But it must be remembered that if this man were honest, moral and true, his power would be still greater, and he would enjoy far better the beauties of his delightful surroundings.

The best man in the world will be a failure if he does not employ his ability constructively. There is a belief among many that honest people ought to have the best that life can give; but the mere state of being honest is not enough. It is doing things that count.

Virtues do not create, but they have the power to properly direct the process of creation. The mind that is pure, honest and just, can accomplish far more with a given ability than one who does not have these virtues. It is constructive ability that does things.

Character simply guides the doing so that the products may be of the highest order and the greatest worth. The person who has character only but no constructive ability, will accomplish nothing in the world, and will have to submit to the inconsistencies of fate.

Combine ability with character, and turn all your powers towards the attainment of some definite goal, and you are going to rise out of your present conditions, and enter into superior ones just as surely as you have life. It is your active nature that counts; therefore, the more development, power and superiority that you can express through this nature, the greater will be the results in the external world.

All the qualities of your active nature must have worth and must work together. Superior qualities working at variance with each other will take you down into inferior environments; while inferior qualities, if constructive and united in action, will take you into a better environment than the one you are in at present.

The whole problem is, therefore, to express your best in action, and to train the active powers and faculties in your being to work in harmony; to work together for the same purpose, and with the same attitude. Conflicting tendencies of mind have given poverty, distress and misfortune to many of great ability and superior goodness; while properly united tendencies have given success to many a man that was neither able nor true.

Nature is just; we receive according to what we have accomplished, not according to what we have tried to do, but what we actually have done.

We will receive material success and delightful exterior surroundings if we have worked properly for these things. But if we have neglected to work for the inner things of life, we will receive nothing that has permanent value in life.

The wise man works for all that is beautiful and true, and will receive riches both in the without and the within. Such is the full life, the complete life, the life that is really worth living.

If things are not right in your world, you are to blame.

Accept the blame and resolve to take things into your own hands and make them right. You can; because your environment will be exactly as your active nature is; and you can change your active nature as you like.

CONCERNING EVIL

Concerning evil, there are many doctrines; some declaring that it is a real and permanent power, battling with the good; others declaring that it is nothing, simply the absence of the good; while between these two extremes, almost any number of beliefs on the subject may be found. To prove that evil is an actual principle, personified in the Prince of Darkness, is not only difficult, but impossible.

On the other hand, to prove to the world that evil is nothing, is by no means simplicity itself.

Nevertheless, this latter doctrine comes very nearly being the truth. However, it is not our purpose to analyze the nature of evil here. That is a subject so large that separate attention will be required. But to make clear what we wish to bring out in connection with the law under consideration, it will be necessary to define, briefly, what evil actually is, that is, what the new psychology has found it to be.

To say evil is the absence of good is correct, though not sufficiently explicit. And to say that evil is undeveloped good, is simply a play upon words. Development is eternal: therefore, the fully developed of today is undeveloped in comparison with the possibilities of tomorrow.

To employ the undeveloped just as if it were developed will produce evil; and this fact has given rise to the idea that evil is undeveloped good. When we look closely at these things that are called evil, we find that in every case, force has been employed contrary to the natural laws involved.

We can, therefore, say that evil is misdirected good; or that it is the improper use of a power that is in itself good. In fact, all powers and forces and elements are good in themselves. All that is real is good. Everything is created for a good purpose, and is actually good, but it is possible to employ it for a purpose that is not in accord with the laws that obtain at present.

Every act is good, proper and useful when performed in its own sphere of action; but when performed outside of its own sphere of action, it is not good; it produces conditions that we call evil. One of the greatest truths in the universe is that every act has its own sphere of action.

We cannot do anything at any place without violating that great law of propriety; and if there were no such law, the universe would be chaos, as one can understand. To simplify the subject as much as possible, we may state that evil is a condition produced by an act that is performed outside of its natural sphere of action, and that the power and effects of that condition depend upon how much life the mind throws into the said act. It is a well-known fact that the mind gives its life to these actions and conditions upon which consciousness is directed; and that consciousness is always directed where reality is supposed to exist.

Therefore, when we consciously admit the existence of evil, we give more life and power to those conditions we call evil; and consequently, make them much worse than they are. That is all very simple; so simple that further elucidation will not be required. But the question is how we can prevent giving our conscious attention to evil.

When evil seems so very real, how can we otherwise but consciously admit its existence? When we know that evil is not a thing, not a principle, not a reality, but simply a certain temporary use of reality; and when we know that the use of that reality has its origin in our own minds, our attention will be at once transferred from the unpleasant condition, and be directed upon our own inner mental domain. Consciousness will be withdrawn from the condition called evil, and will become concerned with the change of mental action.

The power of the evil will at once be diminished, and its effects dwindle into nothing. Actual experience in the life of anyone has demonstrated the fact that a pain, or even a severe disease will disappear instantaneously when consciousness is fully and completely taken into another sphere of thought or action.

This proves that an evil condition can live only so long as we give it life; and we give it life only so long as we consciously admit its existence. When an evil condition is felt, attention should at once be directed upon the opposite good that exists in the inner world of perfection. This action of mind will take consciousness away from the unpleasant condition, and will set all the faculties of mind to work in realizing the absolutely good.

By tracing all perverted action to its inner mental source, consciousness will follow, leaving evil behind, and coming to give its life to the change of the said source. Then, if the desire of the heart is to change the source of that action, and the new, ideal image of the good is at hand, the transformation will be made at once. To illustrate, we will take a depressed condition of mind and body, and proceed by this method to remove it.

First, picture clearly upon mind the perfect image of harmony so that you can almost see harmony with the mind. Second, prove to yourself, by your reason, that this depressed condition is not a thing, but the temporary result of valuable power misdirected; and since this power is directed by your own mind your own mind must contain the origin of the perversion. Third, turn attention upon your own inner mentality, with a view of removing the source of perversion by establishing a state of harmony, and while thus directing attention upon the inner mentality, hold your mind in such an attitude that it is moving directly upon the image of perfect harmony.

The result will be that consciousness will become so absorbed in creating the new state of harmony that it will withdraw completely from the outer evil condition. This outer condition will consequently vanish from the lack of life, while the new state of harmony will be firmly established by receiving all the attention and all the life; a simple process that works perfectly, and that can be employed in removing any evil condition. Before you begin, always picture clearly upon your mind the image of the perfect state that you seek, and proceed as above in the elimination of the wrong and the creation of the right.

A good, clear understanding of the law under consideration will aid remarkably in the turning of your attention. There is nothing like reason, and clear understanding to change the mind.

To fully realize that life and power go wherever consciousness goes is extremely important; and also, that consciousness can be directed anywhere by becoming thoroughly interested elsewhere. People who feel deeply, always have the best results with these methods, because feeling produces deep interest wherever attention is directed.

ALL THINGS WORK TOGETHER FOR GOOD

This law ought to bring cheer into the hearts of everybody, because it certainly declares that the way to better things is not nearly as difficult as we have supposed it to be. The doctrine of the "straight and narrow path" has been misinterpreted, and does not refer to something that is so extremely difficult to pass through. It is not a path that leads straight away from everything that is pleasant in life; neither is it so narrow that only the naked soul can pass through.

The belief that everything in life must be left out if we wish to take this path, is absurd; in fact, the very opposite is the truth.

The path that leads into life, the full life, the complete life, the beautiful life, is straight because it is established upon law. When you take this path, you begin to use properly all the laws of life, and will therefore gain all the good things that life can give.

A law is not a cruel something that punishes, a law is a path to the greater and greater good. When we live according to a law, we are constantly receiving the greater riches that lie in that path; and when we live according to all the laws of life, we receive everything good that life can give. When we violate a law, we go outside of the path, where there is nothing, and receive nothing.

The law does not punish us when we go astray; we simply deprive ourselves of the good things of life by going away from the path where those good things are to be found. The path that leads into life is narrow because it gives room only for your own individuality; and only for the true self. You cannot be a double self, one part good and the other not—when you enter the path.

There is room only for one true self. Neither can you lean on someone else; there is not room. On the path, you must live your own life and give everybody else the freedom to live his own life. Life is given to us to be lived; and to live life, you must live it yourself, and according to your own light.

The path to life, the path to better things; or, to express it otherwise, the advancing path, is not therefore a dismal, disagreeable and difficult path; but the very opposite. It is found by seeking good and the good only. So long as we have only good in mind, we will be on the path; we will live according to the laws of life, and will receive only good things, because the laws of life can give only good things.

But when we begin to desire what is not good, we are at once drawn out of the path; we will be deprived of the essentials to life; emptiness, weakness, perversion, confusion, and all kinds of disasters will follow.

When all our desires are directed upon the good, the creative powers within us will constantly re-create everything about us, and make these things better. Everything in yourself will be made better. You will be in more perfect harmony with your surroundings, and will attract more agreeable persons, circumstances and events. You will become a creator of good; everything that you do will produce good, and everything that you attempt will result in your good. You will meet persons and environments on the better side, and will consequently receive the best things that these can give.

Every change that you make will be an open door to greater good, because you were moving towards the good when the change was made. This is very important, and it is well to remember that when we desire only the good, we are moving towards the good. If we pass through a few unpleasant places while we are moving, that does not matter; the fact that all will be good when we reach the promised land is sufficient. To desire the good, however, does not mean to desire mere self-satisfaction. It is the universal good that must be held in mind; and not only held in mind, but desired with the whole heart and soul.

Desire only the highest good, and then turn your whole life into that desire. Make that desire far stronger than all other desires, and live in it constantly. A multitude of metaphysical laws will come in and promote realization of the good, and you will be absolutely protected from any mishaps. The mistakes of your personal self, while you were not on your guard, will be obliterated before they can produce results.

Should the personal self-attempt to take a misstep, and lead your plans out of the true path, the door will be barred; something will come in the way, and turn attention elsewhere. Having set your heart and soul upon the attainment of the good and the good only, the predominating powers in your being will work only for good, and all lesser powers will, one after the other, be taken into the same path, so that ever long all things in your life will work together for good. We may not all understand at first how this can be true; but it works, and that is sufficient.

EQUAL TO THE OCCASION

The tasks of tomorrow are not one half as difficult as they appear to be today. When thinking of that which is to be, we usually transform our imaginations into mental telescopes.

What we see is made larger and brought nearer. Being so large, we think we must give the matter much thought; and being so near, we think we must attend to the matter at once.

Consequently, we as a rule, give future tasks several times as much thought as necessary; and begin preparation, weeks and months before we have to; wasting time, energy and precious thought simply because we did not see the thing where it is, and in its true size. Sometimes the task looks so large that we fear to begin; or we have doubts as to our ability to carry it through.

We do not feel equal to the occasion because we have magnified that occasion several times over, through a misuse of the imagination. People frequently live for weeks in dread of something that they have to do, because it looks so large and so difficult. But when they come to it, there is nothing to fear at all; no difficulties present; one of the easiest things they were ever called upon to deal with. The magnifying power of the imagination is the cause. And through this very thing, millions of people have either stumbled outright or have started on the down grade.

To be able to see one's self as it really is, and to be able to see one's work as it really is—that is a great attainment indeed. You cannot do justice to yourself today unless you can correctly measure your present capacity. And you cannot properly approach your work unless you can see that work as it actually is—no larger and no smaller than it is.

You may be far greater than your work; you may be equal to far greater occasions than the ones you daily meet; but you may not know it. You may be looking upon your work through the magnifying glass of abnormal imagination; this makes your work look large and difficult, and you fear it.

Consequently, you look upon yourself through fear; and through that glass, you appear to be much smaller than you really are.

Nine people out of ten habitually magnify their work and belittle themselves. They do this unconsciously; in fact, they have inherited the habit, and do not know that they have it. Occasionally we find a person who magnifies himself, and belittles the work that is before him; but he usually does this in the beginning only. The nearer he comes to the real occasion, the more he changes his view, until it is completely changed. He also comes to think that the work is hard, and that he himself is incompetent.

To secure the best results from every action, the actor as well as the thing acted upon, must be seen as they are. The subject is, therefore, of great importance. When the coming task is easy, we cannot afford to give it a great deal of thought and preparation. And when it is hard, we want to know it, so we can prepare ourselves.

But we cannot properly prepare ourselves to meet the difficult so long as we live in dread or fear. And to dispel this fear, it is only necessary to realize that we are equal to every occasion that comes into our path. We are never called upon to do what we are not able to do; that is one of the laws of life. What comes to us, comes because we, ourselves, have sent the invitation.

Things do not come of themselves; and other people can never give to you what you do not willingly accept. When we are equal to great things, we will be called upon to do the great and the difficult.

Therefore, when the difficult comes, we may know that we are equal to it. We can state it as a general rule that every person is the equal of the occasions that come into his life. There may seem to be exceptions, but upon close examination, we find these to be only temporary modifications that are usually too insignificant to change the results.

It is therefore folly for anyone to tremble in the presence of occasions he has never met before. If we were told that we had to tie our shoe strings tomorrow and had never done so before, nor seen anyone else do it, we should possibly lay awake most of the night worrying about how we would ever get through with it.

There are a great many people that spend sleepless nights thinking about how to do things that prove to be just as simple as tying shoestrings.

We frequently spend days, nights and weeks, turning things over in our minds that could be handled perfectly in ten minutes notice. We should never do this if we could see every task in its true nature, and know ourselves sufficiently to know that we are equal to every occasion.

The imagination, of course, is at fault, and the whole matter can be remedied by training the imagination to act in its own legitimate realms only. But the one, who must read while he runs, prefers a simpler method; and we have it. Live constantly in the conviction that you are equal to every occasion that comes your way.

Practice will prove that this is the truth. The man who makes it a practice to meet every occasion with the thought that he is equal to it, will never fail to turn every occasion to good account. When doubt comes up, and you begin to feel that possibly you have met your "Waterloo," remember the great law—like attracts like. You have attracted something difficult because you are able to handle the difficult; you have been called upon to take up the new task because you are ready for it. And going at it in such a spirit will always produce success.

And in addition, your imagination will be daily trained into normal action. But if like attracts like, and we are equal to the occasions that we meet, what causes the "Waterloos" in life? To say that you are equal to an occasion means that you can advantageously cooperate with that occasion, and produce satisfactory results. It does not mean that you have met something to fight, or to resist.

The average person thinks that life is a battle; but he is mistaken. He may be making a battle out of his life by fighting the occasions that are met; and because he fights, he has many "Waterloos."

Failure in constructive work comes only when we are too afraid of the occasions we meet to cooperate with them. And we fear them because we look upon them through the magnifying glass of abnormal imagination. To him who takes advantage of every opportunity; who is always at his best; who views all things correctly; who does not give unnecessary time to trifles; who does not fear the difficult; who knows that he can do whatever his own sphere of existence calls upon him to do—to him there is no defeat. He will not have to turn back nor go down.

We are creatures of habit, though we ought not to be so. What we are used to everyday, comes easy, even though it may be very difficult. But what we have never done before, generally seems hard, though it may actually be simplicity itself. And the reason is this: when we have entered into right relations with things, and have adapted ourselves to the requirements, we are naturally, and constantly prepared.

Such work, therefore, comes easy. The subconscious supply has been made ready; and to fill that place has become second nature. But when we meet something different, we are unable to comply with requirements at once. We are not adapted to the new work; we have not trained the subconscious to respond; we have not found the right relations. And it is necessary to be properly related to your work before you can do it as it should be done. But how can we properly relate ourselves to an occasion that we do not view correctly? This is the entire problem given in a few words.

If you have magnified your work or belittled yourself, you see neither correctly, and cannot bring the two together in proper relationship. Attempts at cooperation under such false conceptions will only result in misfits. And here we find one reason why so many people are in the wrong place; working at things they are not adapted for.

To do your best work, you must properly relate yourself to your work; and to relate yourself to your work, you must see yourself as you are, and you must see your work as it is.

That is simple; and is accomplished by removing all kinds of belittling and magnifying processes. An immense study, if we are to enter all its phases; but if we are not prepared to do this now, we can simplify the matter by living constantly in the conviction that we are equal to every occasion coming to us. This conviction will remove the two processes just mentioned and will establish right relations immediately between yourself and the new occasions you meet.

THE ART OF DEFEATING ADVERSITY

To defeat adversity means to rob it of its power to harm, to be superior to it, to turn it to good account, to extract good from it. Adversity, in its many types and degrees of manifestation, is due to some form of limitation.

Consequently, to gain a correct understanding of the principle of limitation, to become reconciled, to its standards, and to work in harmony with them, deprives adversity of all undesirable effects. Limitation is nature's principle of contraction, condensation, concentration, transformation.

In classic mythology, it is symbolized by Saturn, commonly thought of as God of Time, but, fundamentally typifying nature's universal Law, manifesting as centripetal force, or contracting, crystallizing power.

The beneficence of this great principle is not to be questioned; yet, on all planes, it has its negative, as well as its positive, expression; its unhappy, as well as its happy, manifestations. Carried to extreme or not properly balanced by supplementing qualities, it tends toward disaster and destruction. Given unchecked sway, deprived of the modifying effects of expansion, this contracting, crystallizing tendency of nature would only crystalize to its own ruin.

Considered in its bearing on human life, it is not difficult to see how the principle of contraction and condensation has come to be connected with the idea of adversity, delays, pressure, limitations, restrictions. Nor is it difficult to understand why persons characterized by qualities peculiar to this principle called Saturn traits of character are often regarded as unfortunate. To such a degree is this the ease that Saturn, God of the principle of limitation and concentration, is usually thought of as unkind, even severe and hostile, to human destiny; and the planet, Saturn, by its rings, symbolizes restrictions, limitations, restraint, pressure, and hampering influences.

It is wise to accept it as a fact that the Law of Limitation does manifest itself in these apparently unfortunate ways. Everyone, in some measure, comes under its restraining and its delaying influences; yet many individuals are distinctly marked by Saturn traits, and, at least during a certain period of their lives, seem to be painfully hampered and held in and held down by Saturn barriers. But none the less true is it that emphasis of interpretation is wrongly placed if the Law of Limitation is a reminder of nothing except the undesirable and the unfortunate. That interpretation of the Law has gone far astray, which does not seek to transmute fear and bitterness in regard to the limitations of life, into reverence and deepest respect for the Law itself.

The truth to be emphasized is that the Law of Limitation in its purpose, is beneficent; that Saturn traits of character are in themselves good; that the only way to overcome the afflictive measures of the Law, and to counteract its negative influences, is to recognize its beneficence, and to turn its seeming adversity to good account. To understand the Law and to work in harmony with its principles, will solve all difficulties caused by the Law's unrelenting firmness. "To kick against the pricks," to rail at fate for placing one in the domain of restraint, to cringe under the pressure of circumstances, to shrink from squarely and honestly facing defeat and chagrin—this attitude of mind only tightens Saturn's "rings" of limitation, and intensifies the pinching's of their pressure.

To convince oneself that the Law of Limitation is good, and that the individual richly endowed with Saturn qualities of character is really fortunate, one has only to imagine the absence of this Law in nature and in human life, and to note in human character the effects of a deficiency in its qualities; one has only to point out the desirable features of the Law's expression in nature, and to note the admirable achievements of men gained only by transforming the negative tendencies of limitation into positive virtues.

On all planes of manifestation, definiteness of form and outline is made possible through the working of the Law of Limitation. Shape and figure, individuality and selfhood, likeness and contrast—that which distinguishes one object from another—are due to nature's principle of limitation. Were it not for the functioning of this Law, we would be deprived of the richness of variety that nature presents in her myriad forms, shapes; and figures, in her manifold contrasts of outline and detail; in her multitudinous tints and shades and blending's of color. It is the specific function of the Law of Limitation to mark confines and to determine content, crystallizing each form into its own identity, and separating it from all else, in all realms of material expression, including mineral formation, every department of the vegetable kingdom, all orders and species of animal life, as well as different classes and races of men.

On the human plane, to the Law of Limitation are to be attributed distinctive features of genius, and distinctive talents and gifts that mark men and women as superior in any field of endeavor. It places the stamp of individuality on character, and is the secret of "that peculiar preciousness" which each life possesses, to which each life is entitled, and which gives each life its inherent right to hold a place among its fellow beings.

In individual temperament, the Law of Limitation manifests itself in such qualities as prudence, patience, discrimination, caution, persistency, steadfastness, and faithfulness. These temperamental manifestations, these Saturn traits of character, indicate close connection with time: they suggest regard for time or results of time. They indicate experience, maturity, endurance, superiority of character by virtue of sore testing and long self-training. They enable one to abide by a fixed purpose and to continue in an espoused cause, until the purpose has been attained and the cause has been perfected. They give regard for accuracy and for painstaking attention to details. They give willingness to undergo the severest discipline in the realization of a lofty ideal or in the execution of a worthy motive. "Never give up" is the watchword of Saturn characters.

Quiet, steady persistency in an undertaking insures for them mastery of all difficulties and conquest over all obstacles.

Yet, these Saturn qualities, all admirable in themselves, if unduly accentuated, become undesirable traits of char that delays action. Patience may become indifference or sluggishness of endeavor or even an indulgence that opens the way for others to take undue advantage of situations. Caution may be so encouraged as to interfere with the ability to take the initiative in undertakings. The gift of discrimination may be so emphasized as to lead to faultfinding or a critical disposition. Steadfastness and faithfulness in an endeavor may be so fostered as to hinder fruition or satisfactory completion of the task at hand. Unless held in check and firmly guided by kindly graces of heart, persistency may become stubbornness or obstinacy, and thus may defeat even one's own highest ideals.

Again, if misdirected or unwisely indulged in, these qualities tend toward depression of spirit and a melancholy state of mind. They incline one to hold grudges; to magnify petty personal injuries, by pondering over them. They induce habitual worry. Being lenient toward the time element, these undesirable Saturn characteristics encourage plodding tendencies of mind, inertness, and even lack of responsiveness; soon stamping themselves on the physical organism, they result in sluggish, heavy, clogging vibrations. Reflex influence on the physical organism causes sluggish movement of its functions, and invites chronic disorders.

Likewise, a deficiency of these qualities is also undesirable. Here is one who has the ambition to become a musician. He is apparently qualified with natural ability in musical lines. His temperament demands esthetic interests, and inclines him toward the artistic. In his nature, musical themes and motifs await expression and demand an outlet. His vision of the possibilities of a musical career is, on the one hand, an impetus to attainment; on the other, a source of irritating discontent with his present lot.

Yet, all to no purpose, one thing he lacks: his nature is deficient in the qualities necessary to carry one through an exacting course of training and self-discipline—qualities such as the Law of Limitation in its ideal form alone make possible. To have a vision, a dream, an ideal, is one thing; quite another is it to execute that ideal by overcoming obstacles and meeting every requirement that realization of an ideal demands.

Another is attracted by a literary career. He may be characterized by culture, scholastic attainments of the highest order, and by superior ability and originality. He may be rich in experience and in character and in graces of heart. He may be endowed with wealth of ideas, wealth of material, and fluency of expression.

But, one thing he must not be deficient in if he attains to success as a writer the ability to circumscribe and to define his territory; to limit his theme, his purpose, his development within a definite compass; to extract with precision the essential from the non-essential, both in thought and in expression, in order to meet the demands of his carefully prescribed assignment, which is in itself a self-imposed limitation. In the literary art, as elsewhere, the Law of Limitation must be respected. The Saturn ideal must focus a writer's attention and concentrate his aim until he has a clear vision of exactly what belongs within the circle, "the ring," the radius, of a given requirement.

From these considerations, it is seen that both the Law of Limitation and the qualities that represent the Law are truly beneficent. It rests with the individual himself to turn these admirable qualities to good account rather than to pervert them; it rests with him, by determined effort, to make up for any possible deficiencies of these traits in his character.

The most difficult to reconcile with the idea of beneficence. However, is limitation in the sense of obstacles, barriers, hindrances, delays, adversity. It is asked, Wherein can beneficence be recognized in the midst of undesirable limitation such as these indicate?

In answer, let it be emphasized, first, that limitation in this sense is the training school for maturing and for perfecting just such qualities of character and just such graces of heart as the Law, in its ideal beneficent expression, indicates; second, that man is limited in reality only to such degree as he limits himself. (He who thinks of circumstances as fetters admits himself to be a slave to circumstances.)

He who sees nothing but defeat and chagrin in disaster and misfortune, falls far short of a satisfactory interpretation of life's conditions. Outward limitation, external barriers, prolonged delays—every conceivable type of adversity—all are to be accepted as opportunities for expansion of character; opportunities for wholesome self-discipline and self-mastery; opportunities for development of a unique type of strength and a unique grace of character. (He who is master of himself in the midst of untoward circumstances is master indeed.) From the higher plane of Mastership, he is superior to con¬ditions, he turns them to good account, he extracts good from them; thus, he defeats adversity of all power to harm.

Barriers, pressure of conditions, crushing of fond ideals, delays to cherished hopes—all these, if accepted in sweetness of spirit, should serve as goads to spur one on to more active endeavor. They should serve as a chemical process that dissolves the crusted sediment of selfishness, and transmutes it into qualities of strength and of goodness. And, in proportion as the debris and the dregs of selfishness are removed, or transmuted into goodness and strength, in that proportion does the petty, limited, personal self-rise to its divine inheritance—Consciousness of Freedom.

Recognizing no limitation in the realm of the Higher Consciousness, he ceases to feel crushed and defeated by the happenings of life; thus, his soul attains to superiority over them. Having served his time in the school of Adversity, having experienced the restricting and the restraining effects of "Saturn's rings," yet having held firmly to a lofty ideal of character through it all, and having continued steady in a noble purpose, in due season, he comes to realize that Limitation is, after all, a feature only of the material and the transitory, and that, in the realm of being, in the realm of Soul, in the realm of Consciousness and Realization, there is no limitation—no barrier to achievement. Through limitation, he has learned to transcend limitation.

Thus, the very fact of overcoming barriers and restrictions on the external plane of existence becomes the secret of freedom from them; and, in time, the limited self is led to consciousness of the Higher Self, the Soul, on the plane of Being. But there are other aspects of the Law of Limitation that invite respect and inspire confidence in the Law's inherent goodness.

From one point of view, this principle identifies itself with the Law of Selection, and becomes the basis of discreet choice and wise discrimination in the accomplishment of a purpose. Rather than being a deprivation, it is to be regarded as a mark of wisdom and of superior strength for the athlete under training to exercise restraint in the habits of life; for the artist to refrain from that which interferes with his art, and to use exacting discipline in favor of such details as tend to promote his art. Still again, the Law of Limitation identifies itself with the principle of concentration—concentration, the secret of achievement in all departments of life, the key to unfoldment and attainment in all lines of spiritual growth.

Concentration is the art of limiting oneself, at a given time, to a given object. It is the art of focusing one's attention, of condensing one's ambition, of making one's desire "pointed." It is the art of causing the soul's longing to become a needle-prick of minuteness and definiteness. It is the art of holding one's place as king or as queen on the throne of one's own Cause World, and of issuing and establishing throughout one's own thought-kingdom such decrees as are in harmony with the Christ Ideal. It is the art of piercing the veil that separates the invisible from the visible.

"The master mind dwells on different things at different times: this leads to wisdom. Others miss all things at all times, which brings confusion, never wisdom." An expression more apt than this concerning the art of concentration literature nowhere contains. A subtle, penetrating force is the art of concentration—the most divinely potent of all forces known to man—and yet, it is only a simple, practical feature of the Law of Limitation.

Thus, the very Law under which we chafe, when correctly interpreted, not only furnishes the material and the power needed for accomplishment, but also reveals the requisites of a practical application of the Law itself.

To make friends with Adversity is to transfigure her into an angel of light. Crushing the thistle in one's hand causes pain; touching it lightly stimulates nerve-sensitiveness. "To kick against the pricks" is only to wound and to bruise; to cease resisting the prick of the goad, transforms it into a kindly stimulus for more faithful and more determined endeavor. Let one regard "Saturn's rings" as chains, and one is sure to bear the mien of a culprit or a prisoner. Let one accept them as territory within which mastership is to be attained, and they are transformed into ornaments of grace. From a yoke of bondage, they become "the necklace of pearls" that gives testimony of ripe experience and mellowness of character.

Even to the most adverse situation, there is some redeeming feature. To seek, and to recognize this redeeming feature, marks the wise man. Even the most adverse situation admits of a surprise in the manner of viewing it. To seek, and to recognize this surprise, distinguishes wisdom from folly. One's own need, one's own deficiency, is the magnet that attracts to one's own environment just such conditions as one's own particular stage of development demands.

When one becomes skillful in mastering life's lessons, no longer being so much in need of difficult and painful assignments, the tendency in one's own nature to attract adverse conditions becomes greatly diminished. To be prompt and adept in mastering undesirable conditions, to cultivate a correct attitude of mind toward them, is to defeat Adversity by robbing her of all power to harm.

THE MESSAGE OF THE GREAT INITIATES

ALL down through the ages since the beginning of time great teachers, appointed by the spiritual hierarchies, have come to man to instruct him and reveal to him the next step in his endless path of self-unfoldment. Each of these great messengers has brought a distinct doctrine and when linked together their teachings form a golden chain of ideals which the human race must aspire to even though it may not be able to fully realize the end or the way.

For the benefit of the student of occult philosophy, we list below twelve great spiritual teachers, many of them now regarded as allegorical rather than historical personages. However, the deep student realizes that mythology is the truest history of the ancient people that we have and that only in folklore and legend do we find an authentic record of the great Light bringers and their messages to man.

1. Hermes. This great Atlantean demigod, probably if not actually the greatest illuminator of mortal man, taught as the key to his philosophy-Analogy. The relationships existing between the inferior and the superior worlds was the basis of his doctrine, and the knowledge of the simile was man's first revelation. Hermes is often called the first messenger of God because he is the oldest that we know, and his law of analogical reasoning is the basis of every philosophy of modern times. The essence of his teaching was that God and man were made in the same mold and that all things in the lower world and the lesser sphere are made after the same pattern as the greater thing in the superior world. He taught that the realization of this was the fundamental principle of wisdom.

2. Orpheus, the Grecian demigod, taught man the law of Harmo-

ny and the great work of harmonizing the spiritual and material qualities within his own soul. The seven-stringed lyre of Orpheus represents the seven major rates of vibration known to consciousness at this time. Upon these rates of vibration, which are the basis of form, thought, growth and culture, his philosophy was based, his seven-stringed lyre representing the solar system and the seven centers in the human body and upon this he taught man to play the harmony of nature and the music of the spheres. This harmonization of the centers of consciousness was the redemption of the human soul (Eurydice).

3. Krishna, the great Indian Christ and the most beloved deity of Brahman theology, is said to have had Love as the keynote of his teaching. He taught man of the love of God for His creations, the love of the spirit within for its bodies, and the love existing always between the spiritual and the human. He taught man to live in peace with his neighbor and to recognize the fundamental duty of regard and respect for all other created things. Krishna, the Christ-child of India, is symbolical of the sun, who is in love with Radha, the East Indian symbol of nature. The marriage of the sun to nature and the love of God for His outpourings was the center ground of his divine message to man. He taught immortality and the nonexistence of death, that ignorance was the basis of oblivion and that those who love only the Light would never be in darkness.

4. Buddha, the world's most eminent reformer and regenerator of ideals, brought mankind the doctrine of Renunciation and Non-attachment as the basis of immortality. He told man to renounce the temporal for the eternal, the illusion for the reality, the lower for the higher, and the outer for the inner. He taught that attachment was the basis of sorrow and that freedom from attachment was the basis of peace. Upon his doctrines has been based the greatest religion upon the earth at the present time, a creed which has influenced the destiny of half the people of the earth.

5. Mohammed. The essence of the faith of Islam is the necessity for Obedience and man's perfect willingness to leave his destiny in the hands of the Immortal. Mohammed taught that the greatest glory was for him who obeyed the laws rather than for one who creates a law; that those who leave their destiny with the powers of the Divine and follow those laws in simplicity and trust, obeying them to the letter, shall never want for the treasures of the eternal.

6. Moses taught the children of Israel and the ancient world the om-

nipotence of Law; the justice without mercy of law, the impersonality of law and that those who would break law are themselves broken upon it. He delivered the tablets of the ten laws to the children of Israel, teaching them that law is the voice of God and that those who keep His laws are the ones He blesses and preserves.

7. Zoroaster, the great founder of the faith of the Parsees and the Fire king of Persia, taught the doctrine of Light and said that the sun and flame were the most precious things in the universe. He taught the building of that Fire within the soul of the individual; that the fire that burns in man is the eldest of all Flames; that man is dependent upon fire and that this fire is the divine essence of God within himself. In other and simpler words, he taught the indwelling presence of the Divine.

8. Confucius, the great un-apotheosized saint of China, a god made so by the love of his people, taught that Morality was the greatest of all virtues and the most acceptable quality in the universe; that the salvation of man depended upon his relationships to his fellow creatures; that purity, chastity and fraternity were the greatest of all qualities and that religion in essence rested upon practical works rather than theoretical dogmas.

9. Plato. Plato's doctrines were based upon the principles of Logic and he taught his disciples the orderly creation, the logical creation and the reasonable in the universe. He taught a geometrical base of all growth and instructed his followers that the universe, God, man, and nature are mathematical units capable of exact analysis.

10. Odin. This great Initiate who illuminated Scandinavia and the Teutonic countries, had as the basis of his teaching the doctrine of Courage. He taught the necessity of stamina and daring; that those who aspired to reach the footstool of light must dare all things, must battle against all opposition; and that reward comes to the victor in the battle and not to the one who remains at home.

11. Hiram Abiff, the great Masonic idol and ideal, taught in his unspoken life the doctrine of human Regeneration. Hiram, representing the spiritual essences in the human body, redeems himself and is redeemed through the path of the Masonic mysteries. Only in transmutation lays the path of immortality, and every human quality must be transmuted into a divine and eternal thing.

12. Jesus. The one teacher who is best known to the Christian world, but whose doctrines are the least understood of any of the great world

teachers, is the Master Jesus. The key to his philosophy is Brotherhood and his ideal was a new faith built out of the mutual understanding and common interests of all of the others. He sought to unite all wisdom into one simple creed and also sought to show man the one simple labor which all creation is trying to achieve, each in its different way. Only those who have found harmony and are living in a state of brotherhood with other living things will ever know the message of the Master Jesus, for he synthesizes all the previous world religions for those who have the eyes to recognize that fact.

These qualities, if you will analyze them closely, you will find are absolutely dependent one upon another. There has never been a complete revelation up to date, but all the revelations of the past gathered together build a monumental temple, which is the expression of all known wisdom. This is the temple whose door is open to the student of the Wisdom Religion when he has learned to forsake dogma and creed, worship God in spirit and in truth rather than in clan and group. The message of the Wisdom Teachings to the modern world is, briefly, one of impartiality in which the student worships God in His many fold expressions rather than his own crystallized concept of divinity, which has so long been the basis of his faith. Only in the universal realization of the one truth, the one Light, the one path, can the student hope to make progress. The Light bearers are incidents and can receive our respect and veneration, but the Light is the thing which we should worship and not the One who brings it.

THE SEVEN NATURAL LAWS

THERE are certain natural laws which are the basis of occult wisdom and a thorough understanding of them will give the student a firm foundation upon which to build his superstructure of reason and logic. Man cannot safely think at random but must first of all bases his philosophies upon some rock of immortal truth. And for the occultist, this rock is Natural Law:

1. The Law of Evolution. Everything in the universe is at some stage of an endless path, leading from absolute nothingness to perfect omnipotence. Everything in the universe is greater today than yesterday and will be greater still tomorrow; all things have within them the opportunity for perfection. The law of Evolution is that gradual process

in nature which brings about this realization of the ideal. Evolution of consciousness and of form is the keystone of the plan and those who reject it never study occultism intelligently. The law of Evolution applies to everything from the smallest electron to the Cosmic God himself and to the occultist God is an evolving Deity rather than a creating God.

2. The Law of Compensation or Karma "As you sow, so shall you reap." Every cause you start in motion, every thought, every action, good or bad, has an unavoidable result and reaction. The position of the individual on the wheel of life and death depends upon the works done and the works undone. The law of Karma says: no man can be greater than his works. Eternal justice works through this great spiritual law.

3. The Law of Polarity. Everything in the universe expresses itself through two pole-positive and negative. The law of Polarity teaches that the work of man is to establish himself at a neutral point exactly between the two poles, which position is the place of balance-hence omnipotence.

4. The Law of Periodicity. The law of Periodicity demands that after every expenditure of energy, there must be a time of repose for the restoration of the lost power. Yet it, in the periods of sleeping and waking, winter and summer, life and death, governs action and repose and there is no the Days and Nights of Brahma. This law escapes from it in any realm of nature where energy is expended. If he labors, he must rest; if he rests, he must labor. And the same is true among gods as among men.

5. The Law of Alternation. Everything alternates between its poles. In successive births, man alternates in his forms from positive to negative for the laws of nature demand that we receive and benefit by the experiences of both the positive and negative paths. Every seventh swing in human evolution, we have a perfect type of a male or female form, for these are the two extremes of the pendulum.

6. The Law of Harmony and Rhythm. Nature's divine plan is Harmony and in harmony is the friction caused by bodies out of place. Harmony for man is the adjustment of his life with the Plan of Being.

7. The Law of Reincarnation. This is the hardest doctrine for most people to accept, but everywhere in nature we see the necessity of it. It is the only law we can find which explains the inequalities of temperament and the degrees of intelligence which we find in the world and at the same time retain a just theology. Either this law must be an actual fact or else the divine plan lacks the principle of justice, and human inequalities

and suffering must have other cause than the whims of deity. This law is taught in three quarters of the world religions. These are the seven laws with which occult students must deal in their daily life and with which they must learn to familiarize themselves that they may adjust their lives to concepts in harmony with them. And the only man or woman who is at peace is the one who is harmonious with the plan of his being.

HARMONY

To be in harmony with everything, at all times, and under all circumstances, is one of the greatest essentials to the new life; and so extremely important is continuous harmony that nothing should be permitted to produce confusion or discord for the slightest moment.

Discord wastes energy while harmony accumulates energy; therefore, if we wish to be strong in mind and body, and be in the best possible condition for the best possible work, harmony is indispensable. The person who lives in perpetual harmony with everything will accomplish from ten to fifty percent more during any given period of time; a fact that certainly makes the subject worthwhile.

When harmony is absent, there is always more or less mental confusion, and a confused mind can never think clearly; therefore, makes mistakes constantly. To establish complete and continuous mental harmony will reduce mistakes to a minimum in any mind. Another fact that makes the subject worthwhile.

The mind that is in harmony is in heaven, whether he knows anything or not, whether he possesses anything or not; because in harmony, there is joy, contentment and real satisfaction. On the other hand, the brainiest, mightiest man in the world who lives in discord, dwells in perpetual torment.

To live the good life, the ideal life, the beautiful life, we must be at peace with all things, including ourselves, and every thought, word and deed must be harmonious. Whatever we may wish to do or be, to sacrifice everything for the sake of harmony is perfect wisdom; though when we do this, we find that what we were willing to sacrifice was not taken away. Nothing is lost by him who gives harmony in the first place, and feels harmonious towards all persons and things.

When we establish ourselves in perfect harmony, we shall be reunited with everything we love; and the new unity will be far sweeter and more beautiful than the one that was. "My own shall come to me," is a favorite expression in these days; and many are waiting and watching for their own to come; wondering, in the meantime, what can be done to hasten the coming.

Many things can be done, but the most important is harmony. The person who lives in perpetual harmony will not be deprived of his own very long, whatever that "own" may be. Whatever you deserve, whatever you are entitled to, whatever belongs to you, will soon appear in your world if you continue to live in perfect harmony.

To enter the state of harmony is to enter a new world, where everything is better; where opportunities are greater and more numerous, and where persons, conditions and things are more agreeable. You will, therefore, live in a better world; but that is not all; you attitude of harmony will relate you so perfectly to the good things in all worlds that the best from every source will naturally gravitate to you. A person who dwells serenely in the beautiful calm, is a perpetual benediction to everybody; to be in his presence is to come one step nearer the Beautiful.

What a privilege it must therefore be to live in the life of a living harmony. Harmony is the foundation of happiness and health, and is one of the greatest essentials to achievement and success. When we look into the past and try to number the good things we failed to secure because we fell into confusion and discord, we shall no longer doubt that harmony is one of the greatest things in the world.

The mind that works in perpetual harmony does more work and far better work; and such work is exercise, conducive to higher development and growth. All harmonious work promotes development of mind and body; while work that is carried on in confused attitudes of mind will weaken the entire system, and produce final failure.

We often complain that we have no time for self-development; but if we live in harmony when we work, we are growing every moment; and this development will not be confined to those muscles or faculties that we use directly, but the entire system, the mentality especially, will steadily gain in power and worth. In the presence of these facts, it is certainly folly to permit discord, disturbance or confusion at all; but the majority declare they cannot help it. However, we must learn to help it, and we can.

There is no reason why our minds should be excited nor our nerves upset at any time. We can prevent this just as easily as we can refuse to eat what we do not want. In the first place, we must apply reason to this subject. We must understand that the wrong will not be righted because we "fly all to pieces;" and that to become nervous over a trouble does not drive the trouble away.

To live in a constant strain will not promote our purpose, nor arrange matters the way we want them; and yet, nearly everyone who has some great undertaking in hand does this very thing. We feel that it is our religious duty to be as excited as possible, and to string up all our nerves as high as possible whenever we are passing through some uncommon event; therefore, we spoil most of it, and bring all sorts of ills upon ourselves.

It is seldom that an extraordinary occasion passes off smoothly; there is nearly always something that turns out wrong, falls flat, or disgraces the participants. The reason is discord, confusion and the absence of perfect harmony. It is not difficult to understand why so many undertakings fail; because the art of being in harmony under all kinds of circumstances, has not, as yet, been acquired by the many.

To be in harmony, and to do your best will give you success every time, and will prepare you for the greater opportunities that are sure to follow. That intelligent, well-educated people almost daily break down over mere trifles, is almost too absurd to believe; but that it is the truth leads us to ask the reason why. They should have known better.

Modern education, however, does not teach us how to use ourselves. We are learning how to mix the material substances so as to satisfy every imaginable taste; and we are learning how to use the tangible forces of nature so as to construct almost anything we like in the physical world, but we have not learned how to combine the elements of mind so as to produce happiness, strength and brilliancy.

A few have made the attempt, but the elements of mind will not combine for greater efficiency unless the mind is in harmony. All of us have learned to remember, but few of us have learned to think. To repeat verbatim what others have thought and said, is counted knowledge; and with such borrowed knowledge, the majority think they are satisfied; the reason is they have not discovered the art of thinking thoughts of their own.

Original thinking is the secret of all greatness, all high attainments and all extraordinary achievements; but no mind can create original thought without being in harmony. But how is harmony to be attained?

We all want to know, and we want methods that all can apply with success. In the first place, we must bear in mind the great fact that it is not what happens that disturbs us, but the way we think about that which happens; and our thought about anything depends upon our point of view.

The way we look at things will determine whether the experience will produce discord or harmony; and it is in our power to view things in any way that we like. When something happens that usually disturbs the mind and upsets things in general, we should immediately turn our attention upon the power back of the event, with a view of finding the better side of that power.

Every power has its better side, its ideal side, its calm, undisturbed side; and the mere desire to gain a glimpse of that better side will turn the mind away from the disturbance and cause attention to be centered upon the calm that is being sought. This will decrease the discord at once if we permitted any discord to be felt; though if we apply this method, the very moment we are aware of confusion in our environment, we will entirely prevent disturbance in our minds.

To meet all circumstances and events in this way, will develop in us a harmonious attitude towards everything; and when we are established in this harmonious attitude towards everything, nothing whatever can disturb us. No matter what may happen, we will remain in harmony; and will consequently be able to deal properly with everything that does happen.

The mind that is upset by confused circumstances will lose his ground and fail; but the mind that continues calmly in harmony with everything, will master every occasion, and steadily rise in the scale of life.

QUESTIONS AND ANSWERS

What is the soul?

The soul is a body built by the thoughts, actions and desires of human life which weave a garment according to their own quality. Later this garment becomes the vehicle of consciousness for the spirit, for within it is incorporated all of the growth of the lower bodies.

Does our life belong to us?

In many ways our life belongs to us - in fact, in the Great Plan it does so entirely. But owing to the fact that in the past we contracted certain debts, our free will is mortgaged in favor of people to whom we owe certain actions and qualities. Therefore, in coming into incarnation, certain things we must do whether we want to or not because of sacred obligations we have made in the past.

What is free will?

God alone has free will. Man has the power of choice. Ignorance is the limiting factor in free will. The greater number of things we know the greater is our area of choice until as gods, knowing all, we have the choice of all.

Are all individual experiences preserved?

Yes. They are the basis of soul growth and are stored up in the centers of bodies until we have built the necessary faculties to read them.

What center of Consciousness is man working on now?

Man is at the present time laboring especially to unfold the mind with its forty-nine centers of sense consciousness. That is the work allotted to him during the earth period of evolution.

Why do spirits return as deformed, idiots and cranks?

Those things are the reward of the abuse of mental and spiritual faculties in previous lives. Abuses of nature bring with them terrible karmic debts and those mentally, spiritually or physically prostitute power, will pay for it as we see in the world so often.

If an employee is obliged to lie to an employer, what is the penalty?

If a person finds out that he must lie for his salary it is a very excellent time to find a new position, for if he consciously does it for gain to himself the penalty will be as heavy as though he were doing so, of his own free will.

What is meant by the Word?

The Word is a center of consciousness around which negative particles gather and forms are built. It is not in the last analysis a sound but a rate of vibration. It is the Life producing and manifesting through form.

What are visions and what causes them?

Two causes. First, temporary attunement of consciousness, either positive or negative, with super physical planes: the result of fine spiritual growth or a general rundown condition of the body. The first is safe, and the second is very dangerous. Excitement, worry, grief and so forth, will deplete the system and produce this result. Third grand cause and the most common, late eating.

Should we use our astrology colors?

We should use everything we can but not spend too much time harmonizing vibrations, etc. If we do, we will have no time left for work and labor produces much better growth than color harmony. Never use any such means, however, as astrology, talismanic magic, etc., to gain over other people in financial, spiritual or material matters. To do so is Black Magic.

Please explain the crucifixion.

The word crucifixion means a crossing. The crossing of spiritual and material currents forms bodies and these bodies crucify and seek to destroy the life which is within or hanging upon them.

FINIS

Author and Managing Editor

Darrell Jordan is an acolyte of the August Fraternity, former Noble Grand-IOOF and Freemason. He is also a member of the Theosophical and Philalethes Societies.

Darrell Jordan

Books by the Author

- Illustrations of Masonry
- Surviving Document of the Widow's Son
- The Undiscovered Teachings of Jesus
- The Initiates
- Jefferson's Bible
- Master Masons Handbook
- Forgotten Essays - W.L. Wilmshurst
- Forgotten Essays - Waite
- Forgotten Essays - H. Stanley Redgrove
- The Writings of Sigismond Bacstrom M.D.
- Forgotten Essays – Reincarnation
- Masonic Writings of George Oliver
- Masonic Lectures by Wellins Calcott
- The Fellowcraft Handbook
- Secret Societies
- Vibration and Life
- Key to the Rosicrucian Characters
- The Revelation of John
- Life and the Ideal
- The Mystic Key
- The Philosophical History of Freemasonry
- The Magic of the Middle Ages
- Musings of a Chinese Mystic
- The Life of the Soul
- Christian Mysticism
- Krishna and Orpheus
- The Eleusinian Mysteries & Rites
- The Crucifixion Letter
- You Paid What?
- The Illustrated Pioneer History of the America
- Montana Freemasons 19th Century
- Washington Freemasons 19th Century
- Idaho Freemasons 19th Century
- Rock Metaphysics
- Emblems: Jean Jacque Boissard and Otto van Veen
- Emblems: Nicholas M. Meerfeldt
- Alchemy Art: Manly P. Hall
- Emblems: Manly P. Hall
- Alchemy Art & Symbols
- Splendor Solis

For the latest information, please visit author's site: Parallel47North.com/collections/esoteric-books
If you have any question or feedback, please contact: info@Parallel47North.com

The Artist and Illustrator

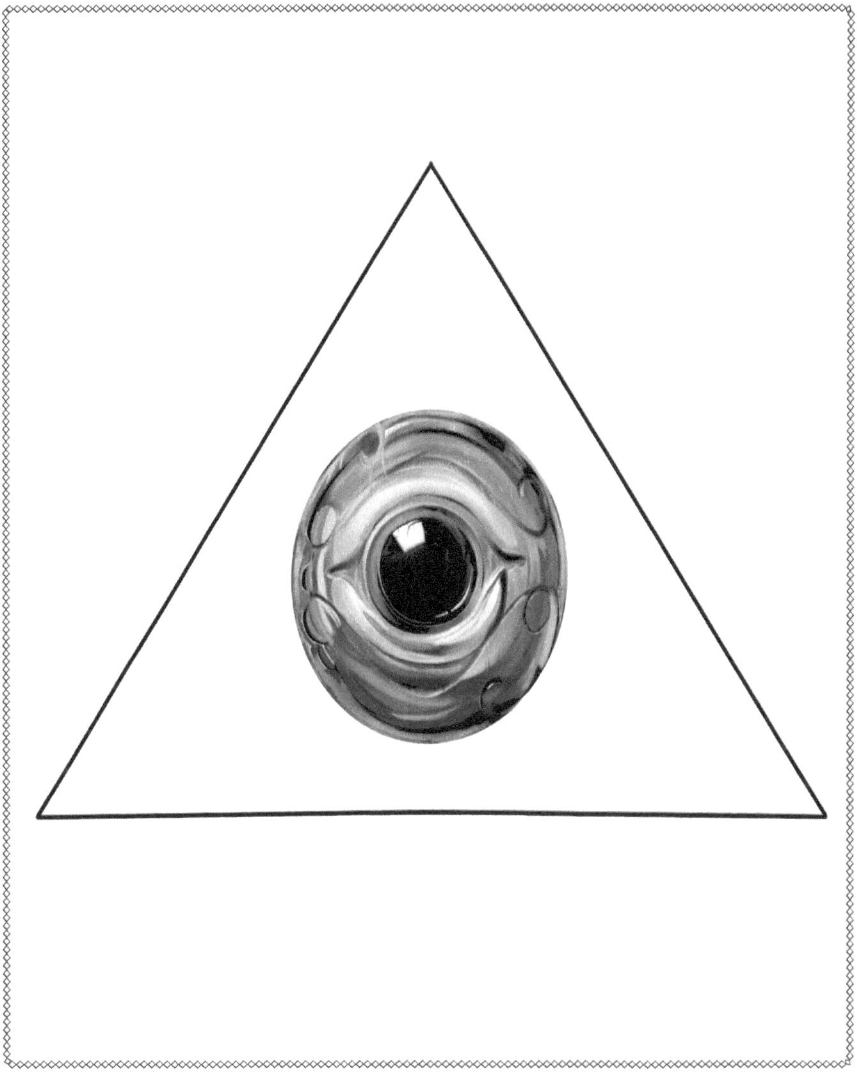

Hand-drawn Illustration of Book Cover Art by Jessica Naomi.
The Artist Portfolio: JessicaNaomiDesigns.com

For those interested in Rosicrucian or similar Esoteric teaching.

Soul.org

Theosophical.org

Whiteaglelodge.org

PTTHfoundation.com

www.ingramcontent.com/pod-product-compliance
Lightning Source LLC
Chambersburg PA
CBHW020311010526
44107CB00001B/67